An Oral History of Tribal Warfare:
The Meru of Mt. Kenya

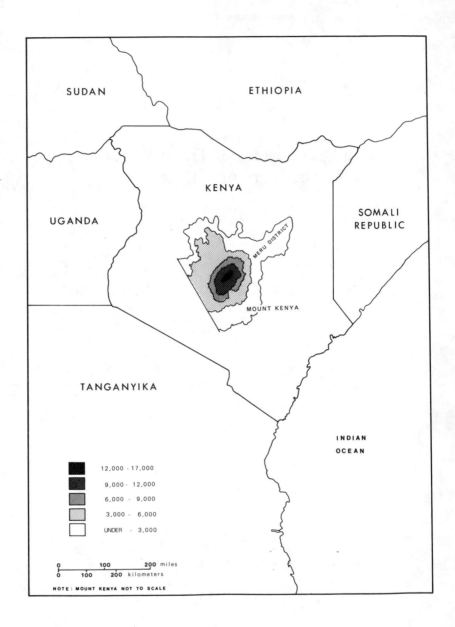

SUDAN

ETHIOPIA

KENYA

UGANDA

SOMALI
REPUBLIC

MERU DISTRICT

MOUNT KENYA

TANGANYIKA

INDIAN
OCEAN

■	12,000 - 17,000
■	9,000 - 12,000
▨	6,000 - 9,000
░	3,000 - 6,000
□	UNDER - 3,000

0   100   200 miles
0   100   200 kilometers

NOTE: MOUNT KENYA NOT TO SCALE

An Oral History of Tribal Warfare:
The Meru of Mt. Kenya

Jeffrey A. Fadiman

Ohio University Press
Athens, Ohio

Library of Congress Cataloging in Publication Data
Fadiman, Jeffrey.
    The Meru of Mt. Kenya.
    Bibliography: p.
    1.   Meru (African tribe)—Social life and customs.
2. Warfare, Primitive—Kenya.   3. Meru (African
tribe)—History.   I. Title.
DT433.545.M47F298   967.6′26   81-16940
ISBN 0-8214-0632-9   AACR2
ISBN 0-8214-0633-7 (pbk.)

DEDICATION

This book is dedicated to the men of Meru, old and young.

To Fabian Njage, Simon P. K. Bengi, Franklin Mugambe, Gerrard Kithinji and a dozen others, all young men in their early twenties, whose total dedication to the Meru people has led to the recovery of this portion of their past.

To M'Mthaara M'Mutani, Matiri wa Kirongo, Heizikiah M'Mukiri, M'Muraa wa Kairanyi and over one hundred others, all men of Miriti and Murungi age-sets. These are the oldest living men of Meru. They are living repositories of the history of their people. It was their willingness to teach their wisdom to a stranger that has preserved so much of it for generations yet to come.

To the men of Meru yet unborn: Remember what those who came before have tried to give you. No gift will prove more precious than your heritage.

Men of Meru, Warriors of Africa, I salute your past.

Jeffrey A. Fadiman
Oral Historian
1981

Table of Contents

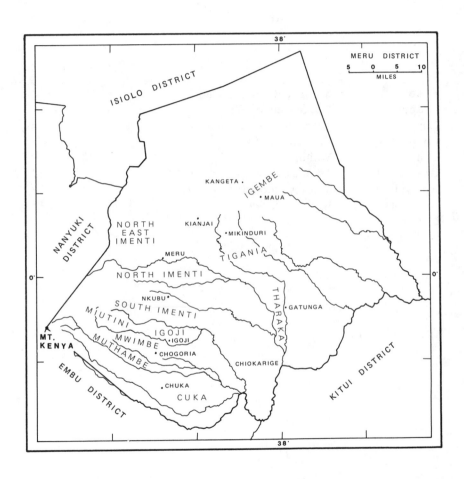

CHAPTER I

Meru: The Final Decade

This is the story of a warrior decade, as reconstructed by men now in their eighties and nineties who once lived it. It was their decade, the peak of their lives, the last decade of tribal warriorhood before its conquest by the West. The tribal warriors still form a shining part of the lore of Africa. Their deeds come alive in the glow of evening cook-fires across the continent, gleaming through tales of raids and ambush revealed by the aged to a circle of wide-eyed children.

Before this century, Europeans also respected the warriorhood of Africa. Practical experience over decades and sometimes centuries had taught them to regard tribal warriors as effective opponents—clever, courageous and highly capable of waging war. During this century, however, the successive defeat and dismantling of warrior organizations across the continent led to the creation of new stereotypes by their conquerors.

Western victories, it was argued, were not merely the result of superior technology, but of the military ineptness of their foes. As individuals, warriors of Africa were admitted to have battled bravely, displaying unquestionable courage against European arms. In groups, however, they proved hopelessly handicapped, not merely by outmoded weapons, but by a complete lack of tactics and strategy. It was this apparent lack of combat formation that caused European observers to perceive their opponents as "hordes" or "savages", capable only of the "ragged frontal charge."

These stereotypes persisted beyond the colonial era. With few exceptions, the historians of Africa have ignored pre-colonial warriorhood, focusing on each society only as it began conflict with Europe. Even the exceptions have largely been restricted to those peoples led by unusual men. Shaka of the Zulu, Toure of Guinea, Mkawawa of Tanzania and the Mahdi

1

of Sudan are four examples. Yet even here, historical attention has focused more on the brilliance of the leader than on the armies that he led.

Even less attention has been paid to the so-called decentralized societies, which waged war at clan level without placing themselves under a single leader. While scholars have sometimes noted their defeats and victories, they have only recently begun to examine the military formations, training, strategies, tactics and psychologies with which this type of society waged war before contact with the West.

One example of this decentralized warfare could be found, until the early 1900s, among the Meru-speaking peoples of Mt. Kenya, who live on and adjoining the northeastern slope of the mountain. Before the colonial era, the name referred to only five of the present nine subdivisions: Igembe, Tigania, Imenti, Miutini and Igoji. British administrators, however, chose to include the Tharaka, on the adjoining eastern plains, and the Mwimbe, Muthambe and Cuka, who border the Meru to their south.

Between 1896 and 1906, the final decade before colonial conquest, the oldest living men of Meru were either children or in their teens. They recall the era as a time when their respective peoples were not formed into a single Meru nation, but had organized into smaller social units known as *miiriga* (singular: *mwiriga*), or ridgetop communities. The *mwiriga* was a composite social group, usually made up of several biologically related clans.[1] They were formed primarily to provide common defense; thus they were composed of whatever number of families might be required to provide warrior sons for a military barrack or *gaaru*. In some regions, the *gaaru* could be filled by the sons of a single clan. In others, several smaller ones would band together for security, creating whatever bonds of kinship might be required.

The *mwiriga* also bound its members by managing their lands. Traditions of land ownership suggest that small bands of Meru-speaking migrants entered the lowest portions of the forests of Mt. Kenya during the first quarter of the eighteenth century. Custom dictated that each band camp initially along the forest edge. On entering the region, the men would mark out ("with axe, red soil and firestick") a hunting area, the fringe of which would subsequently be cultivated by their wives.[2]

Exploitation of the land then followed a predictable pattern. Hunters within each marked section pushed steadily deeper into their portion of the forest, searching continually uphill for wild game and establishing new boundary markers as they marched. Cultivators worked the lowest forest fringes to exhaustion, then also moved upward, clearing new areas as soil fertility diminished or population grew.

Elders compare the pattern of this land occupation to a "line of spears" extending gradually up the mountain slope in parallel formation.[3] In consequence, each migrant band found itself the master of one or more steeply sloping ridges, broad at the base of the mountain, narrowing as they ascended. The boundaries between such units were established at the stream beds or river gorges that divided these ridges. The result was the formation of a series of "ridge-top communities" shaped by mountain topography into self-contained societies.

When necessary, individual *miiriga* could temporarily combine to create larger social units. Such alliances were usually for purposes of war. If these unions became frequent, feelings of *trans-mwiriga* identity appeared, and individuals would define themselves as members not only of their ridge-top but of a region. In turn, two or more of these regions could temporarily combine to form what we today refer to as a major Meru subdivision, such as Mwimbe, Igoji or Tigania.

These larger combinations, however, did not frequently appear. Traditions from every major region recount instances where entire subdivisions were mobilized to meet concerted enemy attacks. Tiganian elders mention the beginnings of peacetime consultations among themselves, Igembe and portions of northern Imenti. Notwithstanding, Meru society functioned at the ridgetop level. The majority of interactions in war and peace took place between single *miiriga*. War, for example, was rarely, if ever, waged between the armies of such theoretical entities as Mwimbe or Imenti, but between two *miiriga*, one from each region, which chose to oppose each other. Identification with the larger units did not become universal until the colonial conquest.

The Secular Councils

Despite the early patterns of land acquisition, few *miiriga* proved able to preserve their territorial integrity. Internal dissensions, ease of migration, military dislocation and other factors contributed to a pattern of fragmentation, in which segments of a once territorially intact *mwiriga* would migrate far beyond its original boundaries. Thus by the 1890s, though the original core areas could still be identified, *mwiriga* membership was defined less in terms of residence within an area than by ties of kin.

This trend toward fragmentation placed new stress on the capacity of *miiriga* to preserve the social order. To insure that the obligations of membership were upheld, a system of secular councils (*kiama*, pl: *biama*) was developed, intended to operate at each level of the Meru life cycle, thus permitting males of every age-set but the youngest to regulate their own affairs.

Entry into this system began in early youth and continued into old age. Application was voluntary at every stage, but peer pressure made non-participation virtually impossible, as every age-mate eventually joined.

Entry into any of the councils was achieved in two steps. The first was through payment of specified fees to existing members, as indication of a candidate's desire to join. The second was by submitting to pain (usually,

3

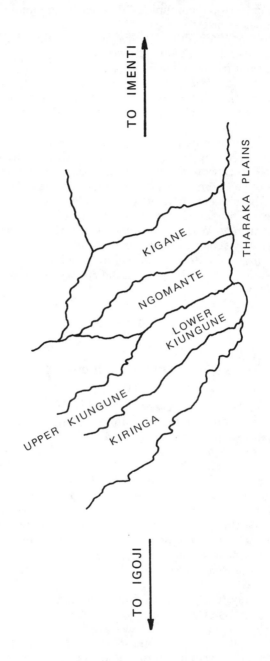

Ridgetop pattern of occupation, South Imenti

prolonged beatings) inflicted by these same members as a gesture of accepting their authority.

Once accepted, persons at every level of the council system entered a period of apprenticeship (*utani*: noviceship). This also was divided into two steps: instruction and service. Instruction was both physical and mental, dealing primarily with the norms of behavior (secrets of the council) to which new members would thereafter be expected to conform. Lessons took the form of enforced mastery of songs, stories, proverbs, riddles, etc., with frequent beatings for those who made mistakes.

During the subsequent period of service, emphasis was placed on silence, obedience and submission to pain. The novice would be compelled either to sit silently in the presence of those members deemed his superiors, or to perform personal services for them, allowing them to beat him for his errors. All three activities were designed to implant the self-discipline and respect for age which were central features of Meru life.

The stage of apprenticeship was eventually followed at every level within the system by one of authority, which gradually increased as the person aged. The lessons learned during his apprenticeship were transmitted at this time to those subordinate to him, utilizing the same techniques of initiation, instruction, silence and servitude that had been imposed on himself.

During this final stage, however, a number of persons would begin to demonstrate either potential or actual qualities of leadership among their age-mates, to the point where they moved informally into positions as spokesmen (*agambe*, sing: *mugambe*) in questions that concerned them all.[4] There were no formal qualifications for this distinction, which instead resulted from a combination of several qualities traditionally held in high esteem. Among these were a pleasing physical appearance, quickness of mind, retentive memory, oratorical ability, physical prowess, and skill in settling the conflicts of age-mates. Adult expectation was another important factor, since sons of those who had achieved this distinction at various stages of their own lives were expected to inherit the requisite qualities from their fathers, and certain families were generally regarded as producing outstanding candidates within every age-set.[5]

At some point during their final stage, certain of these charismatic persons would be encouraged to apply for entry into an elite section of their own *kiama*, known generally as an *njuri*, meaning 'council of the few.'[6] This type of council was composed entirely of persons considered spokesmen for some larger group. All major lineages were represented, and an approximate balance was maintained between members of Kiruka and Ntiba, the two formal halves of the tribe.

Once invited into this more restricted institution, a candidate passed through essentially the same stages he had experienced in the lower council. A period of initiation, marked by payment of fees and by frequent beatings, was followed by a prolonged apprenticeship based on silence and servitude. A final era of authority within the council would last as long as the person remained within that part of his life cycle. He would then move, with cus-

5

tomary rites of transition, into a more mature age level. Thereafter, he would be offered entry into the *kiama* now appropriate to his new status and begin the three-stage cycle once again. If he distinguished himself, he would be lifted once more into the ranks of its *njuri*. Thus a nineteenth century person born into a *mwiriga* in Imenti would pass through the following *biama*:[7]

Age	Kiama	Njuri
7-15+	*kiigumi* (for all)	*kabichu* (for selected few)
15-18+	*uringuri* (for all)	*ramare ba ndinguri* (council for older boys)
18-29+	*uthaka* (warrior-hood for all)	*ramare ba nthaka* (council of warriors)
29-40+	(no councils; possible selection for councils of elders)	
40-51+	*nkomango* (for all ruling elders)	*njuri ya mwiriga* (for selected few)
51-62+	*mbiti* (for ritual elders and aged) (informal consultation with ruling elders as required)	

The institution that was empowered to serve as the administrative instrument for each *mwiriga* was therefore the *kiama* of its ruling set, and ultimately its *njuri*. In practice, ruling elders maintained constant liaison with spokesmen representing both the novice and ritual elders, thus permitting consultation with members of the alternate moietie. In addition, particularly outstanding *agambe* could be selected from among the warriors to sit in on *njuri* deliberations, and contribute on matters relevant to their skill.

Theoretically, problems which arose between two or more *miiriga* were settled by creation of an *njuri* of them all. Actually 'spokesmen of the spokesmen' would be selected from each of the units involved, ideally still representing both of the major segments. In questions involving still wider areas, this pattern would be repeated. Spokesmen from each section would select representatives. These would meet with *agambe* of their area to select still others (*agambe ba agambe ba agambe*). The process could be repeated indefinitely, until an entire subdivision might be represented by *agambe* chosen from a number of such preliminary meetings.[8]

In theory, such selections were temporary. *Njuri* at any level could be convened only to deal with a specific problem. Once it was resolved, the council formed to cope with it would dissolve. However, such questions would arise with considerable regularity, and there was no reason to avoid selection of the same prominent people for these and every other issue, until their status as *njuri* members became permanently accepted by all.

The Supernatural Sphere

To view either the *mwiriga* or its system of councils solely from a secular perspective would be alien to the Meru world view, and thus historically incomplete. Prior to this century, each generation among the Meru peoples saw itself as an integral part of all past generations to which it was linked, not only by bonds of kindship, but also specific ritualized obligations. Thus, in the minds of its members, the *mwiriga* consisted not only of the living but of their ancestors; not merely of a secular community but a related supernatural sphere, each linked to the other to form a single, all-embracing whole.

Similarly, the system of councils existed within both a temporal and a spiritual context. Viewed from a secular perspective, *biama* served their members primarily as centers for conciliation, adjusting conflicts of human interest as they arose. Decisions, however, were based on ancestral precedent, including not only the original traditions of the *mwiriga* concerned, but subsequent interpretations reached by earlier generations of *kiama* elders over similar conflicts. Collective recollection of these earlier judgments supplied a body of oral precedent from which current solutions could be drawn with reasonable expectation of conforming to tradition. The ultimate function of a *kiama*, therefore, was to determine whether conflicts arising among the living had caused those involved to depart from patterns of behavior laid down by their ancestors.

Thus by implication, every facet of human conflict acquired not only temporal but supernatural significance. Since all violations of person or property were defined automatically as departures from custom, they were the concern not only of the direct protagonists, but of their families, clans and ultimately even those ancestors whose traditions were involved. *Biama*, then, were expected to maintain social equilibrium not only among living members of the *mwiriga*, but between those members and their ancestors. Only by so doing could its members uphold both the temporal and spiritual harmony considered essential for the continued survival of the community.

To understand fully the operation of a *mwiriga* one must therefore examine not only its secular structure, but also the supernatural elements related to it. The Meru identified five of these, each capable of altering human existence. The most powerful was the Creator (*Ngai, Murungu*). He was referred to only in the singular, and envisioned as a separate, distant entity, living either in the skies or atop the peak of Mt. Kenya. His primary relationship to man was reflected in the praise names men bestowed upon Him,[9] all of which suggested manifestations of the weather. If angered, *Ngai* could withhold his blessing. If placated, he was beneficent. However, his relationship was with the entire Meru people, and thus beyond the influence of individuals or even a *mwiriga*. He was envisioned as Creator and Upholder of a framework within which humanity could live. Beyond this, no one could say.[10]

7

A second supernatural element was *nkoro* (core, heart). The Meru were well aware of what happened to a body after death. Corpses either rotted or were picked clean by hyenas. Nevertheless, they were equally certain that even after death the *nkoro* inherent within each person remained aware of his surroundings and those that had formed his family. After dissolution of the body, the *nkoro* simply remained in the vicinity, observing the development of his descendants.[11]

The third of these elements was therefore a logical extension of the second. If individual awareness is believed to continue after death, there must also be continuity of kinship beyond the grave. Accordingly, deceased kin whose *nkoro* had entered the supernatural sphere were collectively known as *nkoma* (ancestral spirits). They were believed to be similar in several ways to the living. Physically, they were alleged to look like normal human beings, with each person reflecting his age at death. Geographically, they were believed to reside in dense forest groves near the homesteads of their descendants, particularly those atop high places, such as ridge-backs or hills.[12]

Nkoma were also closely asociated with watering places, whether flowing rivers or certain deep pools, also alleged to harbor nature spirits which would periodically assume the forms of huge snakes.[13] They were also said to frequent specific paths, forest clearings, and areas containing salt (allegedly desired by their cattle), chalk and ochre.[14]

Nkoma differed from other elements of the Meru supernatural in the frequency of their contacts with the living. Contact was believed to occur in four major forms. The first, accidental meeting, happened simply as a result of the normal activities which made up *nkoma* existence. Left undisturbed within their forest groves, *nkoma* were believed to continue the tasks they had followed in life. Informants living on the fringes of such groves have reported hearing sounds of eating, drinking, dancing and the herding of cattle towards water or salt. At certain seasons, the *nkoma* could also be heard singing, particularly songs associated with circumcision and war.[15] Under such circumstances, an accidental encounter could result from gathering wood too near their forested area or walking down a path at an inopportune moment and seeing one or more of them appear. This type of contact, although unintentional, would cause great anxiety to the person concerned, as it was believed to be followed inevitably by some form of personal calamity.[16]

Conversely, communication with *nkoma* could have benevolent consequences. *Nkoma* were believed to live near those families descended from them, observing their daily activities and taking pleasure in the development of their heirs. The living reciprocated this attention by practicing a variety of rituals designed to show the respect due the ancestral dead.

In exchange for such remembrance, individual *nkoma* were believed to appear occasionally to one of their descendants, usually small children or the very old. These appearances occurred most frequently in dreams, but also took the form of disembodied voices speaking in the forest. The purpose of this type of visitation was invariably to offer advice, either a warning of an impending calamity or guidance as to mitigating its effects.[17]

The third form of contact was for purposes of transmitting some aspect of supernatural lore. It most frequently occurred during times set aside for circumcision, when *nkoma* were believed to transmit the knowledge of divination. During this period, songs sung by *nkoma* could be heard clearly from their forests. Families living near such areas would caution one another that *nkoma* were circumcising their young, and enjoin their own children to stay away.

Notwithstanding, certain children within the *mwiriga* would be visited by *nkoma* at night. Traditionally this first occurred in early childhood, before children acquired the second set of teeth. In such instances, weapon-bearing warriors were believed to appear in the child's hut, seize him, and then bear him to a body of water within their forest grove. During this time, they would be singing the songs of their own circumcision, while exhorting the child to be brave.

Mute with a mixture of respect and terror, the child would be circumcised, to the extent that the foreskin of his penis would be folded back to expose the glans. The foreskin would be neither permanently cut, nor left hanging beneath the penis, both actions essential to adult circumcision. However, the folded skin would remain permanently in its new position and resist all subsequent attempts to restore it to the old form.

After completing the circumcision, the *nkoma* would give the boy such articles as were required for his particular type of divination (tobacco, a gourd, etc.). They then commanded him to look at them in order to tell others whatever they required. He was then returned to the hut from which he had been taken, his changed condition to be discovered in the morning. Thereafter, the boy would discover a gift within himself for divination. If he resisted using what he had learned, or concealed his changed condition, subsequent visits from *nkoma* would remind him of his obligation to implement their wish.[18]

Nkoma appeared most frequently, however, to those who had departed from some aspect of ancestral tradition. Such departure, whether intentional or not, was said to disturb the harmony which existed between those persons and their forebears. By departing, violators placed themselves automatically in a condition of ritual impurity (*mugiro*). If not rapidly corrected, the condition itself would invariably bring on some form of personal calamity (illness, death, injury, barrenness, etc.), either to the persons themselves, their property (livestock, etc.), families, lineages or clans.

This condition of *mugiro*, with its attendant assurance of misfortune, formed the fourth supernatural element.[19] While in this condition a person was considered impure (unclean) by other members of the society, and thus barred from many of its normal activities, principally those concerned with sex. The result was a ritualized form of ostracism, which could be terminated only by the person's decision to restore the previous condition of harmony. This in turn could be done only by appropriate ceremony and sacrifice, intended to appease not merely the living he had wronged, but the *nkoma* of his lineage, angry at his departure from their traditions. The condition thus served as the ultimate form of social sanction against potential deviant behavior.

A person could become ritually impure in two ways. One was by inadvertent violation of ancestral customs. Thus *mugiro* could occur during the ordinary course of nature, as when in contact with such customarily unclean activities as menstruation, childbirth, or death. It might also result from certain inadvertent acts, such as the touching of a corpse, or as the consequence of actions by children, animals or even inanimate objects. Thus, a child climbing across its parents' bedding, the discovery of hyena dung before a hut, the collapse of a homestead or the hoot of an owl were all considered indications that those concerned had entered conditions of ritual impurity.[20]

The second, more serious, type of *mugiro* was acquired through deliberate violation of tradition. This could also occur in two ways. Violation of personal or property rights involved automatic departure from ancestral standards of behavior. Thus persons could incur *mugiro* through the wrath of the *nkoma* involved. Alternately, one person could place the condition on another, either by publicly cursing him ("Him who has wronged me, let him sicken . . .") or utilizing the services of an appropriate specialist, skilled in the placing of curses. The consequence in each case was either ritual expiation or personal calamity.

The Ritual Specialists

It is now possible to examine both the secular and supernatural capacities of a *mwiriga* in regard to its function of maintaining social order. The scope of this task was initially delineated by the Meru conception of conflict. Conflict, whether between two living persons or a man and his ancestors, inevitably produced feelings of disharmony, expressed in wishes to harm another person or cause him some form of misfortune. This disharmony was believed in turn to be inevitably followed by natural calamity, usually taking the form of accident, illness or death. The explanation of any form of human misfortune was therefore attainable by seeking the cause of the original disharmony and resolving the conflict that had created it.

When presented with this problem, both potential and actual victims of such misfortune could seek the origins of their troubles through recourse to certain rituals, known only to specialists in the supernatural. A wealthy farmer, for instance, if uneasy that some recent act had provoked either human or ancestral hostility, could try to avert the inevitable retribution by rituals permitting him to foresee the future. A specialist in these practices was called a prophet. In Kimeru, as in English, the term 'prophet' has two meanings. In the Biblical sense, it is defined as one whom God has selected to communicate His words to an entire people. In Meru, this task was fulfilled by a single person, the *mugwe*, who served as intermediary between the Meru peoples and Ngai.[21]

The term 'prophet' can also refer to foretelling the future, usually in an effort to warn those concerned of impending calamity. Most *miiriga* had foretellers (*aroria*, sing: *muroria*), who could be visited by either individuals or representatives of the entire group for consultations regarding possible problems in questions of harvest, travel and war.

Foretelling traditionally took two forms, interpretation of dreams and examination of goats. Both skills were hereditary in that the required knowledge was held within comparatively few families and transmitted from fathers to selected sons. Training was by 'participant observation.' A son would accompany his father as he worked, observing aspects of his technique until he mastered them. 'Foretellers of goats' would learn to recognize certain signs in an animal's flesh, blood and organs which would forecast misfortune for its owners.[22] 'Foretellers of dreams' (*araithe wa iroto*) would interpret them in such a manner as to permit the dreamers to avoid impending harm.[23] If harm appeared likely, both types of seer could provide the potential victim with ritual appropriate to forestall it, thus alleviating the anxiety as it arose.

On occasion, however, calamity would strike despite such precautions: a person fell ill, his livestock sickened, a child died, a wife failed to conceive. In certain instances, specific physical ailments would appear which were universally accepted as supernaturally imposed. The afflicted person, realizing his condition, would immediately suspect that he had been ritually poisoned (Kimeru: cursed), either directly by personal enemies or through the efforts of a ritual-poisoner (*murogi*: the curser, the poisoner; pl: *arogi*).[24]

There could be many ritual poisoners within a *mwiriga*. Knowledge of the craft (*urogi*: cursing, poisoning) was restricted to a limited number of families, but could be passed by fathers to selected sons. Methods of training were similar to those used with other ritual specialties. A son would follow his father into the forests, moving only at night to escape detection. Protected by charms from attacks by wild animals,[25] they would gather the objects required for their task: plants, roots, decayed animal parts, all generally known for their toxic nature.[26] Upon collection, the substances were either burned to ash or ground to powder, then placed in pieces of a ritually broken pot, or within antelope horns. The vessels were then placed in a single hiding place, traditionally a cave far from the ritual poisoner's home, lest their very proximity bring vexation to those within.[27]

To place a curse, the *murogi* would mix his materials (*mithega*, sing., *muthega*: poison, magic)[28] in a ritually broken pot or gourd. This would thereafter be buried near the homestead where an intended victim slept, often with the edge exposed to assure subsequent discovery. The *murogi*

11

would then pass, alone or in the company of other ritual-poisoners, seven times around the victim's sleeping place declaiming the desired curse and chanting the accompanying ritual.

The chant ('Tui . . . tui . . . tui . . . tui') would be loud enough for everyone in the afflicted homestead to hear. Neither the specific affiction nor the particular person was ever named ('Let him who has wronged us . . .'), since the malediction and attendant *mugiro* were believed to fall automatically upon whichever person within the chanting circle of *arogi* had most greatly wronged another.[29]

The final steps in the procedure shed most light upon this ritualist's social role. The partial exposure of the buried *mithega*, as well as the accompanying chant, suggest that the knowledge of having been cursed played a major part in precipitating the subsequent calamity, particularly when this took the form of physical illness or death. Further, the fact that no one within an afflicted homestead could know for certain which person had been singled out must have led all within the chanting circle to search their souls for actions which could have wronged the chanters.

It must be emphasized, however, that the danger of the ritual-poisoner and the fear in which his craft was held by all society, did not lie solely within his own capacity for personal malevolence. In any case these dangers would have been limited to those few persons who crossed his way. It lay instead in the range of services he offered his community, for through his existence every man in the *mwiriga* could be his own *murogi*.

In theory, the rituals of *urogi* were secret and the identity of its practitioners was unknown. In practice, they must have been known to those who used their services, and thus strongly suspected by all. Tradition states that persons convicted of practicing *urogi* have been executed throughout Meru history. Notwithstanding, the executioners' inability to stamp out the practice, despite community knowledge of its practitioners' identity, suggests that it met some deeper social need.

During the fieldwork period of this study, each informant interviewed was quick to suggest others who knew more about (the work of) *arogi* than he, implying that the persons named were either practicing the rituals or had done so in the past. In practice, it was not difficult to determine which persons were considered by their community to be past or present practitioners. It should have been no less difficult in pre-colonial times.

Nonetheless, it does not follow that those under the suspicion of their neighbors are (or were) practitioners in fact. It can even be argued that no actual practitioners existed, except in the collective imagination of society. No informant, for example, proved willing to identify (by full name) a specific practitioner, even one from the historic past. Nor did any admit to having personally seen or heard such practitioners at their work, although they mentioned others that had.

Despite this evidence, however, it appears that the concept of *urogi* was an essential element of the Meru world view, identical to the role played by "evil" within the Christian heritage. Western societies that lacked scientific explanations for the origins of either physical calamity (famine, illness, etc.), or anti-social behavior (violence, adultery, etc.) tended to attribute them to a malevolence beyond their understanding, often personalizing it in the symbolic figure of the devil. Pre-colonial Meru, lacking explanations for the same problems, seem to have projected their origins onto the equally symbolic form of the *murogi*.

Both European and Meru communities have periodically purged themselves of the suspected agents of these symbolic figures, especially after the occurrence of natural calamities (plague, famine, etc.). Usually, this has taken the form of executing aged and isolated members of their societies. Yet no purge, however extensive, sufficed to destroy belief in the alleged agents' continued existence, since survival of the forces they represented (evil, *urogi*) was necessary to explain the continued persistence of calamity and human misbehavior. In short, the symbolic figure of the ritual poisoner survived because its presence served society.

Traditions suggest, for instance, that while *arogi* could indeed be asked to aid in personal vendettas, they could also work to restore the internal harmony of a community which found its social equilibrium endangered. The most frequently cited instance of such action concerns the ability of ritual poisoners to bar the unwarranted or unprecedented emergence of persons to positions of power over their fellows. Such acts, especially if in violation of ancestral precedent, were certain to draw the resentment of those subordinated. This, in turn, could lead to a restoration of the traditional social balance by recourse to the service of *arogi*.

Such instances occurred in several localities during the first years of the colonial era, where young men of inappropriate standing were arbitrarily appointed "chief." In Upper Mwimbe, one of these appointees seized the opportunity to attempt eradication of certain ancestral customs of which both he and the colonial power disapproved, among them the circumcision of females. In this instance, balances which could ordinarily have operated to check the young chief were of no avail, since each attempt to subordinate him to the control of appropriate *biama* was met by appeals to the colonial government and the arrest of all *biama* elders involved. In such circumstances, ritual poisoning seemed the only means available to restore the traditional social equilibrium.[30]

It is inadequate, therefore, to dismiss the rituals of *urogi* with the term 'malevolent.' Nor does it suffice to define the social role of its practitioners as nothing more than a channel for personal vengeance, a Meru parallel to the 'hired gun.' In one sense, *arogi* served as the ultimate stabilizers of secular society, an ever present threat to those attempting change. In another, *arogi* served as catalysts for the entire series of relationships between the living and their ancestors. Not only did their activities provide an explanation for many of the calamities of life, but their continued presence, whether real or imagined, made possible the development of other rituals to overcome them.

Once faced with personal calamity, for instance, a victim first concerned himself with its cause. He learned this by approaching specialists skilled in various rituals of detection (*uringia*: to detect, divine). The origin

13

of this ability differed from that of all other ritual specialists, in that it was not transmitted from fathers to sons, but through selection by *nkoma*. As previously mentioned, *nkoma* would visit the chosen person early in his childhood. They would then circumcise him, present him with the tools of his trade, and command him to practice it. Thereafter, "reflections of what needed to be seen"[31] would come unbidden into the mind of the curse-detector (*muringia*, pl: *aringia*), and he needed only to explain them.

The skill of *uringia* was not necessarily welcomed, either by the chosen one, his family, or his clan. For the latter, circumcision of a member by *nkoma* suggested that not he but the entire social unit might have incurred ancestral wrath. This would in turn suggest the necessity of ceremonial rites and sacrifices, both to assure themselves that the possibility was invalid or to expiate themselves should it be true. Additional sacrifices were required if *nkoma* should visit the individual again. Still others would be needed during the boy's formal circumcision, when the foreskin was finally cut and shaped according to the pattern required by adulthood.[32] The feelings displayed by kin on such occasions were not ones of anger, but embarrassment at having been thrust unwittingly into contact with a condition of ritual impurity, where such sacrifices had to be made.[33]

Selection as a *muringia* was also an embarrassment to the individual involved. This was particularly acute during his time of warriorhood, when peer-group members would taunt him for "reliance on dreams instead of courage."[34] Even when they sought his services, this ability kept him apart from them, and he was always denied full access to their fellowship. Only on reaching maturity did the skill begin to assume positive aspects for those who possessed it, since it permitted acquisition of livestock in return for the services rendered.

Specialists in the rituals of detection performed two tasks, the location of objects lost through calamity and identification of its cause, each requiring a degree of sub-specialization among practitioners. Thus, one *muringia* might be known primarily for his ability to deal with such minor mishaps as the loss or misplacement of objects. A second could specialize in the location of children who had strayed. A third could detect thieves; a fourth, adulterers; a fifth, destroyers of property, etc. Notwithstanding, the purpose underlying all detection was the same: to determine whether the cause of each calamity lay in the anger of *nkoma*, or the malevolence of man.[35]

To accomplish this, the *muringia* would begin by asking each victim to describe the misfortune which had befallen him and his own suspicions as to its origin. As this period of interrogation was a public activity, the victim's own convictions on the subject might be qualified by those accompanying and observing him, often every male member of his *mwiriga*. The questioning could go on for as long as required, often the better part of a day. Its purpose was to establish which (if any) ancestral tradition the afflicted was likely to have broken, and thus which person (or *nkoma*) he was likely to have wronged.[36]

The interrogation was considered complete when the number of potential suspects (whether human or spirit) had been reduced to three or four.

At this point, a single gourd, marked with symbols known only to the *muringia*, was produced, then filled with colored powder. A number of sticks, seeds or stones were selected, each of which was to symbolize one possible originator of the calamity. If men were suspected, each object would be given the name of a man; if *nkoma*, the name of a known ancestor. The objects were placed inside the gourd. It was shaken, and the pattern in which they fell upon the ground determined the final result. Once a decision was reached with one set of objects, a second group was collected and the process repeated. The repetitions continued until victim, onlookers and *muringia* had agreed on three points: the type of *mugiro* that had occurred, the reason for its appearance, and the specific entity (whether human or ancestral) that had caused it.[37]

Only after acquiring this knowledge could the victim seek further assistance, usually a specialist able to assist him in the appropriate "rituals of removal." This class of specialists was generally known as *aga* (sing: *muga*: the curse remover). There could be several within a *mwiriga*, but the skills involved were transferable only between fathers and sons.

A son selected to inherit his father's position would begin during childhood to accompany his father on trips into surrounding forests, helping him gather and prepare the required materials. As was the case with the ritual poisoner, these consisted of roots, plants, animal parts, minerals and certain objects valued only for their scarcity.[38] The process differed from *urogi*, however, in that it took place in daylight, with no attempt to conceal the *muga's* activities from public view. Once collected, the objects were burnt to ash or ground to powder. These were mixed with the blood of a ritually slaughtered goat, then stored in antelope horns, bamboo tubes or gourds. These vessels in turn were placed in an animal skin bag (*kiondo*), which the *muga* kept in his hut until it was needed.

Rituals involving the removal of *mugiro* could take two forms, each of which required the services of a different type of specialist. Victims whose condition had been imposed by a human agency, either directly or with aid from a ritual-poisoner, were sent to the type of *muga* who specialized in counteracting human curses (*muragoli*; pl: *aragoli*). The *muragoli* would effect his cures primarily through the use of plant or animal matter. These mixtures would be not only swallowed, but smeared over portions of the afflicted person's body, thus alleviating both the mental anxiety and physical symptoms the condition of *mugiro* had induced.[39]

Alternately, if the rituals of detection showed that the curse had been placed upon him by *nkoma*, the detector would direct him to a second type of curse-remover (*muraguri*, pl: *araguri*), one who specialized in removing *mugiro* that had been supernaturally imposed (*muraguri*). This type of cure would be effected primarily through the slaughter of a goat. The blood would be mixed with the ash or powders from the *muraguri* stock. Its hoofs would be dipped in the mixture, then licked by the practitioner himself, to indicate that no poison had been used. The goat's intestines were then wrapped around the victim's wrists and arms, then cut, as the *muraguri* chanted the rituals of removal.[40]

Ceremonies of removal were invariably followed by those of redress. No victim's anxiety could be truly alleviated by removal of a *mugiro* if the agent that had imposed it was undetected and thus able to repeat the curse. If the condition had been imposed by *nkoma*, the *muraguri* could arrange appropriate rituals of conciliation. If the agent were a human being, however, the victim had two further choices. He could seek supernatural redress, usually by placing a curse in his turn on the individual detected by the *muringia*. Alternately, he could seek secular redress by turning to the appropriate *kiama*.

However, even the *kiama* would rely as much on supernatural as secular means to conduct its proceedings. Its very decision to meet would be based on the accusations made as the result of curse-detection. Thereafter, the antagonists, accuser and accused, together with elders gathered from both their clans, could be asked to begin the deliberations by the sacrifice of a goat, symbolic of the fact that a condition of conflict (disharmony) existed within two sections of the *mwiriga* as the result of alleged violation of ancestral traditions.[41] Thereafter, the truth of the matter would be determined not only by interpretation of relevant oral precedents, but with spiritual assistance acquired through recourse either to oath or physical ordeal.

If the *kiama* decided to utilize oaths in its search for the truth, units of both the defendant's and plaintiff's livestock would be sacrificed. Various forms were used, which in essence required all concerned to swear that their lives, as well as those of their lineage, clan, etc., would be forfeited if their version of the conflict were incorrect ("If I am lying, let this oath kill me").

The pattern was similar if the *kiama* elected to settle the matter by recourse to ordeal. Having decided, they would request the services of another type of ritual specialist—the 'dispenser of iron' (*mugwatithania-gikama*).[42] In Imenti and Igoji, the iron referred to was a heated bar which protagonists would pass from hand to hand to prove their guilt or innocence. In Mwimbe and Muthambe, it was a heated sword which all involved would lick.

The dispenser of this ordeal could learn the skills necessary for the process only from his father, by observing him in all phases of his work. Preparation involved the collection of certain vegetable products, primarily leaves from which sap could be drawn to rub on the iron, the hands (or lips) of participants and on those of the dispenser himself.

During the ritual, accuser and accused stood on opposite sides of a fire, while the iron was heating. The dispenser would seize it and go through the ritual in the prescribed manner, handling or licking it while chanting the appropriate oath. ("If I am guilty, let this iron burn me . . ."). Each of the antagonists would follow suit, symbolically laying their lives at the disposal of the supernatural by inviting its vengeance as punishment for untruths.

Antagonists choosing to undergo either oaths or ordeals were thereafter considered to be ritually impure; thus they were excluded from certain forms of social contact until the *mugiro* had brought calamity to the guilty. In practice, the condition would endure until a decision was reached on the matter by the *kiama* concerned. Usually, this would occur through the

16

death or illness of one of the contenders or of any male relation who had been included in the oath. If no calamity occurred to either side within a stipulated time, some aspect of the ritual itself was considered to have been at fault, and the entire ordeal would be repeated. The procedure continued until a decision was finally reached and the question of redress was settled.

Rituals of redress would be followed quickly by those of reconciliation. Once a decision was reached on an issue, whether by elders' debate or ancestral vengeance, the person judged at fault would be required to restore the previous condition of harmony which had existed between his social unit (family, clan, etc.) and that of his opponent.

The first step in the process was achieved through payment of some portion of his property to the victim. Usually such payment was in units of livestock, according to the seriousness of the offense.[43] The second step involved another livestock payment, this time to the *kiama* elders who had condemned him. Early European administrators, noting that these animals were immediately devoured by the elders involved, interpreted the practice as either payment of "court fees," "fines," or "bribes to the judges." To the Meru participants, however, such payment was merely symbolic of the desire of all concerned for both communal and spiritual propitiation. The animal delivered was traditionally a sheep, the beast considered symbolic of conciliation because of its peaceful nature.[44] It was eaten by the *kiama* elders and all those who had been most intimately involved.

The act of slaughtering the animal and sharing its meat served as a token affirmation of the willingness of all concerned to restore the condition of harmony which had existed among them prior to the incident. Spiritual concurrence with this decision was assured by obligatory sacrifices of small portions of the meat before the feasting, and continuous invocation of ancestral blessing on all who had been concerned. Only after these rituals of conciliation were complete could the responsible *kiama* and indirectly the *mwiriga* itself be considered to have fulfilled its conciliatory task.

It is now possible to examine the relationship of the ritual specialists to their *mwiriga* as a whole. Obviously, these practitioners did not work in isolation, from either one another or the community at large. Neither did they practice in opposition to society. Even those agents considered malevolent by the Meru themselves played roles identical to those of their benevolent counterparts. Each specialist, regardless of his work, gave other men hope of at least temporary control over the supernatural forces they so feared, yet required as explanations of the calamities that dominated their lives.

It seems possible to conclude, therefore, that the ritual specialists within each *mwiriga* acted together with the elders' councils to make up a single system of both temporal and spiritual redress, at least roughly comparable with our own.[45] Within this framework, various components of the system (*arogi, aga, aringia, biama,* etc.), operated continuously both to create and to conciliate the secular and supernatural conflicts that were inevitable in Meru society. By so doing, they were able to maintain perpetually the social equilibrium of their *mwiriga*, thus assuring its survival.

The Fringe Communities

The authority of the *mwiriga* did not apply equally to all members of Meru society. Certain individuals were either partially or totally beyond its scope, primarily those whose occupations had operated over time to place them on the fringes of traditional life.

Two of these groups seem to have emerged prior to the Meru arrival on Mt. Kenya. Traditions collected from every Meru section suggest that their ancestors originally lived on the island of Manda, adjacent to the northern Kenya coast.[46] During this period the ironsmiths had ready access to the type of iron-sand required for their work. During the early 1700s, the Meru people left their island to begin a migration that would eventually take them to their current area. In consequence, the smiths no longer had access to their traditional supplies and spent much time away from the primary migrant group searching for sources to replace them. In so doing, they cut themselves partially away from the mainstream of Meru social life, developing rites and traditions of their own associated with malevolent curses, which estranged them from agricultural members of the community and placed them and their descendents at its fringe.

A similar pattern developed among those families that, from the beginning of their migration, had chosen to hunt wild game (*aathi ba nyamoo*: meat-hunters) or honey (*aathi ba uuki*: honey-hunters), rather than practice herding or cultivation. Like iron-smiths, males from these groups spent much of their time away from the agricultural community, to the point where their social patterns increasingly diverged. These initial differences were formalized among both hunting and agricultural groups by creation of taboos forbidding members of one occupation to share food with those of the other. People who ate game, for example, were forbidden to drink cow's milk; those who did so were forbidden to hunt wild animals. In consequence, members of hunting groups found themselves in positions similar to those of the iron-smiths—within the Meru community, but restricted to its fringe.

One result of this growing divergence was the development, among both iron-smiths and hunters, of their own systems of social regulation. Each occupational group, for instance, evolved systems of *biama* (*kiama kia aturi*, *kiama kia aathi ba nyamoo*, etc.) modeled along lines established by the agriculturalists, but independent of their influence. Similarly, each group developed its parallel system of ritual specialists, again with functions similar to those who served the agriculturalists, but outside of their control.

Thus, a curse with its attendant condition of ritual impurity could be imposed by members (or ancestral spirits) of an agricultural *mwiriga* (*mugiro jwa mwiriga*), one of the hunting groups (*mugiro jwa aathi*), or the community of smiths (*mugiro jwa aturi*). A victim, on applying to the curse-detector for the cause, would be referred to a curse-remover appropriate to the circumstances. Such a person would be referred to by his contemporaries as a *muga jwa mwiriga*, *muga jwa aathi*, or *muga jwa aturi*, depending on whether he specialized in removal of *mugiro* imposed by agriculturalists, hunters or smiths.

During the period of migration, traditions suggest that both smiths and hunters relied on a system of verbal curses, proclaimed publicly against those who wronged one or more of their members. In effect, these were imposed by convening all male members of the group, who would then march through the agricultural community chanting the conditions of the *mugiro* ("Let him who has wronged us be . . .") to be placed upon the persons involved.[47]

After the Meru arrived on Mt. Kenya the system of verbal cursing used by the *aturi* remained essentially unchanged. That of the *aathi*, however, continued to evolve in a manner that affected not only their own groups but those of the agrarian *miiriga* as well. During the migration, neither hunters nor honey-gatherers felt the need to protect specific areas of land for their exclusive use. Once on the mountain, however, both groups were forced by the pressure of slowly advancing agriculturalists to push farther and farther uphill. An area initially utilized for hunting and gathering, therefore, would be coveted by increasing numbers of agrarians, forced upward by the exhaustion of previous land, the very presence of which dispersed the initial concentrations of game. In consequence, the *aathi* found themsleves deprived of livelihood and were forced to move on.

Aathi biama reacted initially to this pattern of encroachment with traditional systems of verbal curses. These were partially robbed of their effectiveness, however, by the difficulty of knowing when agriculturalists had actually penetrated regions considered by the *aathi* as their own. Nor were the farmers always aware of such a violation. Thus, with no feelings of anxiety or guilt, they could penetrate territory claimed by *aathi*. The initial system, therefore, was supplemented by a second concept possibly adopted from Ogiek hunting communities with which the *aathi* came in contact when first entering the forests of Mt. Kenya.[48]

This new method involved marking off, with a series of large sticks (*ndindi*: bones), approximately three feet long, areas reserved for either hunting or honey-gathering. These were taken from the wood of a specific tree, intricately carved, and smeared with red ochre, then ritually cursed by the hunter.[49] Each stick would then act automatically to impose a *mugiro* upon every person who passed it, since all who did so would have violated an *aathi* area.

This second system had two advantages over the first. One lay in its service as a warning system, since the mere sight of *ndindi* sticks served to keep agriculturalists away. The second lay in its psychological impact on the victims. Since imposition of *mugiro* was automatic, there was no need for *aathi* to keep watch on their areas nor to tour farming communities proclaiming general curses. Instead, a victim's own sense of guilt proved sufficient to produce the expected physical symptoms or other calamities. He, in turn, had no choice but to divulge his guilt to the *aathi* themselves, since only they could remove their own *mugiro*.

For instances where the threat of *ndindi* proved insufficient, *aathi*

19

communities developed more intensive variations of their initial concept. In cases where individuals began to cultivate in areas protected by *ndindi* a second type of stick (*nguchua*: claws) would be used. *Nguchua* were two inches long, hollowed and shaped like a claw.[50] They were marked and cursed in traditional *aathi* manner, then placed in ground adjacent to an offender's hut. The *aathi* would then pass in procession by the victim's homestead, chanting "Those who eat (the property) of *aathi* let them die." Thus warned, the intended victim would discover the *nguchua* and react accordingly.

In still more serious cases, when an entire agricultural community would begin cultivation in regions *aathi* had designated as their own, the hunters would respond with their most potent form of malediction. In this instance the entire *kiama kia aathi* would circle the agricultural community involved, its leading member carrying the corpse of a small gazelle (*kallai kia aathi*). The animal had been stuffed with a ritual mixture (*mithega*) containing the ashes of a newly burned hyena cub, a local tree-parasite (*keia*), and a monkey. While circling the village, the entire group chanted the curse. The inhabitants then sickened and died, for those cursed with *kallai kia aathi* could never have their *mugiro* removed.[51]

Persons afflicted with less potent forms of *mugiro*, however, could seek removal of their condition in the same manner as previously described. The procedure was similar in all respects but one. The afflicted victim, having learned from a curse-detector that his *mugiro* had originated from the anger of a *mwathi* (*mu-aathi*: man of *aathi*), would then go to the appropriate curse-remover. The *muga jwa aathi* would then remove the *mugiro* in a way initially similar to that used by other *aga*.

The oaths used to complete *aathi* rites of removal, however, differed from those of the agriculturalists in one major respect. They were intended not only to lift the *mugiro*, but to prevent recurrence of the violation which caused it. Prevention was achieved by creating a ritualized kinship (*uthoni*: relationship, kinship) between the victim and all members of the society concerned, a ceremony of mutual adoption, in which the victim became brother to the hunters and they to him. The result was to bind the victim to their *kiama* in such a way as to virtually incorporate him into its membership. Although permitted to remain an agriculturalist, he was required to submit all quarrels to its authority and to contribute to its frequent feasts a share of meat, either wild game or an equivalent amount of domestic livestock.[52] Refusal to meet such obligations or any other action against *aathi* interests would result in re-imposition of the *mugiro* and his subsequent death.

It should be noted that the supernatural systems developed by both the hunters and the iron-smiths were initially defensive, the response of numerical minorities to the threat of encroachment by the more numerous agriculturalists. The curse, whether publicly proclaimed or inherent within a wooden boundary-marker, was reserved only for those who first encroached upon the interests of the fringe community involved. However, the concept inevitably proved attractive to other minorities, specifically agriculturalists whose lands were closest to the forest.

Thus, during the early 1800s, a third form of supernatural protection appeared as groups of agriculturalists applied the earlier *aathi* concepts to their own situations. The result was reflected in the emergence of several new supernatural *biama* (*biama kia mithega*: councils of magic) within every agrarian area of Meru, first within those *mwiriga* closest to the forest and subsequently among those lower down the mountain. These new agrarian groups[53] followed practices similar to those of *aathi*. Each *kiama* collected bundles of sticks from specific trees (or bushes), the wood of which was sacred to its particular ideology. These were placed around an agricultural area to protect it against intrusion in a manner similar to that used by hunters.

A new element was then added. A long vine was selected from a tree held sacred by each society. This would be looped entirely around the area to be protected, except for a single narrow gap known only to the owner. Some groups laid their vine along the ground. Others hung it from tree branches. All made certain that it would touch the ritually prepared sticks, thus reinforcing their initial power. Both sticks and vines were then cursed, either by an elder or by ritual specialists of the society in question. These would then act automatically to impose a condition of *mugiro* on any individual who tried to pass them, ostensibly to steal the agricultural produce within the protected field.

The afflicted person would then suffer increasing physical weakness, as well as specific illnesses which varied from subdivision to subdivision. Seeking aid, he would pass through the procedures previously ascribed to *aathi* and become permanently obligated to the group in question, submitting to its *kiama* and contributing to its feasts.[54]

Initally, membership in these new agricultural societies seems to have been restricted to those whose fields provided them with crops in sufficient quantity to require protection. During the middle 1800s, however, periods of severe famine caused the supernatural methods used by certain of these groups to evolve once more, this time from passive protection of existing crops to active acquisition of whatever food supplies could be found.

During such periods, groups whose lands could no longer provide them with sufficient sustenance[55] further modified the original rituals. Now agrarian *kiama*, whose members had traditionally acquired food only through violation of their farmlands, began to ensure the supply of victims by placing stakes and vines along public paths. Others began to enclose farmlands of wealthier landowners, leaving themselves inside. To obtain their removal, those to whom the fields belonged would be forced to pay the fees (in grain, beer, etc.) traditional for removal of *mugiro*. Refusal led to cursing of the entire group. Still others sought calamity, visiting those whom disaster had struck in order to claim themselves as the originators and thus gain the fees required for expiation.[56]

At least two of these food-acquiring groups, *kagita* and *mwaa*, evolved

21

still further into what can best be described as 'dancing associations.' During periods of crop failure, members of both groups would tour the homesteads of those known to be wealthy, singing for their suppers in a manner reminiscent of the English itinerant minstrels.

Biama of *kagita*, for instance, would send messengers to a wealthy elder announcing that they would dance and sing for him on the following day. Traditional patterns of hospitality required him to return their courtesy by preparing food and beer, out of gratitude for their exertions. The dancers would arrive in elaborate costume ("much admired by all"), and dance as well as they knew how for the spectators' delight. The songs were also intended as entertainment, but would contain sufficiently threatening undertones to remind all present of what might happen should the expected hospitality fail to occur:

> "Kagita ndi rwagi, iiiii, ndi rwagi ndathaga muntu itende . . ." (I, *kagita*, am the mosquito, yessss, the mosquito that pierces the foot . . .)[57]

By the end of the 1800s, certain of the fringe communities had learned to apply their supernatural reputation to problems other than acquisition of food. Two groups, for instance, functioned increasingly in questions of justice, serving as informal pressure groups for those of their members engaged in conflict with outsiders. Members of *kagita*, for example, could always appeal to their own *kiama* for support in any quarrel, certain that its entire membership would respond by moving *en masse* around the opponent's homestead chanting songs intended to remind the latter of their power. In similar situations, members of *mwaa* would surround the homes of persons in conflict with one of their number, expressing their support for his position by defecating over every inch of the grounds.[58]

By the beginning of this century, the newer fringe groups differed from traditional Meru social patterns in several other ways. The *biama* of all agricultural *miiriga*, as well as those of the older *aathi* and *aturi*, had traditionally been composed solely of males. The *biama* of the newer groups[59] were open to both sexes, the only pre-requisites for entry being termination of warriorhood and subsequent marriage.[60]

The position of women also varied considerably within each fringe community. In *kagita*, for example, women held subordinate roles among those of its councils which functioned in North Imenti. In South Imenti they held occasional positions of leadership and practiced the skill of curse-removal (*muga jwa kagita*, etc.). In Mwimbe, Igoji, and Muthambe, the entire organization was referred to as the *kiama* of women, in which women held all positions of authority and men joined only during feasts.[61]

The primary purpose of these younger societies had also evolved. The initial desire to acquire food in order to feast had been supplemented by the pleasures of dancing and intercourse. Among the agricultural Meru, tradition restricted dancing to warriors and unmarried girls, except for certain ritual occasions. The newer groups defied this prohibition, building particular huts for each occasion where married members of both sexes danced and copulated throughout the night.[62]

At least one of the societies (*mwaa*: fools, jesters)[63] was composed either wholly or partially of males who wished to act out the roles of females in some fashion that would win at least minimal social approval. Originally, the *kiama kia mwaa* was formed in the same manner as other new *biama*— out of those whose land could not support them in time of famine. Like *kagita* and perhaps others, it evolved from a society using supernatural means for agricultural protection into a dancing *kiama*, using its power to acquire agricultural supplies.

Initially during periods of famine, but subsequently during the dry seasons of every year, members would form into dancing groups and move from homestead to homestead, singing in exchange for food. Each member wore a cowbell and cowbone tied round his neck, the noise of which was intended to draw large crowds to serve as spectators.

The intentions of *mwaa*, however, were different than those suggested for other dancing associations. Whereas groups such as *kagita* offered little more than entertainment in exchange for supper, *mwaa*-groups used their dances as a means of providing themselves with new recruits.

Recruiting was done by a deliberate attempt to draw loud laughter among the spectators which could be interpreted by those dancing as showing lack of respect for the society. The males, dressed in both the clothing and ornaments of women, would attempt to provoke laughter among observers of both sexes by mimicking female body movements, particularly those of urination, excretion and intercourse.

Once these actions succeeded in inducing laughter, the entire troup would stop the dance and seize the spectator who laughed most. They would then formally curse him, imposing a *mugiro* that could be removed only through payment of sufficient food and beer to feed the entire troup. Thereafter, the victim would be considered a member of the *kiama*, insofar as he would be obligated to submit his quarrels to its judgment and to contribute to its future feasts.[64]

This examination raises several questions concerning the relationships which existed between Meru of the agricultural *miiriga* and those of the various fringe groups. It should be noted, as a preliminary consideration, that neither the two original fringe communities nor their later derivatives were numerically large; thus they posed no large-scale threat to the agriculturalists' existence. Nor did every agricultural *mwiriga* have to cope with the problem to the same degree. Those closer to the forest zone were more likely to be exposed to the *mugiro* of *aathi*; those nearer the plains, to the problems posed by derivative groups.

It must also be emphasized that the two older societies, whether smiths or hunters, had traditionally rendered both economic and military services to the agriculturalists. Smiths, of course, forged the weapons of war. Hunters of meat and honey often traded their catches for beads, vegetables or grain. In war, *aathi* served as the Meru 'eyes,' working as scouts during

23

offensive operations and as a form of early warning system during attack. In peace, *aathi* often served as forecasters of famine. Their studies of game animals and bees gave them often unparalleled knowledge of local systems of ecology and made possible within those systems detection of changes that allowed accurate forecasts of what would grow.[65]

In consequence, *biama* of the agricultural *miiriga* treated those of both iron-smiths and hunters with official indifference. Normally, each side ignored the other.[66] Conflicts between the cultivators and members of either original fringe group were settled only by decision of the latter since only *aga* of the community in question could remove whatever *mugiro* had been imposed. Similarly, ritual specialists serving agricultural *miiriga* were beyond the power of those serving various fringe groups. Neither side could directly curse the other, nor could they remove *mugiro* imposed by any *kiama* but their own.[67] If a farmer violated an *aathi* hunting area, for instance, only a *muga jwa aathi* could remove the subsequent curse. *Aga* of his own *mwiriga* would be powerless.[68] As a result, agriculturalist attitudes toward the older fringe communities wavered somewhere between contempt and fear. Their occupations were considered beneath those practiced in agriculture, but their supernatural abilities were held in awe.

Both these attitudes seem to have been transferred to the younger societies, particularly those which had been formed through experience with famine. The economic activities of these food-acquiring councils were detested by other agriculturalists, who regularly denounced them as "*biama* of the stomach." This contempt was balanced, however, by fear of their supernatural skills, and compounded by the willingness of these later groups to use them in ways outside those dictated by tradition.

In consequence, agrarian *biama* seem to have reacted to the evolution of later groups in the same manner that they had reacted to their earlier counterparts. Officially, they ignored them. No rituals were ever shared, whether in war or in peace. No member of a subsequent fringe society could ever aspire to membership in their *mwiriga* council. All privileges and honors that would usually accrue with eldership were denied. On the other hand, no mainstream agriculturalist could appeal to his *kiama* for support in disputes with members of the fringe; nor could protection be given to those forced to join their ranks.

Traditions dealing with the end of the nineteenth century, however, suggest exceptions to this pattern of indifference. During the 1880s and 1890s, warrior *magaaru* in certain areas of Imenti and Mwimbe began to disobey the injunctions of their respective elders' councils and attack one or more of the newer fringe groups. This disobedience occurred most frequently during the feasts of *kagita* and *mwaa*. In these instances, warriors, angry at the appearance of one or more of their own members in the ranks of the group, would attack and burn the dance-huts of the societies and temporarily disperse the membership with clubs and spears. The group would always re-form and rebuild, however, while the *kiama* concerned would unfailingly reimpose its authority on its warriors.[69]

In considering these exceptions, one must first ask why *kiama* elders were so cautious. If agriculturalists everywhere disapproved of the deviant groups that had developed within their ranks, why did they not use their numerical superiority to eliminate them? Why could the mainstream of a war-oriented society not simply stamp out its deviant fringe?

When pressed on this issue, informants reply that the fringe communities were allowed to survive because of fear of their supernatural powers. Both the original and derivative societies, for instance, protected their meeting huts with traditionally accepted forms of defensive magic, intended to impose automatic conditions of *mugiro* upon all members who approached. In Northeast Imenti, for example, meeting places of the *aathi* were defended by *nkima*, rounded objects made of bones, wax and interwoven pieces of animal skin. One of these was placed inside each hut on completion of its construction. Thereafter, it functioned in the same manner as *ndindi*, placing automatic *mugiro* upon any non-member who entered.[70] Other societies used similar objects for the same purpose. Nevertheless, these replies seem incomplete. They explain the behavior of *biama* elders, but not that of warriors, who would have been equally fearful of the supernatural deterrent of the societies, yet periodically attacked them. Nor do informants explain the ease with which these groups survived such persecution as did occur, recommencing their activities without fear of subsequent attacks.

It seems more plausible, therefore, to suggest that the mainstream, while prepared to chastise periodically groups along its fringe, never truly wished for their extermination. Instead, a society as rigidly structured as that of Meru would seem to have required the survival of such groups as a series of psychological options permitted to persons unable to perform correctly within their traditional roles.

From a Meru perspective, these options seem always to have appeared within the supernatural sphere. Thus, those unable to cope with some aspect of their secular role could opt psychologically for some form of ritual specialization, either as a single practitioner or through membership in one of the fringe communities.[71] People of both sexes who proved unwilling to endure the restrictions imposed upon marriage, for instance, opted for entry into *kagita*. Males who failed to conform to traditional masculine expectations—whether as warrior, husband or elder—could choose the limited female role play offered by *mwaa*, combining the characteristics of woman, jester, and *murogi* in such a manner as to win at least minimal social approval and awe. Additional research may suggest other examples.

It can be argued that agriculturalists could still have acted to restrict such psychological options to those considered beneficial to the community, such as the curse-detector, etc. However, the very intangibility of supernatural manipulation will inevitably suggest anti-social options to those who seek and use it. These malevolent uses, in turn, can evolve with time into practices far more devastating in their impact on society than had ever been envisioned at the moment of their birth.

This would seem to reflect the Meru experience. An initially beneficial concept, the protection of hunting zones, evolved gradually into a series of practices that grew increasingly destructive to society at large.[72] The refusal of that society to move against these practices, despite their ability to destroy them and regardless of the social dislocation they caused, suggests that these deviations were permitted alternatives to the traditional social roles. As such they served as a safety valve in a community where few other alternatives were available, thereby helping to facilitate social survival.

CHAPTER II

The Setting of War

Geographic Setting

War, like other activities, is shaped by the geography with which its practitioners must cope. In Meru, military concepts and strategies have always been primarily influenced by the surface features and ecological patterns of Mt. Kenya. Ecologically, the mountain can be divided into eight zones. The ice-capped peaks stand over 17,000 feet high; until this century they were beyond the reach of men. Below them lies a belt of open moor, circling the mountain between 11,000 and 12,000 feet. The Meru knew this region as a place of swamps, lakes and rocky ledges, which offered little protection against the icy wind. Tufted grass grew in the swampy areas, but the cold water that oozed into men's footsteps and chilling mists that obscured their way made it a region that both people and livestock preferred to avoid.

At approximately 11,000 feet, the moor changed to a zone of bamboo, which extended around the mountain to a depth of several miles. This zone was virtually impenetrable except along paths made by movements of wild game. In some areas, plants stood over twenty feet high, and so close together as to block out the sun. In others, older bamboo stalks had been pushed or blown over to form an apparently endless barrier of rotting, tangled poles, through which new shoots fought to grow. The Meru also avoided this zone. The occasional traveler willing to carve his way through found his progress hindered not only by wild game, but by thin, sharp leaves of the bamboo plant which cut human skin like a razor.[1]

Between 9,000 and 10,000 feet, the bamboo gave way in turn to a zone of "moist montane evergreen forest," referred to locally as the "black forest

27

belt."[2] Currently, this zone extends down to approximately 7,000 to 8,000 feet, but may originally have reached to the base of the mountain. It was characterized by a wide range of trees, some of which reached 150 feet, and a multi-level continuous canopy.[3] This zone provided wild game and honey for the Meru hunter-gatherers, as well as firewood for those living near its lower fringe. Notwithstanding, most Meru communities regarded it primarily as an obstacle, to be cut or burned away to make space for grazing and cultivation.

By the 1890s, the forest had already been at least partially cleared up to the 8,000 foot level in Imenti, and somewhat lower to the south.[4] The area most recently cleared had reverted to bracken, a fern of use to neither man nor livestock. This bracken zone extended along the lower fringe of the forest between 5,000 to 7,000 feet. It was a region of low fertility, particularly for nineteenth century agriculturalists. Maize yielded one limited crop per year. Bananas, pulse and root crops grew in the lowest (low bracken) areas, but came up weak and stunted.[5] In consequence, attempts at permanent habitation were rare, not only because of the infertility of the zone, but because of its constant low temperatures which the Meru found difficult to bear.

In certain sections of the bracken zone, however, the clearing of its original forest cover had allowed the growth of a species of grass known colloquially as "kikuyu grass."[6] This growth was most frequently found at an altitude of 5,500 feet, bounded both above and below by areas of "high" and "low" bracken. Unlike the bracken, however, areas dominated by kikuyu grass were of economic value to the Meru, who believed it particularly palatable to cattle. Since these areas were of slight agricultural value, no permanent habitation occurred. At certain seasons, however, entire *miiriga* would send their herds upwards into these tracts of graze.

Below 5,000 feet, the bracken zone gave way to an area originally covered by intermediate ('mixed') forest. Trees in this zone ranged from 30 to 90 feet, taking both evergreen and deciduous forms. Many years of human habitation had partially cleared the original forest cover. At this altitude, however, depletion of the original cover had permitted the appearance of "star grass," a species indicative of high soil fertility.[7]

This star grass zone was the most favorable for agriculture. It was relatively narrow, occurring in most Meru areas only between 4,000 to 5,000 feet. It was known for highly fertile soils, moderate temperatures and adequate, if irregular, rainfall. It thus permitted successful cultivation of a wide range of traditional crops, primarily millet, bananas and yams. In consequence, it became the most densely populated zone on the mountain, where a large majority of the Meru people preferred to establish homesteads.

The star grass region, however, was also marked by giant gorges which fanned radially out across the face of the mountain. Although the gradient of Mt. Kenya was gentle at this altitude, water run offs, beginning at the higher levels, had cut deep clefts into the bedrock. Many of these, by the time they reached the star grass zone, were several hundred feet deep, with slopes sufficiently steep to discourage travellers. Even the smaller streams were often up to thirty feet deep and all but impassable during rainy periods of the year.[8]

From a Meru perspective, the depth, steepness and periodic impassability of these gorges had several consequences. Their precipitous, frequently rain-swept sides made irrigation impossible, and the population was forced to rely almost wholly on rainfall.[9] Socially, they isolated the various *miiriga* from one another to a much greater extent than was the case with other Mt. Kenya societies. Large parts of Kikuyu land, for instance, were relatively devoid of such gorges. Peoples settling those areas, therefore, tended to preserve communications, retaining in consequence a greater sense of mutual identity than was possible for those in Meru. In contrast, Meru settlers divided into isolated groups, settling along narrow pockets of agriculturally desirable soil between two such gorges, then progressively losing contact with other segments of their people.

Relatively few settlers, however, chose to establish their homesteads below 4,000 feet. Below this altitude the star grass disappeared. The original vegetation, where not cleared, changed initially to dry, semi-deciduous woodland, then to thornbush and thicket around 2,000 feet. Agricultural possibilities were limited by poor soils, light rainfall and high temperatures, while the presence of both malarial mosquitoes and tsetse flies precluded either extensive herding or settlement.[10]

This woodland area, however, was of certain economic value. Millet, peas and beans could be grown between 3,000 and 4,000 feet, although the yields were far inferior to those higher up the mountain. Goats and sheep could graze portions of the lower zone in relative safety, while hunting and honey collection were extensively practiced. In addition, alkaline deposits had formed on the floors of certain swampy areas near the base of the mountain, creating a salty soil (*mwonyo*) indispensable to the survival of Meru cattle.

Beyond the woodlands zone lay virtual wasteland. Poor soils, inadequate rainfall and consistently high temperatures permitted little more than subsistence cultivation and herding small numbers of livestock. The peoples of Tharaka maintained themselves within this area, chiefly by cultivating a few more favored sections, but the larger portion was uninhabited except when traversed by herding societies, such as the Galla (Orma) or Maasai.

Military Considerations

From a military perspective the geography of Mt. Kenya offered the Meru unusual problems. One concerned the selection of targets. The highest zones offered none. The barren nature of the surrounding lowlands, unless temporarily inhabited by nomadic herders, suggested that the more permanent occupants might possess little to plunder. The more tempting communities—those holding sizeable quantities of livestock—were those living on (or near) other sections of Mt. Kenya, at altitudes approximately equal to their own.

In practice, this meant that a certain percentage of the annual raids were launched against non-Meru societies to the south: the Cuka, Embu, Mberre and Kikuyu. These "target-communities" were far distant, however, and it was often preferable to war against another Meru group, either in the adjoining Nyambeni areas (Tigania, Igembe) or on Mt. Kenya itself.[11]

The decision to attack another Meru unit, however, could also pose unusual problems. Obviously, the moor, bamboo and montane forest belts would prove difficult to traverse, particularly if raiders burdened themselves with captured herds. Nor could potential attackers hope to cross the heavily populated star grass zone without losing the element of surprise, as word of their passage would always precede them. For the same reason, no raiding party could expect to return through the star grass area, particularly if driving captured livestock. Not only would raiders be slowed by the need to negotiate numerous gorges, but their escape route could be continuously observed and transmitted both to pursuers and their possible allies. These, in turn, might collaborate to ambush and thus eliminate the raiding force.

There were also objections to traversing the woodlands zone. The upper portion, while infrequently inhabited, was still used for agriculture, hunting and gathering. Potential raiders, therefore, might lose the chance to surprise their victims through chance encounter with either cultivators or *aathi*-hunters. Discovery by the latter almost guaranteed the failure of an expedition, since most *miiriga* actively relied on *aathi* related to their members to expose surprise attacks.[12]

Alternatively, if raiders chose to traverse the thornbush and thicket areas at the base of the mountain, the chance of accidental encounter would decrease. This was offset, however, by the increased possibility of contracting either sleeping sickness or malaria. Most Meru lived above the regions infested by malarial mosquitoes and had little natural resistance to malaria. They thus considered themselves unusually subject to its effects while in the lowlands, fearing it to the point where pursuit of lowland raiders was often abandoned at the base of the mountain.[13]

Similarly, the passage of captured livestock through lowlands regions inhabited by tsetse flies could cause infection of an entire herd.[14] This in turn might spread to livestock already in the raiders' possession, leading to losses far greater than the originally anticipated gains.

In sum, the only zone favorable to both surprise attack and return with captured herds was that dominated by bracken. There were several reasons for this. Decimation of the original forest cover had provided an area permitting relatively rapid transit for both men and livestock. Low temperatures and infertile soil made the zone unfavorable to either agriculture or permanent habitation and minimized potential raiders' chances of accidental exposure.

At the same time domination of parts of this area by Kikuyu grass encouraged grazing, a practice which allowed periodic access to opponents' herds without requiring entry into their place of habitation. Finally, it was within this zone that the streams and river gorges offered least difficulty to raiders, not yet having reached the depths that they attained at lower altitudes.

Therefore, the tactics of war-leaders in every *mwiriga* were shaped by the force of geography. Most war plans called for attack on opponents in the star grass zone, whose herds were reputed to be larger than those tending them could protect. In such cases, raiders would climb from their own point in the star grass area up to the bracken, pass silently along the montane forest fringes, then descend on their victims from above. Their return followed the same pattern. Captured herds would initially be driven upwards, then sent racing along the forest edge, with attackers helping to guide them along routes unknown to their pursuers, while the latter raced ahead of them in efforts to cut them off.[15]

Historical Setting

The insecurity engendered by topographical conditions was intensified by the circumstances of Meru history. Oral evidence suggests that ancestors of the contemporary Meru approached their current area as a single group, united at least to the extent of possessing common cultural institutions. On reaching Mt. Kenya, the migrants divided at first into two units, then several.

During this period, known throughout Meru as *kagairo* (the dividing), small bands moved continually away from the main body of their compatriots. Some went north toward the western slopes of the Nyambeni mountains.[16] Others moved onto the Tigania plains. Still other groups moved into the foothills of today's Imenti, Igoji and Mwimbe regions, following river lines up the mountain slope while continuing to subdivide as circumstances required.

Traditions give no reason for this process of division, other than declaring that it occurred without war. Its cause may lie simply in the fact that various components of the original migrant group were faced with a totally new type of topography. In their efforts to exploit it, each group may have drifted gradually out of the contact with others, until acceptance of their common identity and even their common name had disappeared.

Existing oral evidence supports this possibility. Traditions concerned with either Meru origins or their period of migration consistently describe the society as a unit. In contrast, those dealing with the period on Mt. Kenya report only from the narrower perspective of single *miiriga*, a condition which continued until the era of colonial conquest.

This process of fragmentation created two problems for the males of every *mwiriga*. One concerned the drawing of wives from groups in distant areas. Although two *miiriga* might settle far apart geographically, the existence of common ancestors would still make them kin. Taking wives among such people would therefore be tantamount to incest. The root of the problem lay in the fear that time and distance would combine to erase all memory of common ancestry, and suitors might be led into unwitting violations of tradition. Conversely, the second problem was simply to avoid warfare with these same *miiriga*, since the killing of their warriors would be like slaying kin.

Both problems were compounded by the rugged nature of the terrain of Mt. Kenya, which discouraged long distance contacts of any kind. Yet even inadvertent violations, whether in regard to wives or war, were considered certain to draw supernatural vegeance. Oral literature within every Meru subdivision is filled with tales (imagined or otherwise) of such occurrences, recounted in order to emphasize the gravity of the issue involved. The pattern most frequently encountered in such narrations is as follows:[17]

1. *Warriors lie in wait to ambush strangers passing through their own territory*:
   "A party of Kiriene (a *gaaru* in Tigania) warriors set out to raid Mbere. The Cuka heard of their intention, and their warriors lay in ambush. The Kiriene scouts passed through the ambush, but when the main body came up the Cuka attacked it.

2. *No warrior able to harm another*:
   In the ensuing fight, not a single man was hurt, all the spears and other weapons having been deflected by some unknown power. (Alternate version: . . . no blood having flowed from the bodies into which the spears were stuck.)

3. *Warriors learn of past Gichiaro*:
   When both sides were utterly worn out without result, one Kiriene warrior called out "We are Kiriene; who are you that we cannot harm each other?" They sent for some Cuka elders, who slaughtered a goat and said 'There is only one answer. These Kiriene must be our brothers—sons of our mother.' And so it was forever afterwards."

In response to this problem, the Meru developed a system of identifying rituals known collectively as *gichiaro*.[18] In Kimeru, *gichiaro* means 'birth,' carrying with it the added implication that something larger than a single person was born. In the past, the expression was primarily used to suggest the birth of a degree of kinship, involving more than one person, through a process of mutual adoption. Thus, if two persons chose mutually to adopt each other, the subsequent ritual (*gichiaro*) created a condition of brotherhood between them. Thereafter, the two would be known as *ba-gichiaro*

(*gichiaro* brothers). They would address each other as brothers ('son of our mother,' 'son of our father'), and regard each other as members of a ritually created common ancestry.

Gichiaro could also be used to reaffirm a pre-existing condition of common ancestry, created at some point in the past, then forgotten by the descendants of those concerned. Thus, by proposing a mutual adoption, two persons proclaimed their own belief in descent from a common ancestor. In Kimeru, this would be expressed as the possession of common blood, which would make them kin. In practice, the common ancestry could be historically real, or ritually created by the ceremony itself. In either case, the sense of kinship forged thereby bound not only the direct participants, but their descendants in perpetuity.[19]

It is the transmission of this obligation to one's heirs that permits *gichiaro* to be discussed within the context of war and peace. Over time, the descendants of the two ritually created brothers might expand to form sizeable clans, *miiriga* or even subdivisions. By creating this type of kinship with peoples of several other areas, each group gained an increasing degree of protection. Thus, in practice, the rite of mutual adoption served the purpose of military alliance by a created sense of common ancestry sufficient to deter participants from military attack.[20]

It should be recalled, however, that a *gichiaro* relationship imposed still other obligations upon those it bound. If "brothers of one blood" could not make war on one another, neither could they seek wives (or even sex play) among the women of those recognized as distant kin. With this restriction, there was no possibility of a single *mwiriga* systematically creating conditions of ritual alliance with every other in the area. Instead, the system required that certain groups remain potentially hostile (ritually unrelated) in order to provide sufficient marriageable population.[21]

It was realized, of course, that a relationship based on the memory of distant mutual ancestry would run increasing risk of being forgotten as the population of each group increased and spread. This was particularly true in periods where unfavorable circumstances such as war or drought might cause entire *miiriga* to leave settled areas and lead relatively nomadic lives. To avoid accidental bloodshed between such groups, the original *gichiaro* required periodic reinforcement, to remind each generation of warriors of their obligations toward kin.

Alternatively, a *gichiaro* relationship might be artificially created for mutual convenience. In such instances, no genuine common ancestor would exist. Notwithstanding, a condition of permanent hostility between two *miiriga* might become increasingly irksome to both. On an appropriate occasion, spokesmen from one side would approach those of the other, to suggest the possibility of ritual alliance. They would then separate to discuss the proposed arrangement with their respective elders, while spokesmen for both groups of warriors did the same within each *gaaru*. If agreement were reached, two warriors were chosen to represent each *mwiriga* during the ritual. If they were considered leaders, it was taken as evidence

33

that the agreement was intended to bind everyone within both age-sets, and thereby their respective communities.

Details of the ritual varied only slightly throughout the area. Basically, both warriors began by sitting on the hide of an ox which had been slaughtered for the occasion. Two elders, each the spokesman of his own group, then killed a sheep, symbolic of the harmony they intended to create. The intestines of the animals were then dragged once around the seated warriors. Thereafter, two strips of skin were cut from its hind legs and wrapped by the warriors around each other's wrists. Both elders then slashed the intestines with their knives, proclaiming similar slashes as punishment for violation of the bond thus formed. Each elder then lifted the warrior representing his own group from the ox-hide and the ritual was complete.[22]

Patterns of Alliance

Two types of *gichiaro* operated within the area of this study. In the South, Muthambe and Miutini used the term to denote the existence of a distant female ancestor.[23] Thus two persons involved in this type of relationship would refer to each other as 'son of our mother' (*mutanochia*), as would their descendants. The reference would not be to an immediate biological parent, but some distant (or ritually created) 'mother' in the past. Those bound by this type of alliance (mother-*gichiaro*) were forbidden to wage war against each other. However, they could seek wives among their brothers' women.

The second form of this relationship was used by the other Meru subdivisions, as well as Miutini and Muthambe in relations with them. It was based on the existence of a real or ritually created male ancestor. Two people involved in this type of relationship would therefore refer to each other as 'son of our father' (*mutanoba*), as would their descendants. Those bound by this type of alliance (father-*gichiaro*) were forbidden to spill the blood of those considered kin, nor could they draw wives from among their women.[24]

Since the obligations incurred by *gichiaro* passed on automatically to descendants, the relationships could operate concurrently at several levels within a social unit. Individuals, families, clans, *magaaru*, *miiriga* and even entire subdivisions might be bound by differing ritual alliances with units of radically different size.

The Imenti subdivision, for example, was traditionally hostile to that of neighboring Tigania. One of its larger *miiriga*, however, (Igoki) had at one point in its past declared *gichiaro* with a single Tiganian *mwiriga* (Athuana). Within the Igoki *gaaru*, nevertheless, warriors of a single clan (Tharungai) did not share in the Athuana alliance, their ancestors having made

34

gichiaro with a different Tiganian *gaaru* (Kirieni).[25] In theory, a single family within this clan could continue the pattern by making *gichiaro* with still a different Tiganian unit, which would be shared by no one but its own descendants.

It is, therefore, oversimplifying to generalize about these relationships as they existed between subdivisions. Lambert's investigations during the early 1940s produced the following compilation of relationships within the unit, which were based on a common male ancestor:

	Imenti	Tigania	Igembe	Tharaka	Mwimbe	Igoji	Muthambe	Cuka
Imenti			G	G		G	G	
Tigania					G	G	G	
Igembe	G				G	G	G	
Tharaka	G					G	G	
Mwimbi		G	G					
Igoji	G	G	G	G			G	
Muthambe	G	G	G	G				
Cuka								

Father-*gichiaro*, Early 1940s[26]

There were many exceptions to this pattern, however, not only within but even across the formal boundaries between subdivisions. In Muthambe, for example, unusual military circumstances acted to create a pattern of ritual alliances that virtually ignored the boundary line with Cuka. In this instance, the Cuka people suffered a series of increasingly damaging attacks during the 1870s and 1880s, with raiders appearing from Imenti, Miutini and Muthambe. By the 1890s, military pressure had become so intense that the northernmost Cuka *miiriga* began gradually to withdraw from their previous boundary behind the River Mara, south, retreating to a new defensive position south of the River Ntungu.

The evacuated area was rapidly filled by the clans of Muthambe, and as their new *magaaru* were built in what had once been Cuka territory, an unusual degree of hostility arose on both sides. Rather than combine, however, individual Cuka *magaaru* tended to narrow their efforts, each focusing on destruction of the single Muthambe *gaaru* which had settled in its former home. In response, each new Muthambe *gaaru* began to direct its raiding efforts against the single Cuka *gaaru* which most threatened its existence.

To free themselves for concentration on a single enemy, each Cuka *gaaru* began to create (or reinforce) *gichiaro* arrangements with their intended victims' immediate neighbors, hoping to destroy the possibility of assistance during their anticipated attacks. Muthambe *magaaru* replied in kind. Thus a pattern emerged which simply ignored both natural bound-aries (the River Ntungu) and traditional subdivisions, creating gichiaro re-lationships solely for military convenience.[27]

In time of war, *ba-gichiaro* (*gichiaro* brothers) in every subdivision had three major obligations. The first was simply to abstain from attack on those with whom one was in ritual alliance. In practice, this was usually redefined as a prohibition against shedding the blood of a ritually created ally. It did not, however, prohibit all forms of hostile activity.

Ba-gichiaro, for instance, could join a *gaaru* to whose warriors they were traditionally hostile in a joint attack against one of their own ritual allies, sharing in the plunder, but taking care to kill no one during the fight. In the 1890s, for example, two *gichiaro* allies, Miutini (then, a single *gaaru* just south of Imenti) and Chure (a South Imenti *gaaru*) joined two groups from North Imenti (Katheri and Kitheruni), to which they were traditional-ly hostile. The four of these launched a concerted attack upon a Cuka *gaaru* that was *gichiaro* to the two southern groups.

In this instance, the southerners claimed to have played 'jackal to the North Imenti lion,' agreeing to accompany them only to assist in frighten-ing Cuka defenders away, rather than actually fighting. The risk for such 'jackal-warriors' was great, since they would be inhibited in defending themselves if attacked by a ritual ally. If the attackers did manage, howev-er, to send the defenders into flight through a display of superior numbers (as occurred in this instance), the 'jackals' might acquire considerable booty.[28]

The second obligation in time of war was to confer the rights of safe passage and sustenance to *ba-gichiaro* traversing one's area. This applied whether the ritual ally was attacking or in full flight. Thus a North Imenti *gaaru* choosing to raid a community in Cuka, could expect to find sanctu-ary in parts of Muthambe and Igoji while enroute. A Mwimbe *gaaru*, at-tacking North Imenti could find safety in parts of Igoji, South Imenti and Tigania.[29]

Aside from refuge, the main benefit to be derived from passage through the territory of a ritual ally was food, which could be "harvested" in limited quantities from the areas through which raiding parties would pass. Such food collection was limited by traditions which bound both transients and hosts. No woman from a "host area," for example, could refuse millet gruel to a party of raiders, even if giving it exhausted her available supplies. The transients, in turn, were permitted to take only as much as needed to satisfy immediate hunger. Nothing could be carried off as future supply for a cam-paign, or for subsequent barter and profit. Nor could every type of food be taken. Milk, gruel, bananas, yams and probably millet beer were permit-ted. Honey, goats, sheep, cattle and honey-beer were not.

The manner in which "permitted" foods might be acquired was also dictated by tradition. Raiders were permitted, for example, to enter an empty hut and take milk and gruel from the gourds stored there. In each instance, however, the lid of the pot from which liquid had been taken had

36

to be replaced upside down, to show that the contents had been drunk by *ba-gichiaro* entitled to it, rather than thieves.[30]

Similar obligations restricted the acqusition of meat. If a transient raider happened to see the carcass of a cow or other animal which had already been slaughtered and hung in a tree, he was forbidden by custom to climb and seize it. He was permitted, however, to unhook it if possible by aid of a long stick. If the owner of the carcass saw him do this, he, too, was required by custom to cut off a special strip of the meat and hand it to him.[31]

The intent of such ritual was to symbolize and thus reaffirm the existence of mutual ancestry in the mind of each person involved. Perhaps the clearest illustration can be found in the behavior expected of transients who wished to take yams. Such persons could dig only on the edge of a garden. The hole could not be filled in, and the yams thus acquired could be roasted only on a public pathway. If children appeared, the transient was to address them as 'son (or daughter) of my father' (*mutanoba, mwaroba*), share the food he had taken and behave generally as one of their family. If girls of marriageable age appeared, he could joke roughly and sensually with them,[32] although physical contact, of course, was forbidden. The intent was to simulate the behavior of a genuine blood relation and thus reaffirm the *gichiaro* between those persons involved.[33]

Punishment for violation of *gichiaro* obligations was believed to lie within the supernatural sphere. The punishing agent was neither God nor ancestral spirits, but the common blood itself, which had the power to retaliate against those who transgressed against it.

Traditions declare that retaliation was automatic and inevitable. Occasionally it would take the comparatively mild form of warning an offender. Thus, if a woman refused to give gruel to transient raiders with whom her husband's unit had *gichiaro*, it was believed that the lid of the gruel-gourd would pop into the air in muted protest. If she protested the raiders' consumption of milk, her calves would react by refusing to suckle their mothers. Alternatively, her adult livestock would develop human traits, dropping their dung in the privacy of the bush in silent warning that calamity was near.[34]

Supernatural punishments for violating the taboo against killing a ritual ally were more severe. Basically, it would seem that the portion of one's body which committed the deed was expected to endure the punishment: usually a form of disease. Thus, the most frequent form of punishment mentioned by informants was the affliction of leprosy (*mutigiri*) or leucoderma (*rwanga*) on the hand (or hands) which actually killed a ritual ally, whether by intent or accident.[35]

Nor could the shedding of common blood be indirect. In North Imenti and Tigania, for example, traditions illustrate this by recalling the fate of a Tiganian warrior, whose clan had *gichiaro* with a *mwiriga* in Imenti. Despite this, he agreed to act as the 'eyes' (to scout, spy for) of a second Tiganian *mwiriga* that wished to raid his ritual ally. Unexpectedly, his decision led several women of the potential target area to their deaths. They had approached him without fear, knowing that his group was *gichiaro* to their own, then caught sight of the accompanying raiders. Startled, these killed the women, to prevent their own exposure and death. The punishment, however, fell on the *gichiaro*-brother, whose initial decision to act as the raiders' 'eyes' had led to the women's deaths. Thereafter, the warrior's vision began to fail, and he eventually went blind, a circumstance which was unanimously attributed to his actions during the raid.[36]

It should be noted that the passage of time provided a violator no security. Punishments were considered inevitable, but could be delayed until the second or even subsequent generations, falling on the heirs of an individual instead of on himself. A transgressor who escaped physical or biological calamity, therefore, could expect few if any children, after his time as a warrior. Those which he did have would emerge deformed or suffer the calamity meant for him. Those which missed these fates could be expected to go mad, and would certainly have few children themselves. Eventually, the seed of the offender could be expected to disappear, thus wiping out the original offense.[37]

Two paths were open, however, to those who had committed this type of violation. One took the form of a ritual cleansing. This was performed at the offending warrior's request by elders of both sides. These jointly slaughtered a ram that the offender had provided, then sprinkled the blood where he had walked. Thereafter, both sides would negotiate an adequate amount of compensation, to be paid from the offender's livestock (or that of his relatives) to the victim's family. Such actions might not permit the slayer to escape his punishment completely, but could considerably lighten whatever it would be.[38]

In summary, it appears that the Meru system of ritual alliances, by operating primarily at the level of individual *mwiriga* (rather than between subdivisions, etc.), was intended both to limit and to encourage war. By its emphasis on identification of common ancestry, it protected participants against the dangers of incest and fratricide. From a military perspective, it served to cope with Meru geographic conditions, which required fragmentation into relatively small communities while at the same time it precluded the possibility of defense behind natural barriers.

It achieved this by limiting the possible number of attackers, through ritually defining groups between which such attacks were forbidden. Yet, in so doing, the system invariably defined permitted opponents as well, actually encouraging conflict among them by its provisions for sanctuary, supplies while in transit and acts of supernatural vengeance against those failing to comply.

What emerged, in consequence, was an attempt both to provoke conflict and to limit its intensity to acceptable levels. In effect, the system did little more than follow the patterns of Meru domestic behavior. In childhood, youths were trained to provoke conflict with those slightly older than themselves, yet were restricted in the ways they could express it.[39] In adolescence permission to begin the rite of circumcision could be acquired only through limited provocation of male kinsmen.[40] For novice warriors, status within the *gaaru* was acquired only by challenging their seniors in a circumscribed form of single combat.[41] In all these instances, limited conflict was considered a precondition for the subsequent emergence of harmony, in the same fashion that mutual adoption was considered prerequisite to the subsequent emergence of kinship.

Relations between *miiriga*, therefore, did little more than reflect these attitudes on a larger scale. Conflict between them was considered not only an inevitability, but a necessary prerequisite to the continued function of society. At the same time, such conflict had to be limited, in both scope and intensity, to the point where it would remain acceptable to the community as a whole. The result provided individual *miiriga* with both a sense of security and the prospect of limited war. In sum, *gichiaro* provided the essential setting for Meru warfare, by delineating where, how, and with whom it might be waged.

Economic Setting

The reasons for warfare, however, lay within the economic structure of Meru society. Like other activities, war was regulated by the cyclical pattern of the seasons. Because Meru straddles the Equator, seasons were not determined by fluctuations in temperature as in the temperate regions, but through variations in rainfall. A complete cycle, approximating our calendar year consisted of four seasons: two rainy and two dry.[42]

The first rainy season (*Uthima*), began during the last portion of March. It increased in intensity during April, then tapered slowly off in May. June, July, August marked the first dry season (*Thano*), marked by dense mists in many highland areas and chilly temperatures at night. The second, shorter rainy season (*Uragura*), began in mid or late October, continuing till well into December. The last days of that month, through January, February and mid-March, marked the second dry period (*Munyaro*), when temperatures at every altitude reached their peak.[43]

The seasonal cycle was reflected in the patterns of herding and cultivation. To protect themselves against famine, the Meru utilized four of Mt. Kenya's ecological zones. Those portions of the forest fringe that had reverted to Kikuyu grass, it will be recalled, were used for grazing, while the forest itself provided opportunity to hunt and gather honey. The star grass zone was intensively cultivated for millet, bananas and yams, while the upper portion of the woodlands zone yielded a second variety of millet, beans and peas. Since neither the woodlands nor the Kikuyu grass regions were considered habitable, cultivation and herding were carried on by means of daily trips from middle-zone homesteads, to clear, plant, weed, harvest or guard as the season required.[44]

The agricultural cycle began in March, at a time marked by the appearance of the *Pleiades* (Kimeru: *Kalimira*) on the horizon,[45] which signaled the beginning of the rains. By this time, most seed crops had been planted in both the middle and lower zones. During the rainy period, men had no formal agricultural obligations, other than caring for their banana groves. Women, however, were occupied in weeding, an activity which called for daily trips between their homesteads and the cultivated areas.

In May the rains gradually decreased, and great flocks of birds appeared in the lower regions. Both the men and older boys were forced to spend much time in the lower zones, guarding the ripening crops against both birds and animals.[46] During this period, boys would stand guard throughout the day, perching on small wooden platforms to hurl rocks and curses at the descending birds. At night, the men would take over, using shouts, torches, back-fires and pans of glowing coals to drive off encroaching game.[47]

June and July marked a period of minimal agricultural activity. The termination of the rains permitted the daily dispatch of family herds up into the Kikuyu grass areas, since the shoots would be green, tender and particularly palatable to livestock.[48] This was also the time when attention could be turned to repairs, crafts and trade. Most of these activities were restricted to women, although men were responsible for leather work and (if ironsmiths) the production of weapons and tools. Such trade as existed—with exceptions occurring primarily during periods of famine—was strictly local, women traveling no farther than their own or adjacent village markets.[49]

August was a period of harvest, both in highland and lowland areas. Thereafter, new fields had to be cleared in both zones for preparation of those crops to be grown during the second rains. Heavy clearing was the responsibility of males; thus once again much time could be lost walking between homesteads and fields scattered in the lower region. Women, meanwhile, began threshing and winnowing the crop which had been taken.[50]

September and most of October were consumed by planting in both the middle and lower zones. Pulse, millet, sorghum and sweet potatoes were planted, entirely by the women, in anticipation of the coming rains. The rainy period, as before, was devoted primarily to weeding and guarding. During December and January, the highland millets were particularly susceptible to pillage by both animals and birds, and guards had once again to be mounted day and night. By February, the millet, along with other seasonal crops, was ready to harvest. Thereafter, women began their second period of threshing and winnowing, while men engaged once more in heavy clearing of those fields which would be needed to begin the cycle once again. Final planting occurred in early March, and the coming of the first rains signaled a welcome relief for all.

The cycle of military action was dependent in turn upon that of economic activity. In years when there were sufficient candidates, circumcisions could begin as early as December. It was more common, however, for the ceremonies to begin in February, March or early April, when the clearing, planting and related activities had been completed and all members of a community could give time to the rituals. Since the ensuing rainy period inhibited travel to distant areas, most communities felt relatively safe from attack. The period was, therefore, devoted to completing formation of a novice warrior subset, intensifying their training and developing to the desired pitch their desire for battle.

These preparations were intended to reach a peak as the rains waned in May. June through July, the time when livestock herds were sent up to the Kikuyu grass areas to graze, was thus the favored period for raids. The necessity to traverse the mountain along the lower fringe of the forest combined with the presence of livestock within the same area to provide ample opportunity for combat.

August, September and early October were also favorable raiding periods, although less so than the months preceding them. During this period, the men (junior elders) of an entire community might be engaged in clearing their lowland areas, an activity which might leave their homesteads relatively undefended and permit the plundering of sheep and goats. The coming of the second rains, however, signalled opportunity for the circumcision of still another group of older boys and the cessation of all military activity until the subsequent dry season.[51]

Raids were possible during late December, January and February, but the intense heat inhibited travel in the lowlands. In addition, this was the time that both bird and animal predators were most active in destroying the highland millet, and the need to guard fields during night and day served as effective warning against surprise attack. In consequence, raiding was only intermittent during the remainder of the cycle.

Economic activities affected the waging of war in several other ways. One was through the operation of certain military conventions, which were mutually accepted and enforced by all sides. Several of these concerned the extent to which combatants were permitted to destroy agricultural produce. Ripening crops were protected by warriors on both sides. Raiders passing through their opponents' banana groves were permitted to snatch what they required at the moment, but were forbidden to cut down or otherwise harm the trees. If such an incident occurred, whether by accident or intention, it would be taken up by a council of elders representing both sides, after the conclusion of the battle. Eventually, the offender would be compelled to pay compensation to those whom he was judged to have wronged.

The same principle applied to fields of grain, yams, arrow-root and similar crops. These could not be willfully destroyed. Compensation could be claimed only if raiders decided to drive livestock through such a field, in the interests of rapid escape. Similarly, huts, boundary markers, bridges and other property damaged by livestock driven in these circumstances were considered the consequences of war, for which no compensation was permitted.[52]

Existing homesteads were also secure. A raiding party might move swiftly through a group of huts, peering into each and seizing whatever could be swiftly carried. However, the structures themselves could be neither burned nor cut down merely to make an enemy suffer. Convention also restricted what might be honorably seized. Swords, spears and similar weapons were considered trophies of war. Agricultural and economic implements (axes, pots, etc.) were not, nor were salt, beads, cloth and similar items. These things were to be obtained not by war but through trade.[53]

Warriors were also forbidden to interfere with existing trade routes, whether local or linked with non-Meru societies. In many cases, for instance, a river or large stream formed a mutually recognized border between two potentially hostile *miiriga*. In such instances several crossing places (usually three) were set aside at the upper, middle, and lower sections of the star-grass (homestead) zone.

During periods of peace they were sanctified by livestock sacrifices and formal proclamations by the leading spokesmen of both sides, as crossings reserved for the passage of trade. In war, they would remain open to any member of either group except warriors fully dressed for battle. The intent was to permit inter-area barter to continue without restriction, even during periods when hostility between both sides was at its height.[54]

Certain specified paths were also set aside for the passage of non-Meru, whether women or men. Traditionally, these were intended for use during periods of famine. In a typical instance, bands of alien warriors whose communities had been struck by famine or disease would approach unarmed along the specified path. In each hand they would hold up a tuft of grass as a sign of their intention to approach in peace.

They would be met by ruling elders of the *mwiriga* in question, while its warriors stood attentively in the background. Negotiations would begin between the two parties, usually leading to an agreement permitting their women to trade. Alternatively, the aliens might negotiate pasturage rights for their remaining livestock on *mwiriga* lands. In exchange for a percentage of the young born during the agreed period, Meru warriors would forswear attack on the herds in question, regardless of the raiding usually practiced between the alien community and themselves.[55]

In summary, the Meru seem to have intended that the spheres of agricultural and commercial productivity remain as distant as possible from the sphere of war, which was to be waged neither for land nor for its material produce. Nor was it to be fought for control of either natural resources[56] or trade routes. Instead it revolved around problems of status, livestock and the place of each within the Meru social setting.

Social Setting

In Meru, war was allegedly fought for a single purpose, to capture livestock, preferably cattle. In theory, a warrior fought to acquire praise-names and status. In practice, these came as he successfully enlarged his father's herds. Ostensibly, the warrior also benefitted from his efforts, as certain of the animals acquired would be set aside for his eventual bride-wealth. In fact, the reasons for his actions lay deeper than the economic value of the animals involved.

It is true that the major species of livestock—cattle, goats and sheep—were conceived of in the first instance as wealth because they provided security against famine. Cattle were valued for their milk, which was primarily given to smaller children. They were also periodically bled using a tiny bow and arrow. The resulting liquid was mixed with milk or millet and given to women in childbirth.[57] Cattle could also be slaughtered for their meat, although such killing was usually restricted to ceremonial occasions. Those dying of natural causes were consumed immediately, however, and the remainder were always available in case of famine.

Goats and sheep appear to have had considerable economic value. Their skins were used to make clothing for both men and women, with goat skins considered the more durable. The hair and sinews could be twisted to form ropes of considerable strength, and both animals could occasionally be used for milk. Goats were also frequently killed and eaten by people recovering from illness, their blood in such cases being considered medicine rather than food.[58] Their meat was also available in case of famine.

Goats also served a second function. In every area they formed the principal unit of economic exchange by means of which other animals (or objects) could be divided among a group. In Imenti, for instance, a cow was worth five goats; in Mwimbe, six. The ratio varied somewhat in other areas, but the principle was accepted by all.

It must be emphasized, however, that the social functions of Meru live-stock far outstripped their economic value. As such, the animals were considered 'wealth' in a second sense, that of having the potential to create binding relationships among individuals.

One example of this can be found in the Meru pattern of negotiating bridewealth. The arrangement itself was considered merely part of a larger process of creating a lifelong relationship (*uthoni*) between the two families whose children were involved. Superficially, it involved little more than the transfer of five specified items—a cow, a bull, a ram, a ewe and a gourd of honey—by the father of the warrior to the father of the bride.[59]

The symbolic value of these items, however, lay not in what they commanded in exchange (a wife), but in the feelings of goodwill, reciprocity and mutual obligation inspired in both parties by the transactions involved. Custom demanded, for example, that a large quantity of beer be sent ahead of the actual bride-price items, intended as a gesture of respect to the bride's father. The latter would reciprocate, however, by making the gift the basis of a general beer-drink, to which the father of the warrior was then invited. Similarly, delivery by the warrior's family of the traditional large gourd of honey was followed by its transformation into honey-wine (*uuki*) by the relatives of the bride. Once this was ready, another drinking party was proclaimed at which the groom's father was again an honored guest, joined this time by other elders of his lineage.[60]

This same principle of reciprocity was applied to the two "male" elements within the bridewealth. The bull and ram would pass first from the hands of the groom's father to those of the bride's. Thereafter, the latter was obligated by tradition to invite the elders and warriors of both families to a meat-feast, including both the suitor and his father. If a ram had been delivered, the family would slaughter a bull; if a bull had been given, they would slaughter a ram. In either case, the guests were entitled to two-fifths of the meat and the hosts three-fifths. However, the hide was returned to the warrior's father to equalize the division.[61]

The female portion of the bridewealth was often deliberately kept back by the warrior's family. Final payment might be delayed years and even lifetimes, as it was not uncommon for a man to hand the remaining portion of a bridewealth debt over to his son. The intent in this was tacitly understood by both sides. A relationship between the two families, if not yet concluded, was still alive. Therefore, the feelings of good will which the mutual exchange of gifts had brought into existence were still worth preserving. If the arrangement was completed, such feelings might die away.

The same pattern occurred if the female elements were paid. The burden of obligation then shifted to the bride's father who was required to present his daughter (and her children) with livestock of equivalent value during her subsequent years of marriage. Thus, in time the value inherent in each of the bridewealth elements returned to the family from which it came. What should have remained between the families was a tradition of harmony, for which the specific items of livestock had been no more than a required catalyst.

The presence of livestock was also required for the rituals used to reinforce existing relationships. Each stage in a man's life, for instance, was marked by appropriate feasting, for which numerous animals were slaughtered. The subsequent division of meat was done in a manner that reflected the comparative status of every individual at the feast. The act of accepting the meat and consuming it together symbolized acceptance of that status and a consequent condition of harmony among all concerned. It should also be noted that such events were often commemorated in the names of cows. Famines, marriages, payments of compensation, and similar events were often symbolized by the animals which appeared as the result of each occurrences.[62]

Livestock was also conceived of as wealth in a third sense, that of its potential to create or restore harmonious relationships between living individuals and the supernatural. The slaughter of a goat, for instance, was considered prerequisite to such restoration, as it was believed able to indicate a condition of conflict (disharmony) between its owner and the spirit world. On occasion, goats would act in such a manner as to warn owners that disharmony had occurred. Allegedly, the animal in question would do this by either eating hot ashes or attempting to lick air.[63] Thereafter, it would be regarded as having become ritually blemished (*ntang'uru*) through some action of its owner. In consequence, the latter could avoid the subsequent onset of calamity only by sacrificing the animal at once.

The sheep, in contrast, was believed to have the capacity to restore conditions of harmony between man and the supernatural. The owner of a goat such as that previously described, having been warned of his conflict, would realize that he had entered into a condition of ritual impurity (*mugiro*). To restore harmony and thus rid himself of his *mugiro*, the man would be required to visit various ritual specialists each calling for the sacrifice of further goats in order that he might learn which of the supernatural forces he had offended and how adequate restitution could be made. The final sacrifice, however, would be that of a sheep intended to symbolize the termination of conflict and restoration of harmony between the supernatural and the individual concerned.

The same principles were expressed in cases where conflict occurred between two members of the community. If the dispute concerned the violation of ancestral tradition (e.g., theft, assault), a goat would be sacrificed to expresss the condition of disharmony (conflict) which had appeared between the antagonists and by implication thcir lineages. Each person then swore on the body of the goat that his version of the dispute was correct. Since conditions of disharmony were inevitably believed to be followed by calamity, those judging the incident had only to wait until one of the antagonists was struck down. The claim of the other was then declared justified, compensation was arranged, and a sheep would be sacrificed to symbolize transformation of the conflict into a condition of harmony.[64] Here again, specific items of livestock were required as catalysts. Without them, the machinery of conciliation could not function.

In summary, possession of livestock was tantamount to owning the means to create, reinforce or restore harmonious relationships, should instances of conflict arise. They were the ultimate form of personal security; protection against either secular or supernatural disharmony, and the accompanying calamity in any form. The larger a man's herds, in consequence, the greater his sense of personal security, and therefore his status within the community at large.

Conversely, lack of livestock would leave the individual impoverished in several ways. Not only would he and his dependents lack the most rudimentary protection against periods of crop famine, but he would be comparatively limited in his ability to create and maintain harmonious relationships with those around him. Similarly, such a person would be comparatively ill-prepared to cope with situations of conflict, and could expect to avert the inevitable calamities only through the charity of kinsmen. It follows that both he and his dependents would have little chance to marry well after the termination of their warriorhood. Nor could they expect to rise to positions of importance during their years as ruling elders.

Each warrior, therefore, was expected to do far more during his period in the *gaaru* than provide himself with bridewealth for a wife. He was expected to earn progressively greater status for both himself and his family by forcibly acquiring as much livestock as possible during his warrior period. The importance of such acquisition was reflected in many of the conventions by which this form of warfare might be waged, traditions established not to limit cattle stealing but facilitate it.

If two warriors fought, for example, the weaker could save his life by shouting 'Take Cattle!' which was accepted as a declaration of surrender. Alternatively, he could place all of his weapons in both hands, points upwards, and push them towards his opponent. The victor would then seize the weapons, tear off his own skin cloak and place it over his captive's shoulders, thereby symbolically eliminating him from the fight. In other instances, herdsmen refusing to resist seizure of their cattle were frequently ignored by raiders, provided they chose neither to run nor to fight.[65]

The point of such capture, however, was ultimately to exchange the male captive for as much livestock as his freedom would bring. After a battle in which warriors had been captured, elders from the victorious *mwiriga* would send a spokesman to the recent victims to see whether negotiations could be arranged. If both antagonists were Meru, the elder selected would carry a special '*kiama* staff' on one shoulder as a sign that he was negotiating and should not be attacked.

Ideally, the spokesman approached the elders of the defeated *mwiriga* through an intermediary, one whose community was hostile to neither side. The two would travel together to the enemy boundary, where the negotiator would conceal himself. The intermediary would then approach ruling elders of the defeated group and ascertain whether the atmosphere was ripe for negotiations. If the elders replied that their warriors sought only vengeance, the intermediary would return to the negotiator and the mission would fail. If the reply were favorable, the negotiator would himself come forward and bargaining would begin. Eventually, a certain number of livestock would be exchanged for each captive, and they would be allowed to return unharmed.[66]

Female captives were also ultimately redeemable in terms of livestock. Neither uncircumcised girls nor those that had been 'cut' but were still unmarried could be claimed by their captors as concubines or wives.[67] Instead, they, as well as brides who had not yet conceived, could be exchanged for livestock in the same manner as males. Alternatively, the female would be regarded as her captor's daughter. After a reasonable interval, she would be married to a man of another clan, with the warrior and his father acting jointly during the negotiations. The warrior was rewarded by the gradual receipt of livestock as part of the bridewealth, and his family was permitted to enter harmonious relations with that of the man who ultimately received her.[68]

This body of conventions, together with those previously considered, reflects the primary concern within Meru military thought; to create a social setting which both provoked and regulated a specific form of war.

Regulation was provided by the traditions intended to focus warrior attention on the herds. Certain of these acted to separate military from agricultural activities. Others did the same with regard to trade. Still others inhibited the taking of female lives (or captives) by restricting the areas of actual combat to those inhabited by males—since only these were allowed to herd. Other conventions rewarded the warrior who spared a life (by exchanging captives for cattle) and punished one who killed.[69] In sum, such warfare as existed was stringently controlled.

Yet, this form of war also needed encouragement since acquisition of livestock was essential to society's continued operation. This was achieved, ultimately, through development of a social ethic which defined "maleness" primarily in terms of success in war, then permitted males during the first thirty years of their lives to acquire personal security and community status only through the acquisition of livestock by military means.[70]

In theory, these countervailing tendencies should have acted to cancel one another. In practice, they operated to provide a cultural and social setting in which war could be waged at a level acceptable to all. The geographic setting in which the Meru found themselves invited internecine conflict. They reacted, in keeping with beliefs motivating other aspects of society, by regarding conflict as an inevitable prerequisite to whatever form of harmony might ultimately emerge.

CHAPTER III

Learning Warriorhood

The Military Ideals

Meru conceptions of warriorhood were based on five abstract military ideals, the mastery of which was essential to the warrior role. Introduction to these began in early childhood and continued through the first three decades of a male's life.

The first of these dealt with the ideal of self-development, an expression which was interpreted to include both physical and mental abilities. It was to be achieved by continuous application of two techniques, which were expressed as 'hardening' and 'quickening.' The 'hardening' of a potential warrior took place in two ways. One lay in the continual development of physical strength through exercise and diet. The second was through increasing the body's ability to endure physical pain, whether imposed by an individual's own *mwiriga* or the necessities of war.

The process of 'quickening' also took two forms. A potential warrior strove to quicken his physical reflexes through mastering tasks needing swiftness or stealth. He was to work in similar fashion with his mental processes, quickening them by increasing his powers of observation, wit and memory. Only by growing both 'hard' and 'quick' could a male hope for success as a warrior.

The second military ideal was the development of self-control, which related to the hardening process, since much of the pain potential warriors expected to endure was inflicted by members of their own community, either as instructional or disciplinary beatings. A true warrior, therefore, was expected to show neither weakness in the face of pain, nor resistance to those who applied it. If in authority he was to regulate the degree of pain inflicted, limiting its extent to that sanctioned by tradition.

Similarly, sexual self-control was taught from puberty, since warriors were expected to remain celibate for all but the final portion of their military careers. The ideal also applied to material possessions. Warriors were expected to own nothing but their weapons. Cattle, captives and similar booty were delivered to their fathers. Land utilization was the prerogative of family heads. Ornaments (with exceptions) were for women. A warrior was never to fight for possessions, but for honor, reputation and community esteem.[1]

A third ideal emphasized the subordination of individuality to the authority of a group, defined in this instance as the age-mates within each warrior's *mwiriga*. A warrior defined his personal military development in terms not of his own success, but that of his age-set. Boys who aspired to a military role were taught from childhood that achievement was possible only through the united effort of a set, and that individual deviations were, therefore, unthinkable. To reinforce this, every effort was made to develop feelings of 'set-solidarity' among the young, which would counteract every tendency toward individualism. Thus from early childhood, male age-mates were guided into increasing isolation from other members of the community and taught that feelings of obedience and loyalty belonged to their corporate unit alone.

Aspirants to warriorhood were also taught the ideal of subordination to age. The term applied not only to those in age-sets higher in the social hierarchy, but even to age-mates, who were ranked within a set by their moment of entry. Internalization of this concept was crucial to the military system. Tradition permitted its younger members to provoke conditions of conflict, both among themselves and in the sets immediately above them. However, they were never permitted to resolve them. Resolution of all conflict was the prerogative of the aged, defined as anyone older than the antagonists. Youthful submission to such authority was therefore prerequisite to the settlement of military conflicts, whether between neighboring *miiriga* or within a single *gaaru*. In consequence, subordination to the aged was taught constantly from early childhood, and made up by far the largest part of military training.

The fifth and most important of these ideals dealt with subordination to tradition. Obedience to the aged, as previously mentioned, was ultimately rooted in their ability to recall and interpret tradition in such a manner as to protect the young from the supernatural consequences of its violation. A warrior would therefore find it in his own interest to submit to his elders' wisdom and authority, until such time as he grew sufficiently old and wise to interpret such traditions on his own.

The Role of Elder Kinsmen

Formal introduction to the military ideals occurred in early childhood, soon after the appearance of the second teeth. At that time, boys were transferred from their mothers' huts to their fathers' in order to increase their exposure to the world of men. Their primary instructors at this time, however, were usually elder kinsmen, most frequently their paternal grandfathers or other biological relatives of the same age-set. In the daytime, the appropriate elder would accompany a boy as he herded the family livestock. Evenings, the two would sit together at the fire, the older man speaking of his own warrior past, in order to raise the youth's interest in what was to come.

An elder could nourish this interest in several ways. Initially he would provide assistance in creating and using the boy's earliest toys of war— small spears, bows, arrows—as well as in the construction of snares and pit-traps for small game. With the toys would come advice in the arts of shooting, stalking, concealment and related skills which would make up the rudiments of later warriorhood.

Elders would also instruct their charges by relating tales of the past. These usually took three forms. Tales of success would usually deal with a military victory because of the quickness of a leader's wit:

> . . . Each night Kaura Bechau (a Meru hero) led the (Meru) captives out to dance for their (Mberre) captors, speaking to them in a language the Mberre could not understand. Each night, the circle of dancers grew larger, till it finally surrounded the Mberre. Then Kaura Bechau gave the secret signal and. . . .[2]

Less frequently, such tales dealt with victory resulting solely from their courage of numbers:

> . . . a single cow-skin was cast upon the ground. Each Meru *njuuri* (war-units) stamped over and upon it in turn. Only after it had been torn to shreds did the *njuri* (council of councils) decide that the Meru had sufficient warriors to defeat the Maasai. . . ."[3]

> ". . . When the Maasai attacked they struck at two places at once; one near the forest, one near the plains. The (Mwimbe) warriors in the neighboring *magaaru* were confused, not knowing whom to help first. Seeing this, Mbogori set off after the raiders himself. . . .[4]

The tales also dealt with military failure. Invariably this was due to departure from tradition:

> The prophet (*muroria*) had warned the raiders (from Tigania) to turn back if they saw a tree that had been felled so that it lay across their path. When they came to it, the warriors from Athuana (*mwiriga* in Tigania) were for turning back. Those of Kianjai (adjoining *mwiriga*) mocked them for their weakness, declaring that no prophecy was strong enough to bind their (spear) arms. Thus, the entire group went forward . . . (to disaster).[5]

The respect with which the institution of warriorhood itself was treated was further impressed upon youngsters by their grandfathers' insistence on obedience to certain customs concerning the warriors themselves, chiefly those compelling them to display exaggerated forms of respect. No boy, for instance, could remain standing on a path after catching sight of an approaching warrior. His duty was to scurry off and conceal himself from view. Failure to move quickly, or to hide oneself completely, was punished with a beating from the warrior concerned. Nor might a boy, out of fondness for warlike ways, imitate aspects of the warrior dress or hairstyle. Failure to observe this prohibition led to further beating. Protest or resistance to such chastisement led to still more violent punishment, applied by as many warriors as was considered necessary.[6]

The Role of Peer Groups

Peer group training also began with the appearance of the second teeth. It operated primarily through the device of 'boyhood councils' (*biama bia biiji*). Both the structure and activities of these *biama* were intended, by their members, to imitate corresponding institutions among adults, insofar as these could be learned by the boys concerned. In consequence, they served as the primary means through which youngsters could internalize those aspects of the military ethic that would be required of them in later life.

Traditionally, a *mwiriga* would have three types of boyhood council, each intended to teach a different aspect of adulthood. The first, a *kiama* for the youngest boys (*kiama kia kiigumi*),[7] was intended to introduce them to the basic concepts of warriorhood. Rites of entry into this society were intended as lessons in self-control and subordination of each individual to the authority of the group. Boys were thus permitted to apply for membership (Kimeru: 'buy,' *kiigumi*) at any time after their second teeth appeared. The choice was voluntary, but no one could evade it without exposing himself to the ridicule of more daring comrades.

Each step of the entry procedure was rigorously formalized, in order to enhance its significance in the candidates' minds. In imitation of adult practice, each candidate would beg an existing member to serve as his sponsor, acknowledging him with the title of 'father' throughout his boyhood. The sponsor's task was to support the applicant during the moments of pain he would be called upon to bear, as well as to make sure that it remained within permitted limits.

Candidates would then appear before the council members, bearing gifts in imitation of adult practices. Entry into a warrior *kiama*, for example, required potential applicants to provide senior members with lengths of iron chain ('to the length of an arm'), iron being believed to provide its wearers with supernatural protection.[8] In imitation, boys were expected to provide their own *kiama* seniors with chain long enough to wrap around a finger. Other gifts were also modeled (and prorated) after the corresponding custom of adults.[9]

If the gifts were accepted, candidates were then informed that to join the council, they must 'be swept of the bedbugs they had brought.' In imitation of procedures used on entry into the warrior ranks, candidates were forced to run between two lines of boys, each armed with light sticks. The candidates, naked except for leather aprons, then ran the lines from end to end, receiving blows from each person as they passed.[10]

There were several restrictions on the intensity of the beating, al' illustrative of its ultimate purpose. The length and thickness of the 'beating stick' were regulated by tradition. No member of a boy's *kiama* might choose his own. Blows were forbidden on certain parts of the body, notably the face, abdomen and genitals. Ritual sponsors were always present to see that the pain remained within limits, yet the beating could be repeated as often as older initiates desired.

The purpose of such repetition was to evaluate accurately each candidate's reactions. Often several of the warriors themselves would be present as observers of both the beaters and the beaten, an indication of the value placed upon the process. Beaters were scrutinized for signs of immoderation or cruelty; candidates, for indications of temper or weakness. Signs of anger or resistance produced further beatings. Boys who showed weakness, however, were untouched. Instead, they were formally proclaimed to be too young (Kimeru: unripe) for the society, then allowed to return in silence to their fathers' homesteads.

The reprieve was only temporary, for the system permitted no one to remain outside its control. In practice, this meant that *kiigumi* members would act to shame recalcitrants into acceptance of their authority. Soon after each boy's physical recovery, he would be visited regularly by those of his peers who had learned of his failure. These would taunt him with song and derisive nicknames (e.g. *ncuna*: whip), a method of rejection which virtually ensured that each youngster would decide to try again. Once a boy had decided he could endure the required beating, he would reappear before the members, bearing the same fees as before, and undergo the pain.[11]

Boys who passed successfully through the rites of entry were admitted to a second (teaching) stage. In practice, this meant that a boy who successfully ran the line of beaters found himself at the entrance of the official meeting-hut of the group (*nyumba ya kiigumi*: house of *kiigumi*). In reality, such a hut might be little more than a storage place for grain, but its very use by older initiates invested it with the proper atmosphere of awe. On entering, the candidate would squat silently, while *kiigumi* spokesmen would instruct him as to the specific patterns of behavior ('secrets of the *kiama*') he would be expected to follow as a member of the group.

These secrets were intended to strengthen and internalize the concept of age-set solidarity at the expense of ties with all other groups in the community. In imitation of the warriors, members of the boyhood *biama* were forbidden to eat alone. Instead, they were permitted to receive food from their mothers only when in company with their age-mates. Like warriors, they were also forbidden to sleep in the huts of their homestead. Rather, they were compelled to remain with their age-mates in the barrack for boys (*gaaru ya biiji*),[12] usually the same hut in which they had received their initial instruction.

Upon completion of their teaching, boys passed into a third stage, best defined as one of service. Life within their *gaaru* was made to resemble that of the warrior rank and file. In consequence, it placed most emphasis on the ideals of physical 'hardening' and subordination to age. Rank was established from the beginning, based on the time of entry into the group. Older boys continually imposed their authority upon those junior to them, beating them, commanding small services or forcing them to sit in silence in order to absorb their elders' wisdom. It was an existence based on unquestioned acceptance, by both the candidates and their instructors, of the need for continuous control and regulation. For most boys it was their willingness to accept this need that constituted the first step towards their attainment of their warriorhood; hence it was an experience of which they grew increasingly proud.

The second type of boyhood council was intended to train a selected few of the most promising youngsters for future positions of leadership (*ugambe*: spokesmanship). In Imenti, this more exclusive society was called *kabichu*. It served as a higher council for *kiigumi*, in imitation of adult patterns among both warriors and elders. In consequence, where *kiigumi* had sought to train warriors of the rank and file, *kabichu* focused on the development of leaders. Where the former placed emphasis on physical hardening and acceptance of authority, the latter was interested in quickening the mind.

This is most clearly illustrated by comparing the rites of entry into the more elite council with those previously described for *kiigumi*.[13] Instead of the abuse and beating that had marked their initiation into the former group, candidates chosen for *kabichu* were greeted with respectful demonstrations, intended to convince them of the wisdom and power of the society. During one of these, two older members would maintain that the youths of *kabichu* had the power to read thoughts. This they would demonstrate, aided by a series of verbal or physical clues that were unknown to the candidates, but assured accurate replies.[14] After several of these demonstrations, applicants were told they could acquire the same powers upon payment of the traditional fees required for entry.

Once accepted, candidates passed through a period of instruction and apprenticeship similar to that undertaken for *kiigumi*. The skills taught in this instance were intended primarily to develop the powers of observation and memory required to master the visual clues and verbal symbols by which group-members communicated. In time, the boys learned sufficient riddles, metaphors, euphemisms and the like to communicate fluently before non-members without being understood. To observant elders, the comparative ability of youngsters to master these problems proved essential in the eventual selection of spokesmen for the councils of adulthood.

This more elite group taught other leadership skills. Among adults, for example, each slaughter of a beast was followed by distribution of the meat according to rigidly observed traditions. Variations of these customs were practiced by *kabichu*, both among themselves and in the division of the meat for members of *kiigumi*. Thus, if a bird was shot by a member of the elite society, only its chest would go to the boy who killed it. Its head would go to the oldest boy present, its back to the next oldest and so on. In the process, the boys concerned not only internalized the rules concerning division of communal property, but the traditions on which such division was based, knowledge essential to their training as *agambe*.

Notice should also be taken of a third type of *kiama*, one which served as an alternative to both *kiigumi* and *kabichu*. Between the ages of ten to fourteen, a youth might opt for entry into a boyhood version of one of the fringe societies. These were named and modeled after their respective parent-groups, to whose rites and traditions they attempted to conform. That of the iron-smiths (*aturi*), for instance, was named *gaturi* (little smiths); that of the hunters, (*aathi*), *nkima ya aathi* (twigs of *aathi*). All of the fringe societies were open to youths at whatever age they chose to join. Recruitment might occur merely through accident of birth, as when the sons of an iron-smith or hunter would inevitably follow his profession. Among adults, it could also take place by involuntary entrapment, as would occur through violation of a supernaturally protected agricultural or hunting/gathering zone.[15]

Entry could also be voluntary, whether for children or adults inclined toward supernatural practice. Within the fringe groups of boyhood no compulsion was used, each band relying instead on the lure of its supernatural claims.[16] It should be emphasized that the claims of these councils to vast extramundane abilities were simply ignored by the adult community. They did, however, generate considerable awe among children of their own age, providing thereby a large, impressionable supply of potential victims. For this reason, such groups served as effective instruments for infusing the basic principles of supernatural manipulation into those who aspired to master them.

Rites of entry into these boyhood fringe groups were similar to those of *kiigumi*, as was the underlying intention of assuring submission of each individual to group authority. Potential candidates would initially subordinate themselves through pleas and gifts to older members of the *kiama* they wished to join. After agreeing to become their sponsors, these older members would lead them to the appropriate meeting place. There the candidates would indicate their submission to other members of the society through distributing additional gifts and enduring the obligatory beatings.

As with *kiigumi*, the initiation was followed by a period of instruction. The initial lessons were intended to isolate new members, both from the company of other age-sets and those of their own age-mates who had joined other societies. Isolation was achieved in traditional fashion through a series of injunctions to perform all social functions (eating, sleeping, etc.) only in the company of society-mates, and a second set of behavioral taboos requiring evasive actions (silence, dropping eyes, withdrawal, etc.) in the present of outsiders. Obedience to such instruction was characterized as adult behavior; refusal to do so, as childish ways.

Subsequent instruction departed from the pattern of the mainstream. Instead, it was intended to demonstrate and teach the techniques each fringe group used for manipulation of the supernatural, primarily the powers of defensive ritual, cursing and curse-removal. Societies modeled after the *aathi*, for instance, constructed smaller versions of the *ndindi* sticks, which they placed along paths leading to their meeting places, thereby proclaiming them as forbidden (hunting) zones.[17] Other groups taught equally appropriate imitations.

Boys were also taught to guard their meeting huts in a manner intended to imitate their elders. It will be recalled, for instance, that adult *aathi* protected their own meeting places with objects (*nkima*) made of bones, strips of animal hide and wax. Young *aathi*, seeking to imitate them, constructed similar objects, using twigs and various types of vegetable fiber in place of the animals they were too young to hunt.[18]

New members were finally taught to respond to violations of their property or against one of their number in a manner as similar as possible to that practiced by their adult counterparts. Young *aathi*, for example, would respond to alleged violations of their property by removing the protective charm from its place in the meeting hut. Raising the object on a pole, they then carried it around the homesteads of potential offenders, while the boys chanted curses at the top of their lungs:

> May the head of the person who has wronged us be carried like this . . .
> May the head of the person who has wronged us be picked at by *mutitu* (a river bird). May the mother of the person who has wronged us no longer have pot fragments with which to cook (i.e., may her children all die). . . .[19]

The wording of the chant and the manner in which it was delivered imitated the respective adult societies as far as possible. The reaction of potential victims was also essentially the same. Any boy who felt sufficiently certain of having wronged some member of the chanting group would approach it, bearing an appropriate gift. He would then beg for removal of the *mugiro* he believed to have been imposed upon him for past actions. An older member of the society would then assume the role of its curse-remover. The *mugiro* would be symbolically brushed (or beaten) from the body of the offender. The fee—usually a hen—would be shared among the members, with the victim receiving a symbolic portion. Unlike adult practices, however, a victim of boyhood *biama* would be under no further obligation and would be free to go.

The existence of alternatives to the processes of militarization in a society as war-oriented as Meru raises a question as to their ultimate purpose. Available data suggest that boys drawn to such fringe groups came primarily from the level of *kiigumi* (rank and file) rather than that of *kabichu* (leaders). Boys were accepted into these groups at any age, and no barrier was put before sons of agriculturalists wishing to join boyhood versions of non-agricultural groups, or vice-versa. The element of compulsion was also lacking after removal of boyhood *mugiro*, no one having been forced to join this type of group as the price of his cure.

Available information suggests that these boyhood *biama*—again in imitation of adults—existed as limited, but nonetheless permitted, alternatives to the rigors of militarization in the *gaaru* of *kiigumi*. Informants emphasize that membership in such a fringe group did not excuse a person from his basic pre-military obligations, whether dietary, social or physical. It did serve, however, to minimize the impact of these obligations by providing an alternate environment in which a limited number of boys, perhaps those least able to adjust to traditional militarization, could find new ways to regenerate their self-respect.

These new abilities, once mastered, would serve, in turn, to protect this minority from persecution by their more military-minded age-mates, since the latter would fear supernatural retribution for their taunts. It was this self-protection, plus the voluntary nature of these societies, which seems to have allowed them to survive.

It seems possible, therefore, that all three types of boyhood councils formed an informal but nonetheless unified system. Within it, a majority of each age-set trained throughout boyhood for service in the rank and file. A small percentage of these were then allowed to develop capacities for leadership, while a final, perhaps deviant, minority could incline towards practice of the supernatural without harassment from the community at large.

The Role of War-Leaders

War leadership took two forms. A man of unusual physical strength, courage or tactical skills could aspire to the title of *ncamba* (war-leader),[20] a position which carried the actual responsibility for conducting raids. Alternately, a man possessing unusual gifts of tact, sensitivity and judgment might gain renown as a conciliator. As such he would be able to exert his own form of leadership in such a manner as to reconcile conflicts among his age-mates. Such men aspired to the title of *mugambe* (spokesman), in this instance for the warriors. Both types of war-leader, as well as former holders of each title who had entered the ranks of elderhood, continued to concern themselves with the militarization of the young. This concern became increasingly evident after a youth reached puberty. At that time, he was encouraged to leave the ranks of whichever youngsters' *kiama* he had chosen, and enter one more appropriate to his new physical status. *Biama* at this second level were known generally in Imenti by the name *uringuri* (eldest boyhood) and in the southern areas as *ncibi*. Members of such groups in all areas were known as *ndinguri* (eldest boys).[21]

Initially, entry into *uringuri* served merely to reinforce the patterns of behavior already learned within the earlier *biama*. Rituals of entry were the same, except that the traditional gifts required from candidates were such as to oblige them to perform and thereby master tasks which would be required of them at later stages of their lives. Boys joining *uringuri* in Imenti or Igoji, for example, were required to brew and provide sugar-cane beer for all who were already members, a task which required much time and labor, but one which the warriors would demand of them many times as a prerequisite to their eventual circumcision.[22]

Similarly, the pain each candidate bore during his period of initiation was intended to test and thus reinforce the powers of self-control. In Muthambe, for example, boys who were *uringuri* members collected large piles of 'itch-leaves,' (locally known as *baatha* and *nchegeni*) which were piled between four stakes, planted firmly in the ground. These were linked by lengths of iron chain, which were then buried under an inch of loose soil. Candidates entering the hut were made to sit silently among the leaves, during every period of instruction. If they shifted position sufficiently to expose the chain, or even indicated awareness of the leaves, they were considered 'unripe' for membership in the society, and ordered to return when they were sufficiently mature.[23]

Initial patterns of instruction were also similar to those the boys had previously experienced. Songs, proverbs, maxims and the like were usually presented as a guide to assist them in avoiding their former childish ways in favor of the adult behavior demanded by the society. In practice, these amounted to little more than an extension of their former restrictions and privileges. The earlier pattern of utilizing food-taboos, conversational restrictions, physical avoidance and required night time attendance in the *kiama* hut was reinforced in such a manner as to isolate the members from contact from any age-set but their own. At this stage, however, additional emphasis was placed on avoidance of contact with women and girls, a forerunner of the requirement for chastity that they would bear as warriors.

Subsequent instruction, however, was carried out under the indirect guidance of the war-leaders and other appropriate elders. These had three responsibilities. One was to extend the original concept of age-set solidarity into traditionally approved channels of conflict. A second was to regulate that conflict, so that the spirit of hostility thus generated could be used to motivate the development of military skills. A third was to provide situations in which these skills could be tested under maximum conditions of stress, in order that those most likely to serve as war-leaders of the future would be selected.

It was for these reasons that new *ndinguri* soon found that a new dimension had been added to their ideas of solidarity among age-mates. Previously, they had been able to win adult approval merely by isolating themselves from other segments of the community. At this stage, such behavior was no longer enough. Instead, they were encouraged by taunts from the appropriate adult observers to band together and then to seek out similar groups of *ndinguri* from adjacent *miiriga*, in order to provoke them into conflict.

The creation of such conflict was rigidly controlled. It could not be sought by individuals, but only the entire group. Nor could such a group provoke women, children or men in age-sets higher than their own. Only neighboring *ndinguri* groups were allowed to roam the villages in search of prospective opponents. Once confronted with them, however, they were allowed to use little more than song to express their hostility. In consequence, the songs had developed into elaborate forms of insult and served to strengthen group solidarity against outsiders. Each society had its own traditional songs, all jealously guarded as the wealth of the *kiama* concerned. The singing of one of these by a nonmember, or the twisting of traditional words by an opposing group would bring the entire society into battle against the offenders. Each effort to actually engage in conflict, however, was thwarted by the intervention of observant adults, in such a manner as deliberately to leave the hostility of both sides unresolved.

These feelings were then channeled into traditional forms of premilitary training. Wrestling, for instance, had always been practiced on an individual basis. Among *ndinguri*, it was elevated to a group activity permitted only when practiced by entire societies. Such matches were usually planned for specific periods, traditionally nights of full moon, when agricultural activities were at a minimum. Prior to the actual announcement, conflict between two or more groups of *ndinguri* was allowed to reach unusual peaks, with all efforts at violent resolution blocked by the adults involved. Only when the tension between such groups reached a point where the daily activities of older age-sets were disturbed, would the elders meet to proclaim formally a wrestling night.

When the date was formally announced, *ndinguri* of the appropriate areas would converge upon an open field usually reserved for the dances of warriors and thus a place of awe to older boys. On such occasions, members of every age-set in the area might turn out as spectators, especially prominent among whom were the warriors whose interest in the contest often drove them to the point of blows among themselves. Women were particularly welcomed, since their ululation and shouts served as the reward for potential victors and punishment for the defeated. Even the younger children, although not usually allowed to roam at night, would accompany the wrestlers from their *mwiriga*, dancing around them and chanting songs intended to raise combatants' spirits to a fighting peak.

As the full moon rose, *ndinguri* from a specified *mwiriga* would gather at one edge of the cleared field. Others from the society selected as their opponents would appear at the other side. Each group was accompanied by war-leaders and elders to see that order was kept. When all were present, the group which had prepared the wrestling field by clearing out the roots, stumps and similar obstructions would begin the contest with a song along the lines of this one:

Urinara ku Kithunku Makuma
Mucii ukugia ndiu?

Where will you dance *Kithunku Makuma* (an ironic name for their opponents)
Is there an eagle in the family?

The question was sung many times, each louder than the last. It was intended as a chanted challenge to their opponents, informing them in the instance selected, that as only the singers had bothered to clear it, the wrestling field was theirs. If their opponents wished to remain there, they would be required to fight.[24]

The opposing side sang back to the challengers in a similar vein, moving gradually into the field as they did so. As the groups edged toward one another, a pre-selected challenger stood out in front of each. Both of these, by pre-arrangement, would be of approximately equal height and strength. Each would sing out to the other in turn:

Iiii baaba ng'ombe nyingi; Itu baaba ng'ombe nyingi.
Ari ma nani ndimukinde; aitie ruu akarie ndeqwa,
Akarie rucii nam mutongu. Uuuu, Kibaru, thira rambu

My father has many cows; Yes my father has many cows;
If I am wrestled down by you, I will take you home to
    eat a bull with us, we rich ones; So, *Kibaru* (his
    opponent),
Beware of me. . . .

The two boys would then spring at each other and stand momentarily locked together like bulls. In the interval, dancers would form two moving rings around them: an inner circle composed of *ndinguri* and occasional warrior observers, an outer one made up of girls and younger women. These would circle the combatants, singing praises and taunts until one boy was thrown to the ground. A second pair would then step forward and grapple, then a third. Usually, the younger boys would pair off earlier in the evening, so that the balance of the fighting would remain with the eldest and strongest on both sides. Periodically, whole groups of *ndinguri* would break off the dancing and lunge at one another, scattering spectators on every side. In such cases, warriors or elders were supposed to restore some semblance of order, but these, too, would often be carried away by the occasion and leap into the struggling mass. Gradually, the superior strength, cunning or numbers of one side would force the others off the field, and the victors would plunge triumphantly towards the girls and women of their clan to receive an ovation in the form of louder singing, ululation and mention in the words of the songs.[25]

War-leaders also used the hostility engendered among *uringuri* groups to intensify their training in the tools of war. One example can be drawn from the techniques used to instill mastery of the Meru throwing-club and shield. The throwing-club of a full-grown warrior was from eighteen to twenty-four inches long. It was cut from the branch of a particular tree, then specially hardened over a charcoal fire. It was widened at both ends, partially to assure a stable grip, but primarily to facilitate the act of throwing it end over end at an enemy.[26]

Ndinguri, of course, were not allowed to use such clubs in any instance short of actual battle. When going to contend with other groups, however, they were permitted to arm themselves with large numbers of *mpangua*, a hard twelve-inch-long fruit which served admirably for throwing, or *ntongu*, a round, poisonous fruit about the size and shape of a tangerine, which was hard enough to raise a lump on any head it hit.

They were also permitted to carry small shields. These were essentially imitations of those carried by warriors. Adult shields were oval and about forty inches long, large enough to fully protect a kneeling man. They were made up of a wooden mid-rib and frame, onto which was stitched a covering of rhinoceros or buffalo hide. The shields of *ndinguri* were smaller and narrower, but otherwise identically shaped. They were made either of thick bark or from the wood of a specific tree, known for its flexibility and lightness.[27]

Training took place in large groups, ideally between *ndinguri* of traditionally competitive *miiriga*, who were already on the verge of open conflict. When all had assembled, two lines were formed of approximately equal size. In some areas contestants' bodies would be covered with chalk dust to allow those watching to note where the blows landed. Each boy would be identically armed, the left hand holding a shield; the right, one of the two throwing-weapons. Adult war clubs and stones were forbidden. Left-handed persons were permitted or even encouraged to shift their positions, holding the shield in the right hand and the throwing objects in the left. This transfer was thought to make them particularly dangerous, as their opponents, acting from habit, would defend themselves against attack from the right side, a mistake they would rarely have a chance to correct.[28]

The two ranks would face each other and slowly advance. Each group would hurl what would usually be considered as deadly insults at the other, with the intention of causing them to throw and thus expend their weapons at the maximum possible range. As the groups closed, a hail of fruits would begin to thud down on the upraised shields, and the contest would transform itself into a shoving match in which each group united in an effort to push its opponent from the field. At some point, war-leaders intervened to stop the conflict and inspect each boy's body for evidence of injury. Those who emerged unscathed would be rewarded with songs of praise.

War-leaders applied the same techniques in teaching mastery of other weapons, notably bows, arrows and spears. Meru boys, of course, had been encouraged to use tiny weapons since they could walk, and to compete with one another individually in contests of accuracy and skill. On becoming *ndinguri*, however, they trained only in groups, and in ways intended to increase hostility between competitors. Archery, for instance, was taught primarily by permitting groups of *ndinguri* to shoot blunted arrows at one another or at groups opposing their own during the shield-training exercise previously mentioned. War-leaders and elders were always present at such training, primarily to ensure that combatants remained at such a distance from one another as to preclude the possibility of injury. However, the occasion inevitably provided opportunities for persons to display their skill at the cost of an opponent, and honors were reserved once more for those who emerged unscathed.

Conflict was also introduced into training with spears. Younger boys had been taught to master the weapon by a game called 'spearing the wheel' (*thigu*). A group would line up in single file. An older boy would roll a wheel, usually made from branches tied with fiber, on the ground before them. Each boy would cast three spears at the moving target with honor going to the one who stopped its flight.

For *ndinguri*, a second version of the game was introduced. Boys from hostile groups would be arranged in two lines, facing each other at a distance of 15 feet. A war-leader would roll the wheel between them and each boy would cast his weapon. Once the wheel was halted, however, the successful spearman would be required to charge directly toward a distant specified point, breaking through the masked ranks of his opponents to do so. The other side would then attempt to intercept and capture him, while his own mates attempted to provide protection.[29] The game would continue until every boy had run the course, or an outbreak of violence forced adult observers to intervene.

It must be re-emphasized that the roles played by war-leaders during each phase of *ndinguri* training were not restricted to mere regulation of group conflicts. Rather the skirmishes resulting from these exercises, like the beatings which preceded them, were intended to provide these observers with the opportunity to exercise their third and most important responsibility of evaluating youngsters under conditions of stress in order to identify possible future candidates for positions of war-leadership, either as *agambe* or *ncamba*. It will be recalled that potential *agambe* were sought primarily for their sense of judgment and moderation. Thus, during skirmishes or beatings, observers evaluated the actions of beaters as well as the beaten, noting the degree of self-control among those inflicting pain as well as those bearing it.

Potential *ncamba*, however, were sought primarily for their daring, physical strength and personal courage. Those responsible for their selection, therefore, made every effort to provide situations wherein these qualities might be tested. In certain areas, the oldest and bravest of *ndinguri* were given the chance to test their valor against wild beasts. In North and Northeast Imenti, for instance, areas much influenced by Maasai cultural patterns,[30] *ndinguri* would be sent against a single lion. When reports of such a beast were brought to the warrior *gaaru*, no effort would be made to kill the animal. Instead, war-leaders would confer to see whether any of the *ndinguri* were worthy of the honor of attacking it. If none were found worthy, the idea was dropped and the beast driven off by the warriors themselves. Otherwise eight to ten youths were chosen, unobtrusively separated from their fellows and taken to a remote place. Preference was given not only to those who had excelled throughout their training, but also to those whose fathers had been *ncamba*, because of the belief that inherited blood would display its true qualities when under maximum stress.

The group was then informed of the lion's existence and asked which of them wished to kill him. Boys' initial responses were closely observed by the adults present, who attempted to identify those most likely to succeed. No compulsion was used. Those possessing the qualities of war-leadership (*uchamba*) were expected automatically to accept. If too many refused, the plan was abandoned and the boys returned without comment to their age-mates.

Several precautions were taken to protect the volunteers from serious harm. Only individual lions were singled out for combat; pairs and prides were driven off. Boys agreeing to the struggle were accompanied by many times their number of warriors, who stood ready to protect them if their own efforts failed. Nor were single individuals allowed to fight, regardless of their desire. No fewer than ten were usually required if the combat was to take place at all.

On relocating the beast, the more numerous warriors encircled it, keeping far enough away to avoid alarming it. The *ndinguri* were then formed into a single line, then told to maintain it if they valued their lives, a pragmatic reflection of the Meru ideal that success could come only through the unity of age-mates. The youths then advanced, shields high, spears in position. Usually, the lion responded to the attack by escaping into the bush. Only if cornered would it charge the line of spears. If charged directly, a youth was instructed to duck his head beneath the shield and then crouch on one knee behind it, bearing the lion's weight on both the shield and his body until his friends could spear it. If this occurred, honor went to the boy who struck first, even when the blow failed to prove fatal. Thereafter, warriors were permitted to aid the youths until the lion was either driven off or killed.[31] The successful *ndinguri* were thereafter praised in song throughout the area and were remembered years later in the subsequent selection of *ncamba*.

The Role of Circumcisers

In theory, the title of 'circumciser' included only the few persons who actually trimmed the penis foreskin of the candidates for warriorhood. In practice, the title was often expanded to include two other groups which were equally essential to the circumcising process. One of these consisted of the warriors within the candidates' *mwiriga*, whose ranks they aspired to join. The second was that of the novice elders (*aruau*), whose ranks at this stage of the candidates' existence included their fathers, fathers' brothers, and other male kin.

The initial stages of circumcision were marked by the deliberate creation of tension between adjacent age-sets. During this period the *ndinguri* played the role of catalysts, promoting their own group interest by provoking conflicts with the two sets immediately above their own. The warrior age-set played the role of their opponents, acting to obstruct the aspirations of those beneath them for reasons of their own. The novice elders, after initially opposing their sons' wishes, functioned subsequently as conciliators, acting in conjunction with the ruling elders to harmonize conflicting interests for both warriors and candidates.

The Meru referred to this first period as the 'crying time,' suggesting the moment when young people cried out for the rights of adulthood. The first problem faced by a candidate who had reached the stage was to gain the permission of his family elders to initiate his formal circumcision. In principle, this included only the blessing of his father and father's brothers, all to be acquired through presentation of traditional gifts. In fact, it also meant concurrence by the other members of his father's age-set, as well as that of appropriate ritual specialists whom they would subsequently consult.

There were several reasons for the novice elders to refuse their sons' requests. A father might prefer to delay circumcision of his first-born indefinitely, since completion of the ritual would terminate his right to produce more children,[32] and therefore to have intercourse with his wife. Alternately, a refusal could be based on lack of wealth. The ceremonies were costly, drawing upon both the annual harvest and the family herds. Men with few material goods might therefore delay permission as long as possible, lest their poverty be displayed for all to see.

Similarly, an entire *mwiriga* could be temporarily impoverished by the impact of raiders, drought or other disasters. If the millet crop failed, for instance, there could be no brewing of millet beer and no way for the rites to be performed in traditional fashion. If the livestock had been driven off by raiders, there would be no chance to pass on the required gifts and no method of resolving the tensions circumcision inevitably produced.

The *ndinguri* reaction to such delays was conducted according to tradition. Balked as individuals, they retreated into the company of their age-mates seeking solace for long periods in distant portions of the bush. As additional candidates matured sufficiently to join their ranks, they began to apply the techniques they had learned, banding together in unison to provoke conflict, this time not with other bands of *ndinguri*, but with the age-set of their parents. They had been instructed, of course, that conflict within their own communities could be expressed only in song. Thus, each evening the aggrieved youths would paint their faces and bodies with charcoal and castor oil, then decorate themselves with feathers. Thus attired, they gathered nightly to dance and cry out songs which were rude and abusive to each person who had refused their pleas.

At first, when their numbers were few, these dances took place far from the homesteads of those concerned. As the candidates grew more numerous, they moved gradually to a point where the words of each song could be easily heard. Finally, they would leave the dancing place together, moving from homestead to homestead, singing the most abusive songs they could invent.[33] These were mingled with 'crying songs,' intended to shame the appropriate elders into reversing their decision:

> I will die without having been circumcised
> since even an old man (the boy's father) who will not
> circumcise his son can get a place to live (i.e., be
> accepted by the tribe).

> I will die without having been circumcised
> If I am denied, I will escape and find a place (outside the tribe)
> Because my parent has ill-used me.

> I will die without having been circumcised
> I am like an adopted son
> whose parents have died.[34]

The purpose of such songs was less to generate feelings of shame among the particular parents involved than in the minds of their age-mates. As the abuse grew more pointed, feelings of hostility between the boys and their parents reached a point where age-mates of the latter felt compelled to step in and restore harmony among all concerned. In extreme cases, restoration of such harmony became a matter of honor to members of the age-set concerned, thereby making it nearly impossible for recalcitrant persons to resist the collective will.

The boys' next problem was to secure permission from the warriors. Here, the pattern was repeated. Youths seeking circumcision would initially approach the warrior *gaaru* individually, bringing traditional gifts with which to announce their purpose. The earliest candidates would invariably be driven away, usually with threats, taunts, and beatings for those who permitted themselves to be caught.

Warriors had even stronger reasons for refusing their permission than the youngsters' biological kin had. Usually, each war barrack contained members of two[35] separate sub-sets at any given time. Whereas the ranks of the eldest set would be continually thinned, as warrior after warrior left the structure to marry, those of the younger group were continually swelled by new recruits. Eventually, the youngsters would find themselves with sufficient numbers to defeat the remaining members of the older group in a limited form of combat. According to tradition, they were then permitted to expel them physically, thus terminating their period of warriorhood, and seize the *gaaru* for themselves. This position could be maintained until the arrival of still younger warriors dispossessed them in their turn. No senior warriors wished to hasten the moment of their own expulsion; therefore it was in their interest to delay as long as possible the circumcision of persons in the age-set beneath their own.

Thus blocked, the younger boys resorted to the same tactics which had overcome the opposition of their parents. Grouping into their own *biama*, they would carry their cry to the warriors' ranks. When they were few, the traditional dancing and abusive songs took place some distance away from the *gaaru* itself, well outside the range at which warriors might be able to catch and beat the singers. As their numbers grew, they moved closer, sang longer and grew increasingly abusive.

Boys in this position also showed less and less respect for the warriors' status, evading or refusing the customary gestures of submission and respect they had practiced since childhood. Instead of fleeing from the path at a warrior's approach, a group of *ndinguri* might choose to stand and fight. When asked to brew beer for the warrior dances, a request traditional at this stage, boys would evade the work, delay the completion of the task or even refuse. In one instance, frequently recalled by elders throughout Meru, a group of *ndinguri* is alleged to have thrown a chameleon, a harbinger of death, among the warriors of their own *mwiriga* as the latter danced—a deadly insult that nearly precipitated warfare between the two groups concerned.[36]

It must be emphasized that the *ndinguri* intended, by such behavior, to provoke just this type of conflict between the warriors and themselves. Less serious incidents, of course, generally ended with angry *nthaka* catching and beating every boy concerned. This was usually done with such severity that the boys' fathers were forced to intervene and buy off the warriors' anger with gifts of livestock. However, incidents of the same type would be repeated continually, until eventually conflict between the two age-sets would reach a point where the ruling elders themselves might intervene to re-establish harmony. In subsequent negotiations, warriors would reluctantly grant the required permission, in exchange for additional gifts of livestock from the youngsters' parents, a process which reconciled the desires of all three groups to the degree needed to establish harmonious relations among them.

The candidates' experiences so far were intended to reinforce several of the lessons they had learned as younger boys. One was that each upward advance through the Meru social hierarchy could be achieved only by permission of the sets above one's own. A second was that advancement was possible only by united action with one's age-mates. Individual efforts were of no avail. A third lay in realization of the necessity for conflict between one's own age-set and those above. If conducted within the restraints established by custom, such conflict would force intervention by still higher authority and thereby prove an effective means of advancing the interests of one's group.

The subsequent stages of circumcision, however, were intended to undermine whatever feelings of progress had been attained, thereby refocusing the candidates' attention on still higher goals. Having received formal permission from the warriors to enter their ranks, they had next to acquire their informal acceptance as equals. Initially, such efforts took the form of accepting traditional tasks which warriors were permitted to impose on each boy, particularly those who had flaunted their authority in the past. The most common of these was the demand to brew millet beer, a job requiring considerable time and labor.

Deprived by the warriors' formal permission of their right to united protest, individual youths had no choice but to submit, suffering the warriors' taunts and demands in respectful silence. Disrespect or disobedience at this stage might cause the warriors to force a boy to continue brewing until the intercession of his elders was required once more to gain their consent to the completion of the tasks.

Completion of this period of servitude was symbolized by the warriors' partial acceptance of the candidates for circumcision. This was demonstrated by the participation of both age-sets in an *nkibata*, a dance held on the night before circumcision in which only warriors and candidates might join.

Nkibata was extremely popular and *nthaka* from several areas might travel considerable distances in order to participate. Traditionally, the dance was begun by leading warriors, each of whom danced nude and in full armor, shield gripped in the left hand, spear in the right. Headdresses of colobus monkey skin, tufted with ostrich feathers were woven carefully into their hair, which was dyed red and plaited to the shoulders. Additional monkey skins were wrapped around their legs, while their ankles were ringed with wooden bells. The new initiates were also nude, with the exception of loosely wrapped bands of goatskin around their waists. They were unarmed, carrying in their right hands long staves tipped with rooster feathers.

Leading warriors would announce the dance by sounding long, one-note blasts on the war-horn (*coro, rugoji*), an instrument traditionally made from either the horn of a forest bongo (*ndongoro*) or greater *kudu* (*kamaaru*).[37] Having gathered at the customary dancing field, the *nthaka* then formed into a single circle, facing outward toward the spectators, and began to chant and dance. The candidates responded by forming a circle of their own, facing inwards towards the warriors. Each group then revolved around the other.

It was at this point that candidates were intended to realize that their acceptance by the warriors was incomplete. Instead of greeting them with songs of welcome the veterans showered their fellow dancers with abuse, taunting the group for its youth, military inexperience and lack of manhood, reflected by their fears of the approaching ordeal:

> How can children (such as you) seek the tasks of men;
> You who are too small to be cut (circumcised);
> You who will cry (cry out) at the pain (which is to come).[38]

Such actions were not intended to overawe the youths, but to provoke them into appropriately angry verbal responses, which would in turn stimulate their courage for the final test to come. In practice, it must have deeply shaken the sense of security derived from their earlier efforts, replacing it with increasing awareness of their final obstacle, the circumciser's blade.[39]

The insecurity felt by candidates was intentionally heightened by their experience with the singers of *kirarire*. These were special songs of instruction sung only on the night before the actual cutting. In theory, they were

67

intended as a form of encouragement to the candidates, warning them of the pain which awaited them in such a manner as to stimulate their courage. In practice, such songs must have created unusually intense feelings of personal insecurity and fear.

Kirarire were also intended to amuse and stimulate the community at large. At one point during the final evening, large crowds would gather before the homesteads of each candidate's parents. While dancing continued in the background, self-proclaimed experts (*itharia*) would begin to chant the first sallies, calling out the most philosophical, witty or simply vulgar verses that they could muster, in an attempt to amuse and thus obtain food and beer for the listening crowd from the initiate's parents. On this evening, there were no limits and any form of verbal abuse was permitted, most of which was directed at the women (primarily the candidates' mothers) responsible for providing food.

When the *itharia* had raised the laughter and bantering of the crowd to a sufficiently high level, their position of leadership would be gradually usurped by the 'beater of *kirarire*' (*muringi wa kirarire*), or song-instructor of the youth.[40] The *muringi* had no special qualifications, other than being a respected elder who had attained the position of spokesman (*mugambe*) among the people of his area. However, one man among these elders generally attained a particular reputation for wit and repartee of the type demanded by *kirarire*, and it was he who generally gained the post by general agreement.

Like the *itharia* who preceded him, he had as his first task coaxing continual amounts of beer and food from the mistress of the homestead where he sang, either by cajoling her with praise-songs or taunting her with abuse. This accomplished, the *muringi* turned to his primary function, songs for the instruction of youth. In these instances, both traditional and extemporized verses would be chanted out by the instructor, and the candidates alone would make replies, usually nothing more than a long, drawn-out 'iiiiii,' signifying agreement. Some of the verses dealt with patterns of behavior the candidates would be expected to assume after their circumcision was complete:

> Tanwa niuntu gwaitanirwa ukarumage nyakwa ja mwano mwari,
> ukarumage bagu ja mwano mware.

> Be circumcised so that you may insult your mother
> like your father's daughter. (i.e. respect your elders)[41]

Others were sung merely to inspire community enthusiasm:

> Kirindi kia Mbugi na Murutu,
> mbitikirieni Kirariri na Mkia
> na mutue

> This gathering of Mbugi and Murutu (mythological ancestors of Meru)
> Respond to my Kirariri
> With the sinews of your head

(Sing the responses so strongly that the veins in your foreheads fill to bursting).[42]

Most, however, were intended solely to remind the candidates of their approaching pain, thereby raising them to a peak of inner tension:

Iiiiii, Uuuuu, mwiji,
I ru i nkware egamba

Yesss, you, boy!
It is tomorrow that the spur fowl cries

[Tomorrow, at the moment when the spur fowl cries
(dawn), you will feel the pain.][43]

Kirariri continued till dawn. When the sun rose, each initiate was daubed on the forehead with red ochre by his father, then delivered by the latter to a waiting warrior. By so doing, the parent symbolically reaffirmed his tie with the child one final time, then passed him into the hands of those who would thereafter have full charge of his welfare.[44]

After leaving the homestead, each initiate joined a small body of singing, dancing warriors. These ran him double-time to the banks of a river. The boy then bathed his entire body in the water ('washing childhood away'), while the warriors sang songs on the bank, exhorting courage. The boy remained only a short time in the water; when he emerged, the accompanying group of warriors ran him double time towards the large open field where the cutting would take place, and a jubilant, chanting crowd awaited his arrival.

The arrival of the first initiates from the river caused the spectators to redouble their noise. Each boy ran to the center of the circumcision area, then squatted, heels well under his buttocks, knees well apart, head thrown back and hands thrust upwards, with the elbows resting on his knees.[45] His sponsor stood directly behind him, holding him under the arms and generally steadying him. As other boys arrived, they assumed the same position, forming a rough line across the field. The sponsors lined up behind them and all waited, faces impassive, for the circumciser to arrive.

Once all candidates were on the field, the warriors formed a ring, shoulder to shoulder around them, their banana-leaf skirts and the motion of their dancing forming a ring through which the remaining spectators could not see. Meanwhile, a selected number of warriors were sent to fetch the circumciser (*mutaani*).

The *mutaani* was presented to the candidates in the most threatening possible manner. In some areas, he was concealed at the edge of the field in such a manner as to appear to have emerged from the ground. If his age permitted, he entered the circle leaping, dancing and swinging his knife near the candidates' impassive faces. He wore a headdress of colobus (monkey) skin, with a single upright feather at the forehead. His eyes and the bridge of his nose were daubed with white chalk, in order to prevent his glance from bringing misfortune upon candidates and spectators alike. He was usually accompanied by an apprentice, often his own son, who held a skin bag or large antelope horn containing various ritual mixtures to rub on his knife, allegedly to make the cutting more (or less) painful.[46]

The circumciser began by seizing the end of the foreskin between finger and thumb, drawing it forward, then cutting off the extreme ends in two cuts, one from each side. He then took a fresh grasp on the remains, pulled it forward and slit it just enough to leave a small opening. The penis was then pushed through this opening, leaving a small tassel of foreskin hanging below its base. The operation lasted less than a minute for each boy.[47]

As the circumciser finished, each candidate leaped backwards into the air, throwing himself into the arms of his sponsor, who then deposited him slowly on the ground. At this moment, the boy's behavior during the actual cutting was proclaimed by a specific shout from the surrounding warriors. If he had born the pain without flinching, it was a shout of triumph. If he had winced, or blinked, the clamor was softer, and held undertones of sorrow or contempt. If he had cried or moved to evade the knife, the cry became hoots of derision. The warriors' reaction would be taken up in turn by the women waiting at the edges of the circumcision field. As with the earlier challenge of wrestling, their ululation and shouts of derision or praise represented the ultimate judgment of male behavior. If a boy had proven worthy, they responded in triumph; if not, with expressions of scorn. People in adjoining areas, hearing their clamor, would pass on the basic message with additions of their own. The clamor would continue until it eventually reached the parents of each candidate who were required by custom to await the news of their respective homesteads.[48]

It must be emphasized that there was no physical punishment for failure, even in this final and most crucial test. Instead, the penalty was identical to that imposed for failure at every stage since early childhood, namely, the contempt of one's age-mates, expressed in taunting songs and derisive nicknames. In this instance, since the ordeal was impossible to repeat, disgrace could be expunged only through later deeds in war. Even then, the incident would never be entirely forgotten, and an individual thus marked would have difficulty gaining a wife.

If a boy's reactions had been correct, however, the subsequent shouts of joy would be transmitted to his waiting parents, who were required by tradition to offer beer to everyone. The subsequent dancing would continue through the evening, the songs which accompanied it now offering congratulations and praise:

Twauma gugaikia i kerikwa i ja mbui
Mwanetu akugura kerikwa ja mbui

We have come from taking it (seeing the circumcision)
May it be straight (ened) with feather
Our boy has bought (manhood through bearing the pain)
May it be straight (ened) with feather.

(May the process of circumcision straighten the life of
this boy as an arrow is straightened in its flight by adding
feathers.)[49]

The ordeal of the circumcised, however, had not yet ended. The final stage was still to come. Now honored with the title of *'ntaani'* (the circumcised, newborn), they were led from the circumcision field to a shady grove, to rest and recover. From here, each youth was subsequently transferred to a special hut, where he remained in seclusion till his wound healed.

It was during this healing period that members of the age-sets that had guided the candidates through earlier stages of their circumcision played out their final roles. From the perspective of the newly circumcised, these final lessons must have seemed like little more than repetition of the instruction they had known since childhood. As before, despite their having borne the pain of circumcision, senior warriors were permitted to visit them at will, in order to beat them again and again for past transgressions against their authority. As before, representatives of their parents' age-set, in this instance their circumcision sponsors, were present to regulate the severity of the beatings, acting to reconcile both sides through discussion and settlement of the past incidents from which each beating sprang.[50] In theory, these acts of conflict and conciliation were intended merely to bind both old and new warriors into a more closely knit fighting unit in order to enhance their military efficiency.

Actually, lessons gained from the experience must have been far more sobering. One lesson was that even attainment of the coveted title of warrior brought its members no personal security. Rather, each obstacle surmounted led only to the realization of still another ahead. As children, these new warriors had been made to feel inadequate through lack of age; as adolescents, by lacking the signs of puberty. On attaining puberty, they were taunted for their lack of circumcision; on achieving it, for their lack of military experience. On entering the *gaaru* this pattern continued. Veteran warriors taunted the newcomers for their lack of praise-names, battle-trophies and military reputation until the newcomers would literally be driven into launching raids. The lesson inherent in this pattern, never explicitly expressed but understood by all, was that personal security could be acquired only by mastery of warriorhood itself.

Learning Warriorhood: How and Why

This analysis would be incomplete without attention to two final points, one dealing with the specific means used to militarize the youth of Meru, the second with the reasons for doing so.

Means used during the early stages of militarization were similar to those used by Western societies. Initially, the intent of those responsible was to undermine each youth's sense of personal self-worth and security. This was achieved through enforcement of stereotyped rituals of submission (silence, service, enduring pain, etc.) calculated to convince the person of his own inadequacy. Youths placed in this position found themselves

71

stripped of the essential ability to protect themselves against either physical or verbal abuse. The consequence, inevitably, must have been rapid erosion of their feelings of individual security, personal worth and self-esteem. This erosion, in turn, must have led to increased willingness to subordinate their individualism to the wishes of authority, whether expressed by a peer-group, the aged or tradition.

The next stage was the provision of a new basis for personal security, by replacing individual self-images with the mentality of the group. Again, the means used were similar to those of the West. Each group was isolated from all other elements of the community, having been taught systematically to feel uncomfortable in their presence. Laughter and expressions of happiness were permitted only among themselves. Deviations in clothing or personal adornment were prohibited. Absence from the group, even for sleeping, became progressively more difficult and finally impossible. In short, members were forced into identical behavior patterns within every conceivable situation. Their reward for conforming was expressed in the conditional approval of their seniors; thus they were permitted an equally conditional reinstatement of personal worth, self-esteem and security which, however, would endure only as long as individuals were prepared to subordinate their individual identities perpetually to their appropriate group.

Such feelings of security, however, could have been only temporary, for the third stage of this process seems to have been intended to place the group-mentality so carefully created, within a larger context of perpetual insecurity against which even solidarity with one's age-mates could offer no protection. At every stage they were taught to yearn for status still higher than that achieved, yet every formal rise within the hierarchy only placed them in situations identical to those they had faced before.

The repetitive nature of this pattern suggests that personal security, in the sense of a stable, accepted place within Meru society, was impossible for any male to attain, at least until he entered elderhood. Instead, the young were taught that life's sole purpose was to strive upward. Since each achievement in that direction led simply to the need for further achievement, the very act of striving became every male's reason for existence. It can be argued, therefore, that Meru society envisioned no other role for its young than their progressive militarization, to be attained through ceaseless pursuit of intangible ideals which they could never fully reach.

This conclusion, however, raises the question of its purpose. Why should this particular society have focused so exclusively upon the militarization of its young? The answer does not lie in fear of extinction. Any people, when threatened with conquest by more powerful enemies, will channel every effort into continued survival. In Meru, however, this was never the case. Each subdivision had attained reasoable security by virtue of its geographic location, the Mt. Kenya forests offering adequate refuge to groups facing extermination. Nor did such prospects actually threaten. Neighboring societies fought on a numerical and technological level equal to their own. Battles were small-scale, usually involving fewer than 100 men. Booty was limited to livestock, war-trophies and occasional captives. No effort was made to seize land or to either enslave or expel the population. Warfare was frequent, but its effects were peripheral, offering no threat to society itself.

A more accurate answer may be found in reconsidering the Meru concept of conflict, whether expressed in individual violence or in large-scale war. Members of contemporary Western societies conceive of conflict as potentially limitless, perhaps because of their experience with its excesses. For that reason, they consider it an abhorrent human behavioral trait to be suppressed.

The Meru, however, seem to have perceived conflict in more positive fashion. It was thought to be limited, therefore susceptible to regulation. More important, it was conceived of as a motivating force, a prerequisite to the establishment of harmony between two segments of society. As such it was regarded as essential to the maintenance of social equilibrium. This can be illustrated by briefly reconsidering each of the military ideals, as defined in this analysis, from the perspective of its potential social rather than military value.

Military Ideal	Social Value
1. Desire for self-development	Necessary to provoke conflict.
2. Self-control and subordination to group	Necessary to limit, regulate conflict.
3. Subordination to age and subordination to tradition	Necessary to resolve conflict, create larger harmony between conflicting units.

This arrangement is intended initially to suggest that the internalization of each of these ideals was required of every Meru generation, as a prerequisite to the creation of *one* portion of the process (conflict/harmony) used in Meru to relieve social tensions. If the assumption is correct, then internalization of all of them would be necessary if the entire process was to function as intended. The military ideals, therefore, appear to have served not merely as motivating abstractions, but as cornerstones, essential prerequisites for a system of domestic conciliation. Viewed in this context, the entire process of 'learning warriorhood' seems to have served not only to protect Meru society against outsiders, but to preserve it against disruption from within.

CHAPTER IV

The Novice Warrior

In theory, warriorhood began at the moment circumcision was complete. In practice, it started only after wounds from the operation had healed sufficiently to permit entry into the *gaaru*. At that time, a single older *muthaka* was selected to escort each new recruit from his homestead into the warrior ranks. This escort assumed the role of sponsor toward the novice, taking subsequent responsibility for his correct behavior within the *gaaru*, as the youth's circumcision-sponsor had done during the operation.

New warriors soon learned, however, that passage into the war-barrack signaled no more than still another cycle of apprenticeship. To those outside the structure, they were warriors and were referred to by the coveted title of *nthaka*. Within it, however, they were still addressed as *ntaani* (sing: *mutaani*). It will be recalled that the term had initially been one of honor, used at the moment of their circumcision to denote that they had been "new born" into the stage of manhood. Within the *gaaru*, however, the same term acquired different undertones, suggesting the ignorance and inexperience of a novice.

Fortunately, the period of apprenticeship (*utaani*) was short, lasting only from the beginning of the rainy season (when circumcisions traditionally began) to the end, when the subsequent dry weather would permit *ntaani* to earn status within the *gaaru* by their behavior during raids.[1] Between the time of their circumcision and the ending of the rains, however, novice warriors passed through the final stages of their training, a process intended to raise their fighting spirit to such a pitch as literally to compel them to wage war.

Entering the Gaaru

For the novices the initial problem posed by this final portion of their training was to gain the acceptance of their seniors regarding their right to act as warriors. The struggle to achieve this began with each youngster's entry into the war-barrack, since his right to a respected place within this structure came under immediate attack.

The resulting conflict was partially due to the physical arrangement of a *gaaru*. In Imenti, the structure was built along the lines of a beehive, with thatched roof reaching almost to the ground. It was large enough to house fifty warriors and sufficiently high to permit occupants to raise six-foot spears against attackers. The framework was supported by four upright poles. Two smaller ones at the front supported a single open door.

To the right and left, as one entered the doorway, were spaces for warriors to stack their spears. The left side, in addition, held a small, deep pit used for urination at night. Beyond these spaces, on either side, were two long sleeping platforms. These were constructed by building a wall of logs, then filling the space between them and the *gaaru* wall with earth. The long platforms were about thirty inches high. A third platform, exactly opposite the doorway, was deliberately built a few inches higher and much narrower than those on the sides.[2]

At any given time, a *gaaru* would be occupied by representatives of two sub-sets.[3] The older of these, having entered the structure before their fellow warriors, were generally referred to as 'the senior ones' (*nchanganabire*). Their juniors, having entered at a later date, acquired the title of 'the junior ones' (*ntimirigwe*).[4] As the senior sub-set passed out of warriorhood, the junior group assumed its title, transferring the other name to a still younger group when its first representatives arrived.

Status within the war-barrack was determined by membership in either of these two groups and reflected in the sleeping place each person could claim. For a brief period, members of the senior group were permitted to claim the structure for themselves alone. In consequence, they could occupy all available sleeping space, spreading along both of the long platforms according to their status. Positions nearest the door were reserved for war-leaders. Those directly behind were taken by members of *ramare*, the council of warriors. The remaining space was used by younger and weaker members of the group, with the least prestigious taking positions at the rear.

As the first *ntaani* of the subsequent sub-set appeared, they were contemptuously relegated to the high sleeping platform. Senior warriors referred to this as the small jumping place of the *ntaani*, and made certain that the novices realized it was the least honorable position. It was drafty, being opposite the open door, and could be reached only by jumping the open fire. It was also felt to be the position most exposed to attack by hyenas, which would occasionally leap at meat hanging from the *gaaru* roof. Finally, it was too short to permit proper leg-room, thus making sleep difficult.

76

As circumcisions continued, more and more novices entered the *gaaru*, to be confined in their turn to the 'jumping place.' Concurrently, increasing numbers of senior warriors began to leave, either occasionally, in search of wives, or completely, because of marriage, in so doing, they left additional sleeping space to their remaining age-mates, at the very time when the high platform grew progressively too crowded for the novices. For *ntaani* the solution lay once more in reversion to the techniques they had learned in prior training, the provoking of limited conflict with their immediate superiors. In practice, the boldest of the newcomers would begin by placing his sword on the sleeping platform to his left, the usual place for it being behind his head. Next, he might lay his elbow on the same spot. This would be followed by his foot, then his leg.

At some stage, those senior warriors occupying the least prestigious portion of the long platform would order him back. If backed by sufficient numbers of his age-mates, he might repeat the infraction or even refuse. Disobedience to a superior was punishable by beatings for all *ntaani* concerned, but the encroachment would begin again almost immediately afterward. In theory, acts of defiance and punishment would alternate at an increasing rate, with the least prestigious senior warriors cast in the role of primary opponents. In time, hostility between these two groups would increase to the point where warriors senior to both of them (members of *ramare*) would intervene, either ordering the *ntaani* back to their original position or commanding the lesser seniors to make room.

Inevitably, either decision would generate the same result, as the process of encroachment would soon begin again. Since new members continued to enter, the space they required had to be won. Winning was possible only by re-creating the pattern of limited conflict. The effect was to reinforce the lessons of their boyhood by demonstrating their continued relevance within warriorhood itself.[5]

Eventually, *ntaani* occupied the entire left side of the *gaaru*, relegating their own newest members to the jumping place and continuing to encroach on veterans' positions along the other side.

At an appropriate time, approximately twelve years after entry of the first *ntaani*, the elders would proclaim an end to the period of subset formation. A short interval would follow during which no circumcision would take place. Thereafter, initiation into still another subset would begin, which in turn would send its first initiates into the *gaaru*. These, known in their turn as *ntimirigwe*, would be forced onto the jumping place to renew the encroachment process.[6]

Approval of Ramare

The second problem faced by *ntaani* was that of acceptance by members of the senior warriors' council (*ramare*). These persons, or others

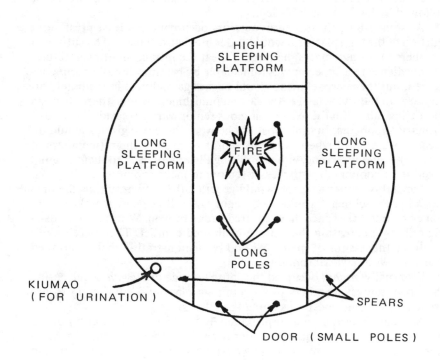

Ground plan of *gaaru*, Imenti

selected by them, were responsible for the more traditional portions of their final military training, since only they were felt to possess sufficient judgment and restraint.

This training began immediately upon entry into the *gaaru*, and continued intermittently throughout the early months of warriorhood. In its initial stages, it consisted of the traditional methods of alternating periods of pain, verbal instruction and required service. The process began as each novice stepped inside the structure. Within moments he was informed of his obligation to 'purchase' a warrior-name, that of his uncircumcised period having been abandoned as unworthy of his new role.

A man's warrior-name was selected by his father. Customarily, it referred to either some facet of the latter's character, reputation in war, or current economic status.[7] Thus, the son of a wealthy man might be referred to as *M'Inoti, M'Ikaria, M'Mbui,* or *M'Mburugo*—all of which suggest possession of large numbers of livestock. One whose father had been noted in war might be known as *M'Ruchio* (taker of the sword), *M'Kiambati* (he who took cattle) or *M'Irandu* (he who has killed). Alternately, a talkative man might name his son *M'Kwaria* (he who speaks swiftly), *Kirathuku* (loud talker) or *Kibuura* (he who quarrels).[8]

The father would pass on his selection to the sponsor who formally fetched his son to the *gaaru*. The novice himself would not be told, nor would he know what to expect on entry. The intent of those responsible for his militarization was to place him once more in a situation of stress, in order to evaluate his potential.

Approval, as always, could be obtained only by submission to deliberately inflicted pain. On entry, therefore, each *mutaani* was told to grasp one of the *gaaru* posts, so that he might 'buy' his name and with it his right to remain inside the structure. The first blows, he was informed, were merely to 'clean off' the red ochre which his father had smeared on his body, so that he might not try to set himself above his fellows.[9] Those following were to force him to accept any one of a number of warrior names other than the one he was given. During the first stage of the ceremony, the new *ntaani* were formed into a circle, then armed with flexible switches. At a signal from the older warriors, they would begin beating their age-mates, continuing until the reeds broke in their hands. If a boy refused to stand the pain, he was tied to one of the *gaaru* uprights and the beating was continued.

During the second stage, beating was done by members of *ramare*. A novice was given a series of names other than that intended for him. The names suggested at this point were usually those of animals regarded with ill favor by all, such as *M'Mbiti* (son of hyena) or *M'Njoka* (son of snake). After each suggestion, the *ntaani* was asked whether he would accept the name proferred. After each refusal he was beaten on the buttocks by two *ramare* spokesmen who stood on either side. If a newcomer was so intransigent as to refuse the name which had been chosen for him, however, he could be beaten all night until he reconsidered. Nor was sleep permitted to any of the novices until all had agreed to 'purchase' the required names.[10]

This stage of training was intended to instruct *ntaani* in two ways. By passively enduring the required beatings they symbolically reaffirmed their desire to remain within the warrior ranks and were thus accepted by those representatives of the warrior council who had beaten them. By accepting a name symbolic of their fathers, each took on the obligation to uphold the father's honor, since the name thus chosen remained with each *mutaani* throughout his warriorhood. If, however, his own exploits eventually overshadowed his father's reputation, the entire community chose for him new names which reflected them. Each man thus remained in the shadow of his father unless able to mold a reputation for himself.

Beating was also the primary means of reinforcing verbal instruction. During such periods, each *mutaani* in turn would be ordered to stand before the supporting post nearest the door. Two members or representatives would stand on either side of him, bearing light, flexible switches. Only the buttocks could be beaten, and then only until both sticks were broken or the lesson was felt to be complete.

The lesson was administered in the following manner:[11]

You will obey the order of your leaders. (Whack from the right)
And never question them. (Whack from the left)
You will never lose your temper. (Whack from the right)
Or use a hasty word. (Whack from the left)
Or raise your spear in anger. (Whack from the right)
Or draw your sword in anger. (Whack from the left)
Or raise your hand in anger. (Whack from the right)
. . . .

The lessons included instruction in certain privileges, acquired only through reaching adulthood. The *mutaani's* word or oath, as well as his curse, was now accepted as potentially harmful to others, since it could evoke conditions of *mugiro*. Therefore, explicit instruction was required concerning circumstances in which these could properly be proclaimed. Nor was a novice required to labor in the fields, even to assist his family during harvests. Instead, he was to direct all efforts toward improving his own economic position by acquiring livestock in raids. He was permitted to listen during elders' council meetings, and in exceptional cases could even join their deliberations. Finally, *ntaani* were permitted to call upon any one of the various ritual specialists for performance of rituals connected with illness, catastrophe or death.[12]

Other lessons added new dimensions to the traditional restrictions on warrior behavior. The rule prohibiting absence from one's age-mates, for instance, assumed new meaning when perceived in terms of possible enemy ambush of the warrior thus isolated. Restrictions against sleeping in (or even entering) huts other than the *gaaru*, while primarily intended to prevent sexual contact, also seemed more relevant when considered in terms of possible surprise attack. Obviously, warriors grouped together within a single structure could react against aggressors more effectively than widely scattered stragglers.

Traditional food taboos also assumed new meaning. Novices were now restricted to foods symbolic of their military status. Birds, eggs and various insects, for example, were considered the food of children. Beans, tomatoes and other vegetables were reserved for women and the aged. The effect was to provide each non-military class with a source of supply during periods of scarcity. By so doing, all available meat could be reserved for consumption of warriors, who could thus symbolically maintain the strength to protect their community.

New dimensions could also be found in the behavior now required with other social classes. Particular stress was laid on reactions to elders. These were to be given the same exaggerated deference that the novices had previously given warriors. Now warriors themselves, they were still expected to stand aside for every elder met along the paths. Silence was required in the presence of the elderly, except for properly respectful greetings, adjusted to various degrees of kinship and status. Bantering and laughter were forbidden, as was questioning without first asking explicit permission of the elder involved. Replies to elders' queries were to be delivered in a soft-voiced monotone, while looking at the ground. Obedience to reasonable requests was mandatory, while insulting or cursing older people individually or as a group led to the severest possible penalties.[13] Such instruction, of course, was intended to reinforce the concept of submission to the aged, thereby assuring that the warriors' spears were used only to benefit the community.

Traditional restrictions against contact with females also gained new meaning. *Ntaani*, of course, were required to go to exaggerated lengths to avoid such contact. When gathering food, for instance, bands of novices would go from homestead to homestead, collecting food from the mothers of their age-mates. No conversation, however, was permitted between them. The warriors' request was made by means of a special whistle. The food was then brought to them by a small child.[14] Similar arrangements applied to unmarried and uncircumcised women. *Ntaani* were forbidden to eat, rest and speak in their presence, or even look at those they met along the paths. Theoretically, the purpose of this instruction was to permit new warriors to maintain their physical peak. In fact, aside from restricting sexual contacts, its effect was to reserve all marriageable women for those senior warriors who had begun to seek wives. The restriction prevented development of disruptive sexual rivalries between veterans and novices.

As in the case of the *biama* of boyhood, periods of verbal instruction were supplemented with times set aside for traditional tasks. These, too, acquired new dimensions, evolving from simple labor into effective training tools. The clearest illustration of this technique can be found in the requirement to collect wood for the *gaaru*. Wood collecting occurred daily and was reserved for the novices, as had been the case in other societies throughout childhood. At this stage, however, an arbitrary restriction was imposed. The *ramare* permitted such collection to take place only at night, a practice intended to increase the difficulty in locating adequate supplies. Since failure to produce the required amounts within a given time led invariably to beating, new warriors once again found themselves placed under conditions of stress.

The most obvious solution was to steal existing supplies of firewood from the homesteads of elders, particularly poles used to support banana trees within each family's groves. This act, in turn, required development of theft and foraging skills, since punishment was administered to any *mutaani* caught (or even seen) within such areas. In consequence, new warriors were literally compelled to develop precisely those abilities—swiftness, stealth, etc.—which would most facilitate their subsequent survival among the enemy.[15]

Restrictions placed by the *ramare* on daily food collections suggest similar training patterns. Custom dictated that food for both novice and veteran warriors was to be collected by the former from their mothers. However, if supplies proved inadequate, fear of the subsequent beatings would drive newcomers once more into foraging. In this instance, tradition required that foodstuffs be taken solely from the groves and gardens of those few older warriors whose approaching marriage permitted cultivation by their prospective wives. Retaliation, of course, was inevitably severe for those careless (or slow) enough to be identified by the property owners, a threat that once more compelled development of the qualities of swiftness and stealth. The result was a system that provided *ntaani* with two satisfactions, one in developing skills appropriate to the acquisition of food, and a second in striking back against those who beat them for failing to provide it.

The task of food collection was also intended to instruct novices in correct forms of diplomacy. One lesson concerned the behavior of warriors forced to forage among the fields of families related to their own. If visits to an appropriate homestead found its womenfolk absent, for instance, *ntaani* were permitted to take what they required from its gardens. The food thus taken, however, had to be cooked and eaten (in part) upon a public path, then shared equally between warriors and whatever local children were nearby. For the same reason, gardens from which produce had been taken were to be carefully weeded by the warriors concerned.[16] As *ntaani*, use of these and similar practices were intended to demonstrate the existence of kinship ties between themselves and the landholders, the gestures indicating that the food had not been seized by thieves, but by warriors acting within the limits of custom. Later, as raiding *nthaka*, they would use these same gestures while traversing *miiriga* with whom their own was militarily allied, demonstrating that such supplies as they had been forced to seize were not stolen but intended for 'kinfolk' acting within the limits prescribed by custom.[17]

New warriors were also allotted tasks intended to train them in the proper use of their new authority. This training was achieved by allowing them responsibility for the teaching of children. Every warrior, of course, was expected to assist in instilling respect for the institution of warriorhood, primarily by beating children whose behavior failed to reflect a proper degree of submissiveness. Novices, however, were taught the limits of such beatings by their own excesses. Failure to beat a disobedient child would lead to beatings of their own on return to the *gaaru*. Failing to provide a specific reason for each beating given led to similar consequences. The same applied to warriors who beat too harshly. The novice whose stick drew the blood of a child, whether by intent or accident, would be beaten in consequence till the switches broke.[18]

A second responsibility of this type was to teach children to fear strangers, especially strange warriors. One method used called for the novice to creep up in darkness to a hut in which children were playing. He would then call one in a soft voice, saying, "Bring me your finger and I'll give it a ring." The child who gave his finger to the soft voice in darkness had it promptly bitten. Thus he learned (ostensibly) to fear strange voices and, in the process, all warriors. A second example called for the *mutaani* to stand outside the child's hut in darkness and ask in a gentle tone for aid, usually in the form of either water or tobacco. The child who responded to the plea was beaten within the limits previously described. In consequence, children everywhere learned the folly of responding to strangers, while the novices found opportunity to explore the nature of their authority.[19]

Initial military responsibilities were also intended to reinforce traditional values. Periodically, *ntaani* were asked to man outposts which guarded the main approaches to each *gaaru*, a practice which increased their isolation from non-military elements of society, and at the same time utilized their desire for responsibility. At other times they were sent to herd cattle near the forest fringes when these areas were particularly tempting to raiders. With these exceptions, however, the only tasks required of novices were the defense of their *miiriga* and preparation for raids.

At this stage of training, however, much preparation was more theoretical than real, for despite taunts of military inexperience by the veterans, *ntaani* were in fact forbidden to wage war. No single novice, for instance, was permitted to leave the *mwiriga* for any reason, whether to scout, forage or seek war trophies. Nor could small groups of them set off to try their skill. The decision to wage war, however small-scale, lay not with individual warriors, but with their *mwiriga*. A raid without the approval of its ruling *kiama* was not viewed as warfare, but as an act of personal vengeance that would dishonor the age-set of those involved. In consequence, the novices were caught between opposing pressures. On one hand, they were taunted individually and as an age-set for military inaction. On the other, they were restricted to minimal domestic responsibilities, and explicitly forbidden to transcend them.

Thus balked, they had no choice but to struggle for what limited security could be obtained within the *gaaru*. This in turn must have proved frustrating, since each effort to extend their own rights brought instant retaliation from their superiors. The traditional beatings might be alternated with demands by the veterans for livestock levies, the cost of which had to be divided equally among every member of the junior group, and borne ultimately by their male kinsmen from whose herds the animals had to come.[20] It was a system against which individual *ntaani* could do nothing, either to protect themselves or advance their corporate interests. Their sole hope lay in subordinating personal differences to the point where they could act in every instance with a single voice. To achieve this, they required spokesmen.

Establishing Spokesmen

New warriors faced three difficulties in selecting spokesmen for their group. One was that its membership was never stable, but increased throughout the apprentice period as new members passed through circumcision. Each of these, in turn, brought with him a potential for leadership which could upset previously established patterns and throw the entire subset into turmoil. A related problem concerned the lack of formal procedures for selection. Leaders emerged as the result of a general consensus by all concerned, a process that required time and was subject to change.

The most serious challenge, however, lay in the very nature of the disciplinary system with which new warriors had to contend. The heart of its authority lay in the tradition of collective punishment for an individual's offense. This meant, in practice, that each attempt by potential leaders to assert themselves could lead to whipping for the entire junior group. In such instances, custom called for the emergent leaders to explain their actions before an ad hoc *kiama* of age-mates, a process which inhibited emergence of leaders, since their individual efforts at assertiveness might bring punishment to all.

To resolve the problem, tradition permitted *ntaani* to resort to the custom of *gituuji*. This was a feast given by each novice soon after he entered the *gaaru*, at which he offered a bull for consumption by his age-mates. Theoretically, the event was intended to symbolize the newcomer's acceptance by those of his own age-set who had entered warriorhood before him. By offering meat, he claimed the right to join their ranks. By eating it, those senior to him accepted his claim. In practice, *gituuji* also provided novices with the opportunity to establish rank among themselves; in this way the emergence of leaders was facilitated. The institution was not a single event, but a recurring series of feasts which stretched out over an entire rainy season. Ideally, each new warrior proclaimed *gituuji* as soon as he recovered from his circumcision wounds.[21] Since youths could be circumcised at any time within a given season, as many as fifty such feasts could be held, with novices moving from one to the other as their numbers increased.

The feasting was rigidly formalized with each portion of the slaughtered animal given out according to status within the group.[22] The result was a continuing series of opportunities, free from the oppressive presence of senior warriors, to adjust that status to the satisfaction of all. Thus, when a potential leader entered the *gaaru*, whether backed by a legacy of family wealth, military courage, or skill at reconciliation this potential would be reflected in each subsequent division of *gituuji* meat. The act of mutually consuming the meat thus divided would symbolize agreement to such adjustments by all concerned.

Selection of spokesmen for the novices was generally followed by their incorporation into the council of warriors. Formal membership was limited to four persons—two from the senior sub-set and two from their juniors.[23] Temporary additions, however, could be made to any warriors' council to aid in resolution of a specific problem. Thus, if a quarrel concerned warriors of two clans, representatives from both sides would be added to the *kiama* to act as 'spokesmen' in seeking its resolution.

Selection was by general agreement among both novice and veteran warriors, with informal concurrence of the *kiama* of ruling elders. Members might be selected for a number of reasons. Some were chosen for their ability to conciliate; others, for their powers of oration. Still others came to prominence by virtue of their physical strength, weapons skills or merely wealth and corresponding social status of their families. Novices whose fathers had held similar positions were closely observed, both by their peers and by interested elders, since the qualities of spokesmanship (*ugambe*) were believed inheritable.[24]

In most areas, *ncamba* of both junior and senior status were also members of the warriors' council. In no instance, however, did they rule it. Rather, they were considered first among equals when the council was concerned with questions of peace or war. In turn, they deferred to their fellows when faced with domestic issues. In short, the warriors' council was intended to serve as an amorphous committee of equals, whose status within it rose and fell according to the need for their abilities.

Persons thus selected would be summoned periodically by the ruling elders to observe such aspects of their own *biama* as were believed instructive to themselves. These warrior spokesmen also served as liaison between the elders and the warrior rank-and-file, communicating wishes voiced on both sides in order to minimize friction within the *mwiriga* as a whole. This type of contact occasionally led spokesmen for the elders to invite leading members of *ramare* into their ruling group. There, they would represent the interests of their own set among the aged, while gradually absorbing the traditions by which society as a whole was controlled.

Ideally, the principles thus learned would be applied in turn to conflicts among the warriors. Disputes within the *gaaru* could be settled only by members of *ramare*, and only according to the principles that they in turn had acquired through association with the aged. Thus council members conceived of themselves as neither rulers nor judges, but merely spokesmen for tradition. By so doing, they created a basis for their eventual future selection to the ruling councils during their own period of eldership.

Leadership could also be established through the institution of single combat, for it was through this that spokesmen for battle (war-leaders)[25] could emerge. Before circumcision, novices fought one another with the traditional weapons of boyhood. When they became warriors, the process evolved into an informal, but continuous, succession of "challenge-combats," encouraged both as military instruction and as a prerequisite of the selection of *ncamba*.

The weapons used in these combats were carefully regulated by tradition. Shields were formed by stitching buffalo or rhinoceros hide to an oval frame of wood long enough to protect the warrior's upper body. A wooden spine was then added, into which a hand-grip had been burned with charcoal. The hair was then shaved from the skin and designs of red, white and black were applied with ochre, chalk and charcoal.

Spears took two forms. The less common had a rounded (leaf-blade) iron head, usually six inches long. It had a roughly formed socket with a mid-rib running towards the point which permitted the attachment of a wooden six-foot shaft. The shaft could be attached in turn to a one-foot hollowed iron butt, which was sharpened at the tip.

The more common type of spear had been borrowed from the Maasai. The blade was usually three feet long and two inches wide. The butt was almost as long and rounded throughout its length except for its end, which was squared. Both pieces of iron fitted into a short wooden shaft, leaving space for only a hand-hold between them.

War-clubs also took two forms. Throwing-clubs (*njuguma*) were carved from the root of a single tree, shaped with an iron knife, then scraped smooth with leaves so rough as to have the effect of sandpaper. The finished product was between two and three feet long. Its rounded head permitted it to be thrown thirty to forty yards with sufficient force to stun an enemy.

Hitting-clubs, in contrast, were intended to remain continuously in a warrior's hand, to be used in beating down an opponent's shield. The most common type (*ntaratuki*) was made from a single rounded stone the size of an orange. This was set on the end of a flexible stick three feet by one inch in diameter. It was initially kept in place by strips of pliant wood bent over the surface and lashed with bits of hide. Thereafter, a piece of wet buffalo skin was folded over it, covering the stone itself and three inches of the wooden shaft. This was then lashed and allowed to shrink into a firm fit.

A second variant of this type (*ngachagacha*) was similarly constructed. In this instance, many small stones were placed inside a piece of wet goatskin. This was attached to a three-foot-long flexible stick, permitted to shrink into position, then firmly lashed with hide bindings. Usually, a warrior would carry no fewer than three war-clubs into battle.

Swords averaged twenty-four inches in length. The blades were hammered from crude iron to a width of one to two inches below the tapered point and perhaps one inch at the base. This base was then finished off into a tang, which was heated and jammed into a four-inch wooden grip. No binding of any sort was used to secure it. A sheath was then fashioned from two strips of wood, which were then stitched together with bits of cowhide. Usually, ochre was then rubbed into the completed sheath to produce its traditional red sheen.

In training, single combats were carefully regulated. No warrior was permitted to seize arms as the result of a quarrel. Nor could any two persons settle disputes in private. If an aspiring novice wished to challenge an opponent, whether in his own age-set or above, he was required to wait until that warrior slept. He then crept towards the sleeper and wrapped a dry banana leaf around his leg. The deliberateness of the action was intended as a barrier against challenges issued in moments of ungoverned rage. On waking and finding the leaf, the sleeper would demand the challenger's identity. Only then could the latter stand forth fully armed before the *gaaru* doorway and call him out.[26]

Such challenge-combats were public events, requiring the presence of spectators favorable to both sides. Tradition also required the attendance of *ramare* members and as many elders as might be near. The purpose was not only to insure fair play, but to allow those responsible to evaluate the fighting qualities of both parties. Beyond that, the occasion was intended as instruction for other novices, with regard to both the fighters' skills and their strategic errors.

After the wakened warrior had armed himself, he would meet his opponent in the open space before the *gaaru*. Usually, each would grasp a four-foot high oval shield in his left hand. The right held a six-foot spear with all four fingers placed under the shaft. A twenty-four-inch sword hung at the right side of each warrior's belt, as did one or possibly two clubs. A third club was held in the fighter's shield hand, grasped in the palm, while his fingers secured the shield itself.

At the beginning of the fight, each warrior knelt, resting on one knee at a range of six feet. In so doing, he was able to conceal his head, body and feet against possible spear thrusts. At a signal, both fighters sidled forward, lunging semi-blindly at one another as they moved within range. Ideally, this initial lunge would cause one of the two to lose balance, exposing him to a spear thrust. If this failed to occur, both warriors would draw back slightly and lunge again. The idea was to maintain one's forward momentum while remaining on one knee. The shield was then wielded in such a manner as to force the opponent off balance and thereby to permit effective use of the spear.[27]

If spear and shield tactics proved unavailing, one or both warriors might shift the spear quickly to the left (shield) hand, and grasp a club (or sword). These weapons would then be used to smash or hack at the opponent's shield, in the hope of destroying the frame to the point where its protection would fail. If this tactic proved unsuccessful, combatants might swiftly return to their spears, hoping always for a successful thrust in the opponent's ribs. Such a thrust might signal an end to the fight.

Antagonists were free to lunge to their feet and fight standing. However, the first to do so generally exposed both head and ankles to the spear of his opponent, thus risking disablement before he could strike. When he was kneeling, the shield was large enough to cover the entire body and protect all extremities from harm.

This type of combat could end in one of three ways. A spear-thrust to the body, if sufficient to draw blood, was considered a victory for its originator. Since combatants, in this case, were of the same *gaaru*, each was expected to control his thrust so that it would draw blood but not kill.

Alternately, if one warrior was obviously losing, the fight could be stopped by a member of *ramare*, or an elder if one was present. He stopped the fight by circling around behind the thrusting combatants and placing a skin bag (*mondo*, pl: *biondo*) over the shoulders of the warrior who had lost. He would then shout '*jukia mondo*' (take the bag), as a sign that the fighting should end.

In instances where neither senior warrior nor elder proved willing to stop this type of combat, a method of self-surrender could be used. In this case, the losing warrior would suddenly leap backwards, away from his opponent, and reverse his shield. In so doing, he risked injury from the victor's final blow, but spectators could usually be relied on to raise sufficient hue and cry to bring the victor to a halt. Further, a victorious warrior who kept striking at an opponent who was attempting to surrender, risked beating by that warrior's age-mates, or discipline by the *ramare*.

As the result of these combats, several persons might rise to positions of prominence. Eventually, one of them would perform with exceptional skill, generally in combat with one of his seniors. At the conclusion, those who favored him would sing out that he was 'truly *ncamba*.' If others took up the cry to the point where it became general, the senior warriors had no choice but to accept the verdict, and the person's new status was acclaimed by all. No formal ceremony accompanied this declaration. Rather, there was simply agreement among those responsible that the *ntaani* had found a spokesman for problems of war.[28]

It must be emphasized that the status of *ncamba* was never permanent, but always open to other warriors. If one person objected to the selection of a second for the coveted title, he had only to challenge his supremacy according to the conventions described. Similarly, warriors of lesser ability could increase their status by challenging those alleged to rank above them in fighting skill. The results of such battles were reflected in the nightly allocation of *gaaru* sleeping places and the division of meat.

The challenge-system fostered little sense of security among participants, since whatever status had been obtained was open to attack from below. It did, however, provide incentive, since honor was available to those who strove. Ideally, the result was a body of warriors in constant action, each struggling ceaselessly to protect or improve his position through the constant honing of military skills.

Conditional Acceptance: The *Authi* of Nudity

Soon after circumcision of its final member, the newly formed sub-set was presented to the community at large. This was done by proclaiming a special dance, the '*authi* of nudity.'[29] Participation was restricted to warriors, although both novices and veterans danced on equal terms, a practice that allowed the former to display both the physical evidence of their newly acquired manhood and symbolic proof of their acceptance by the seniors.

It was also the first occasion for the new warriors to appear fully armed. Ideally, each man carried a shield, spear, three swords, and three clubs. In fact, less wealthy novices were content if they had one of each article.[30]

The day before *authi* was spent in final preparations. Junior and senior warriors alike painted their shields and bodies, smearing the latter with castor oil, then covering it with chalk. *Ntaani* remained naked. The veterans symbolized their higher status by dancing clothed, either in single square capes cut from cowhide, or white cotton cloths[31] tied around their necks and shoulders.

At sunrise, the entire body of warriors burst onto the field at a run. Each novice, nude and fully armed, advanced toward the middle of the dancing area in a series of stiff two-legged bounds. By that time, the edges of the cleared space were ringed with spectators, as no class or age-group of people could be forbidden to see *authi*.

Young women stood in compact groups urging the dancers to higher and longer leaps. If a misstep caused one person to bounce either his body or his shield against those of another, custom required both to stop dancing and fight. In theory, members of *ramare* would rush between them before blood could be spilled, but combatants would then find themselves special targets for the spectators' jeering and abuse. Such skirmishes grew more frequent as the warriors tired, providing entertainment for the audience and ample opportunity for novices to display their skills.

Authi lasted from dawn till dusk. Among civilians, the occasion was accepted as symbolic of the senior warriors' acceptance to their ranks of the *ntaani* age-set. Within the *gaaru*, however, this acceptance remained conditional, dependent upon the novices' continued willingness to conform to their seniors' expectations.

After completing *authi*, however, the novices found themselves faced with what must have seemed like the withdrawal of even such conditional acceptance as had been achieved. At this point in their training, the expectation of their superiors was no less than participation in the act of war. To guide *ntaani* through this final step, the senior warriors, at the instigation of *ramare*, resorted to the tactic of taunting.

The novices, of course, had been taunted by their seniors since circumcision. They had been ridiculed unceasingly as pretenders who took the title of *nthaka* without the wish to fight. This led to intense frustration among those subjected to such treatment, yet the full impact was blunted, since novices knew well that the time for war was months away, and that they would be forbidden to fight even if willing to do so.

When they had completed *authi*, however, the earlier feelings of reassurance disappeared. By this point, the rainy season was almost over, and the earth was nearly hard enough for raids. In consequence, the taunting was systematically intensified, focusing mainly on the alleged lack of manhood of the novices. They were particularly reviled for their appearance in *authi* having "deceived the people (the community) by showing them that which never was there."[32]

The lesson was reinforced by reactions from the civilian community, particularly the younger women. After *authi*, songs reviling the *ntaani* for military inaction sprang up throughout the area. This was particularly evident during community dances. Although formally forbidden to notice the existence of women, new warriors were very much aware of their presence. The women, in turn, made use of such occasions to compete with one another in their taunting. One girl, for instance, might subtly taunt a particular *mutaani* by mistakenly referring to him (in song) by the name of a noted veteran rather than his own, thereby implying that the junior lacked the qualities attributed to his senior. A second might sing of the senior warriors in a manner suggesting their achievements could never be equaled by those now entering their warriorhood.[33] The novices, forbidden by custom to respond to the taunting, could only keep silent.

It must be emphasized that the custom of taunting, particularly when practiced by women, was regarded as a uniquely effective instructional device, perhaps the only one capable of producing such tension and insecurity among new warriors that they would subsequently prove willing to risk their very lives to relieve it. The technique was intended, at this final point in their militarization, to drive them physically away from their relatively secure existence within the *gaaru* and into the isolation of the bush. Only under such conditions could their urge for combat be raised to the pitch required.

The Public Oath

Tradition provided novices with only one solution to this final problem, compliance with community desires in the form of a public oath (*kirugu*, pl: *irugu*). There were several steps in this declaration. The first emerged as the result of the continued taunting. As life within and outside the *gaaru* grew progressively more unbearable, one novice after another would decide to declare an oath. In Imenti, for instance, the vow most frequently resorted to was called 'cutting the heifer' (*rengua mwari*). Having chosen to proclaim it, the novices would flee the *gaaru*, either individually or in small groups. Thereafter, they would gather together in a remote section of the bush and establish a rudimentary camp.

For an unspecified period, they would live a hand-to-mouth existence, foraging for survival among the *mwiriga* gardens, unable to act out the second step of their decision until the birth of a heifer calf. During this time, every hand in the community seemed turned against them. Homeowners grouped together to guard their gardens, while wealthy elders took great pains to conceal the births of such heifers as had been born, as all feared the wildness of these 'bush-warriors' and the harm they might do among their herds.

Eventually, one or more of the waiting *ntaani* would learn of the birth of a heifer calf (*mwari*). He would steal into the homestead of its owner, then silently 'cut the heifer,' traditionally by slicing its ear. Having done so, he would leap up and backwards, shouting out a specific oath, by which he would thereafter be publicly bound, such as:[34]

> May I remain in the bush till I have killed (an enemy warrior). May I neither wash nor shave my head until I have brought (captured) cattle to my father.

The cry and variations of the oath it contained would then be repeated by other runaway novices, who one after another would burst into the elder's homestead and slice the ear of a heifer. By so doing, each passed symbolically into the status of 'oath-warrior' (*muthaka cia kirugu*), the act of proclamation having ritually compelled them to remain outside the *gaaru* till the vow each had taken was fulfilled.[35]

Merely proclaiming an oath, of course, intensified rather than eased *ntaani* insecurities. Having accepted the senior warriors' evaluation of themselves, they responded by setting the highest possible conditions necessary to regain community esteem. Having done so, and still lacking formal permission to wage war, they retreated to their bush shelter, to be joined by increasing numbers of their age-mates, and to wait.

Each step of this behavior had naturally been anticipated by the senior warriors. On returning to their shelter, *ntaani* were met by those of their age-mates who were not under oath. These had been sent by *ramare* to assist them during their isolation. Their first task was to build near a river a communal shelter (*nyumba ya kirugu*: oath-hut) for the oath-warriors, where additional age-mates could gather should they choose to flee the *gaaru*. Thereafter, these assistants served as liaison between oath-takers and veterans, since those under oath were forbidden to speak to anyone not sharing their self-imposed isolation.

Oath-warriors remained in this communal shelter for the balance of the rainy season. During this period, they intensified their resolution and raised their fighting strength by a number of traditionally accepted practices. One was that of isolation. During their weeks in the bush, none but those age-mates designated as liaison might see them. By custom they were forbidden to leave the rough shelter they had constructed except to relieve themselves at night. To insure compliance with this practice, senior warriors stationed members of their own group a respectful distance away from their shelter, but near enough to assure themselves that tradition was observed.

Fighting spirit was also strengthened by the practice of meat-eating. Prolonged consumption of beef particularly was believed to increase both physical strength and mental agility. As a result, *ntaani* spent most of this period inside the shelter feasting on cattle donated by their parents or kinsmen. For the same reasons, they neither shaved their beards nor their hair during this period. Nor did they apply oil, ochre or any other traditional decoration to their bodies.

Martial resolution was further heightened through the use of songs. Some of these were intended as 'songs of sorrow,' in which novices would musically long for the moment when they could burst free of their shelter and win the glory that all knew was to come. Other songs sang proudly of their approaching victories:[36]

Nduina miutini, iiiiiii
Nduina miutine kwa ba karuthia
Ntige gaaru ya ingwa

I will break *miutini* (the smallest Meru subdivision), Yessss
I will break *miutini* at the homestead of Karuthia (an *ncamba*)
I (will) leave the(ir) *gaaru* closed.

It should be noted that the decision to go to the bush was not restricted solely to *ntaani*. Senior warriors might choose to join them, both in seclusion and during the subsequent raid. These men could have several reasons for their action. One person might never have achieved real distinction (a praise-name) during his own novice period. A second might be striving for the title of *ncamba*. A third might hope to increase his livestock herds, prior to negotiating bride-wealth.

On the other hand, not every novice was required (or permitted) to take this type of oath. If an elder had circumcised two sons at once, for example, only one was allowed to 'cut the heifer,' lest both be killed in a single raid. Generally, the elder of the two was first to go. Only when he had earned his praise-name was the other permitted to follow in his path.[37]

Sons of the wealthier elders (*nthaka nkurii*)[38] might also refuse to follow their age-mates into the bush. Some, particularly 'only sons,' were forbidden by their fathers who feared for their lives. Others were told that adequate numbers of livestock existed within their families' herds, and that no desperate efforts to acquire their own were required. Novices of this type would still join raids, but their status made fulfillment of battle-oaths unnecessary and relieved them of the need to seek glory actively. Most males in this position tended to channel their energies towards becoming spokesmen (*agambe*) for their age-set, whereas their poorer comrades dreamed of acquiring the wealth that *nkurii* had already obtained, and with it, the reputation of *ncamba*.

In retrospect, the public oath seems, therefore, to have served as a permitted alternative by which sons of the poorer families within each *mwiriga* could rise to prominence. By first proclaiming and then fulfilling this type of vow (or a series of them) a previously obscure person could swiftly acquire a reputation for military renown, along with sufficient livestock to assure a prestigious marriage. It would also provide the status required for entry into *ramare*, perhaps initially only with regard to questions of war, but eventually into other areas as broader experience was acquired.

For the novices, however, all attempts at immediate fulfillment of proclamations were blocked by custom, for permission to translate their intentions into action was still refused by their superiors. In consequence, they found themselves with no alternative but to return to their bush-camp, forced once more into a situation of stress. Only by increasing their own tension (Kimeru: wildness) to the point where it disrupted the community at large, could they force those responsible into decisive action on their behalf.

As always, their resentment could be expressed only in song. As the rains lessened, the impatience of those confined within the camp reached new heights, and their singing grew steadily more sorrowful and wild. At this time, ever larger numbers of senior warriors were posted silently around the novices, lest they break free from their self-imposed confinement and run amok.[39]

At some point, certain of the novice elders, the age-set representing the fathers of those thus confined, would decide that the oath-warriors had "grown wild enough."[40] They would therefore approach the ruling elders to request their release. These, after consultation with the senior warriors and appropriate ritual specialists, would eventually agree.

Despite this agreement, oath-warriors were never merely released to rampage through the countryside unchecked. Instead, their final period of isolation was used by appropriate war-leaders to plan a raid involving every member of the *gaaru*.[41] The novices, released from their seclusion only after this planning was complete, would emerge from their shelter only to find themselves surrounded by the senior warriors, all fully armed. A senior spokesman would then inform them that their time to fight had not yet come, but that they would be permitted to intensify (Kimeru: strengthen) their oaths by proclaiming them in public.[42]

This process took place in two stages. The earlier was through participation in the feast of *renta*, a ceremony in which the novices were symbolically united with their seniors. *Renta* would usually begin during the final portion of the rainy season, when the earth was still too wet to permit large-scale raids. In cattle-rich areas such as Imenti, each warrior taking part was required to procure a bull, either from his own acquired livestock or the herds of his family or clan. In poorer areas, such as Muthambe, the entire feast might consist of goats, with families of each warrior contributing beasts of approximately equal value to the feasting. If necessary, parents of five or six warriors would group together, one providing the required animal for the feasting, the others reimbursing him with smaller gifts for their portion of the total.[43]

The day of *renta* was proclaimed by the council of ruling elders. During the next few days, bull after bull would be brought to the place of feasting. These were guarded constantly by the most senior warriors until the herd was considered complete, at which time they were driven to a river bank and slaughtered. The meat was then separated from the bones and hung high in the trees.

Thereafter, selected warriors banded together to construct a particular type of 'long hut' (*nyumba ya renta*), to be used for the feast. The construction was done under supervision of a ritual specialist, usually a *muga*, who was charged with selecting the site and providing the completed structure with ritual protection in the form of a bundle of herbs to be hung on its roof.[44]

Once the site had been chosen, the front and sides of the hut were constructed in traditional fashion, with the men retiring periodically to permit girls to complete the required thatching. The rear of the hut, however, was extended backwards by each group to arrive, until the entire structure might reach a length of over fifty feet.[45]

The feasting would begin the same evening. Only warriors were permitted to be present. To emphasize their unity, seniors and juniors alike were forbidden to oil or paint their bodies, nor did they wear the traditional skins. During the feasting itself, there was very little speech or movement. Occasional songs were sung in praise of their own or former age-sets, and of the ritualist, whose powers protected them at their feasting and would continue to do so during their coming campaign.

As with previous feasts, a secondary purpose was to permit the warriors to increase their strength symbolically for the raid to come. At its conclusion, both juniors and seniors were permitted to proclaim their battle oaths. For novices, these were repetitions of those made previously, first alone, and then among their age-mates. Proclaiming the vow during *renta*, however, had the effect of intensifying it in the *mutaani's* mind, since failure to fulfill its conditions would now shame him before the senior warriors as well as his comrades. The next step was to intensify it once again by proclamation before the entire *mwiriga*.

The opportunity to do so was provided by declaration of an *authi* of oaths (*authi ya irugu*), to take place immediately after the completion of *renta*. Preparations were similar to those of the previous *authi*. The warriors, after smearing their bodies with oil and chalk, then raced with weapons in hand towards the dancing field. The actual dancing was also conducted in the same two-legged, bounding fashion previously described. At some point, however, the elders would reassert their control. Singing the 'song of *kiama*' they would dance onto the field waving long green banana stalks as a signal for the warriors to give way.

Movement among the dancers would gradually subside, as both novices and veterans drew together in compact groups. Thereafter, the final proclamations could begin. Each man in turn would bound stiff-legged across the length of the field, halting finally before the assembled ruling elders. Drawing himself to full height, he would raise his spear and shout out the oath at full voice. By so doing, he would be permanently committed to live outside society until the specified conditions were fulfilled.[46]

Not until *ntaani* had completed their vows could the older warriors stand forth. When they did this, their proclamations, like those of the novices, became known to the entire *mwiriga*. Only by fulfilling them could the individuals involved rejoin the community in honor. Proclamation of the final oath signalled the completion of *authi*. Only after its termination could the raiding season begin.

Preparing the Novice: Conclusions

Meru society seems to have relied on two identifiable principles in preparing its novices finally to wage war. The first may be defined as the perpetual denial of earned status. Novice warriors had been conditioned from childhood to believe that the coveted status of warrior would be theirs once they had successfully endured the ultimate pain of circumcision. With the title, youths anticipated the respect, acceptance and authority that they themselves had been taught to render warriors. Instead, they found this status denied them by their seniors from the moment of their entry into warrior ranks. They were relegated to the least honorable place within the *gaaru*. Their advanced training, with its emphasis on beatings, silence and servitude, was conducted along lines identical to that experienced throughout childhood. Their attempts to establish leaders or to improve their collective position were met by livestock fines imposed ultimately upon the herds of their kinsmen. Finally, there seemed no way to alleviate their seniors' constant taunting, each achievement merely leading to its re-appearance in new forms.

The second principle was to create situations of maximum stress, in order to stimulate *ntaani* responses in directions suggested by tradition. This practice had been introduced at several points in precircumcision training. After they had entered warriorhood, it was extended into every facet of daily life. The arbitrary restrictions placed on sleeping space, wood collection and food gathering serve as typical examples. In such instances, routine duties were transformed into stress situations, requiring a choice between military acts (foraging, etc.) or failure and consequent shame. The same principle can be seen in the taunts of women at community dances, the challenge system of single combat, and the final driving of novices into the bush. In each situation, the alternatives were militant action or disgrace.

A partial exception might be made for the sons of wealthy men, since it would seem that a few persons within each sub-set maintained a degree of protection within the *gaaru* social structure. The wealth and position of their families served to blunt the harshness of the senior warriors' inevitable taunting. The herds of their kinsmen proved large enough to provide for either fines or feasting, allowing these sons of the wealthy to gain status above their poorer comrades. Status in turn aided their own efforts to develop the skills of conciliation, which served to provide them with a reputation and praise-names of their own. Members of this group might well decide to seek a reputation for military skill and daring, as well as statesmanship. Most, however, were content to maintain their inherited position and eventually step up into identical roles within the elders' community.

Even sons of the wealthy, however, suffered from the feelings of insecurity their warrior apprenticeship was intended to provide. Tradition offered no permanent means to relieve the tension caused by denial of what had been earned. Initially, each novice sub-set proved able to better their status (and thus, security) by drawing on the teachings of their youth, uniting behind established spokesmen and provoking limited conflicts with those above them. However, these tactics brought no real acceptance of their warriorhood, either from senior warriors, or (after the *authi* of nudity) the civilian community. Faced with the increasing contempt of society and their own rising insecurity, they had no choice but finally to comply with community expectations, setting goals (public oaths) which could be resolved only by waging war.

> . . . we were like bowstrings, drawn always more tightly, so that in the end we had no choice but to either shoot or break.[47]

CHAPTER V

Waging War

The Preparations

After completing the *authi* of oathing, war-leaders gathered within the barracks of every *mwiriga* to select targets for their initial raids. Prime responsibility for this planning lay with *ncamba* of the senior age-set, joined by the few novices who had carned the same title from their age-matcs. Advice was also sought from former war-leaders, novice elders whose accumulated experience was too great to be ignored.

As soon as leading *ncamba* had selected a potential target, their choice was debated by the *gaaru* at large. A designated spokesman for the war-leaders would begin by presenting their conclusions to the assembled group. If there were objections, he would do so again, and might retell a proposed plan several times within a single night. Eventually a general consensus would form. Thereafter, assembled warriors would select still other spokesmen to present the proposal to the ruling elders.[1]

This second presentation was made before the highest elders' council. If more than one *mwiriga* was involved, representative elders from each group would assemble to form an *njuri*. Traditionally, the ruling group would hear the entire proposal in silence. If it lacked merit, they would reject it out of hand, permitting no further warrior debate. If it seemed worthy, they would dismiss the warrior-spokesman and begin deliberation among themselves.

The first step in such discussions was to determine whether the *mwiriga* selected for attack contained members related to any of their own lineages, whether by blood or ritual. This involved culling the memories of the oldest men of the community, to insure that such alliances remained intact.

The second step, once the target-community had been deemed acceptable, was to insure that it held sufficient livestock to make an attack worthwhile. This was particularly important if the *mwiriga* were primarily pastoral, as was frequently the case with neighboring societies influenced by Maasai. In such instances, knowledge of the location of the desired livestock was rarely up to date, and much of the limited dry season period might be lost in searching for them.

To be certain of the availability of a proposed target, spokesmen for the ruling elders would dispatch scouts (*athigaani*, sing: *muthigaani*) to investigate the area. These were usually aliens who had found refuge within the Meru community or had established patterns of residence at its fringes.

In North Imenti, for example, *athigaani* were frequently agricultural *maasai* (Ukwavi, Kimeru: Ukabi), who had fled their own areas during periods of warfare or famine. In Lower Mwimbe and Muthambe, they were refugees from Mberre, Embu or Ukambani who had fled for similar reasons to *miiriga* with which their own had *gichiaro*. Such persons, if they could be trusted, retained the ability to move freely within their former home areas and thus could provide information on the movement of livestock held by units hostile to their own.

For the same reasons, *miiriga* near the montane forest relied on *aathi* hunters or members of the cattle herding Ogiek bands with whom they had established ritual alliance. The relative freedom of movement enjoyed by both these peoples permitted them to gather data from potentially hostile areas without fear of reprisal. Obviously, the potential for double-spying must have occurred to every *muthigaani*, if only to assure his continued welcome in every area. However, most *miiriga* seem to have accepted the risks inherent in this possibility as a matter of course, reasoning that the alternative would be to choke off the available sources of information altogether.[2]

A scout's work was to locate enemy herds, observe their warrior defenders and estimate the difficulty of raiding them. Usually, they left their own communities in groups of ten or more, traveling fully armed through the often hostile regions that separated them from the intended target. At the enemy border, the group dissolved, each man moving off alone in order to cover as much area as possible.

It was not enough merely to see an enemy herd. Much time had to be spent following it, divining the general direction and speed of its movement, in order to lead raiders to its approximate future position. If the herd was stationary, the habits of its defenders had to be studied to estimate the most effective pattern of attack. Alternately, a target-community might have as many as a dozen separate herds, all grazing at constantly variable distances from one another. For the *muthigaani* to ignore even one of these might lead the future raiders to unexpected discovery and defeat. Finally, each scout was required to obtain proof of what he had seen, to be presented at the elders' council as evidence that the herds in question could be seized. Traditionally, the most honored proof was an ear-tip from one of the animals, concrete testimony that he had been able to approach them.[3]

Scouts were also instructed as to their behavior if discovered. If non-Meru, they were simply to state that they had returned to their own society. If Meru, they were to plead famine in their own region, citing the dearth of both livestock and grain that had forced them to leave. If this explanation was accepted, the scout was to remain with his captors until given the opportunity to slip away. In practice, evidence suggests that most scouts led an effective double existence, passing relevant information to hereditary enemies in exchange for protection by them both.[4]

Once a scout returned with favorable reports, the ruling elders generally gave their blessing. To do otherwise might have lessened their influence over the warriors on future occasions, and caused the latter to accuse them of excessive caution.[5] With this permission obtained, warrior spokesmen would then join the leading elders to consult the appropriate ritualist.

The specialist to be consulted varied according to area. Warriors in South Imenti customarily visited the *mugwe* (dispenser of blessings). Traditionally, five senior warriors and an equal number of elders would appear at his homestead before each raid to receive his blessing and prophecy. They would present him with a goat, which he would strangle in order to drain blood from its throat into a small gourd. After peering into the vessel, he would prophesy. The forecasts were always general, dealing with victory or defeat for the entire group, rather than the fate of single warriors. If failure was foreseen, the project would be abandoned. If success, the *mugwe* would deliver this blessing, taking honey in his mouth, then spitting it over the forehead of each warrior in turn.[6]

In theory, the *mugwe* of South Imenti dispensed blessings to every section of Meru society. The period of dispersal at the close of their migration, however, had also fragmented the institution of *ugwe* (blessing), permitting *agwe* of lesser stature to emerge in Tigania and Igembe, as well as Tharaka and Cuka. The remaining areas, as well as those whose warriors were unable to reach a *mugwe* for military reasons, seem to have transferred certain of his traditional functions to other ritual specialists. Thus the war-leaders of North and Northeast Imenti, cut off from ready access to *agwe* in both South Imenti and Tigania, were served in this instance by the *aga* (curse-removers), while those of Muthambe, Mwimbe and parts of Igoji visited *aroria* (foretellers).[7]

The rituals, however, were essentially similar to those of other areas. In Northeast Imenti, for example, two to four war-leaders accompanied by an equal number of ruling elders, would visit a respected curse-remover (*muga*) before each raid. Like the *mugwe*, the curse-remover would prophesy by killing, then opening, a goat. Ignoring the blood, he would ascertain the future of the proposed raid by scanning the entrails. If the forecast was failure, the *muga* would conclude that some action of one (or all) of the warriors present had caused them to enter into a condition of *mugiro* (ritual impurity), and that it was this which caused the entrails to foretell their defeat. The warriors would then provide a second goat, which the *muga* would sacrifice in turn, using the entrails to cleanse them of whatever *mugiro* was obscuring the possibility of success. Thereafter, still another goat would be provided, and the forecast would be repeated. The pattern would continue until a favorable result was obtained.[8]

The *muga* would then advise the warriors of certain actions to be taken at various stages of the raid which were held necessary for its success. In some cases groups would be directed to return if they came across certain reptiles or animals (phython, hyena, etc.) while en route. In other instances, they were ordered to attack from a specific direction and at a stated time. A *muga* might also specify which lineage was to begin the attack, a matter of great honor to the *ncamba* concerned. He might also dictate the types of war-trophy to seek, which to ignore, and those to consider ritually blemished (*ntang'uru*) and thus reserved for the *muga* himself.[9]

Ritual specialists were also responsible for preparing the 'war-magic' (*muthega ya vita*), which was given to leading *ncamba* before each raid. The concept was evidently derived from earlier incantations used by the *aathi* to protect themselves while hunting. In Northeast Imenti, for instance, *aathi* referred to such protective substances as 'bite' and 'blow;' the names of each having been derived from the action used to implement it. 'Bite,' for example, was prepared from a number of plant and animal substances known only to *aathi*. These were boiled in a clay pot that had been sealed to prevent the escape of steam. The residue was then collected and shaped into a small black ball. When hunting, the *mwathi* simply held it in his fingers, then 'bit,' while reciting the proper incantation:[10]

Njira no muthwa aki: Only ants on the paths
Tukona gintu giku: We shall see no bad thing.

'Blow' was prepared in identical fashion, but ground into a fine black powder, which was blown into the air with an equivalent incantation. The hunter would then be safe against discovery by either animals or enemies.

Initially, knowledge of both 'bite' and 'blow' (as well as other variants) was restricted to those *aga* who served the two hunting communities by permitting ordinary *aathi* to seek protection while in the forests. In exchange, the hunters would supply their *aga* with forest products and fermented honey-wine (*uuki*). At some time in the late 1800s, war-leaders from certain *miiriga* in Northeast Imenti are believed to have sought out these forest *aga* with essentially the same request, asking protection from discovery within the forest in exchange for gifts of livestock and millet beer.

Inevitably, the *ncamba* were followed by curse-removers from these same *miiriga*, who approached their forest compatriots ('in the manner of small children') to learn what their warriors required. In consequence, by the 1890s, *aga* from these *miiriga* were preparing their ritual mixtures in the same manner as those serving the hunters, boiling similar ingredients within in sealed clay pots to form a blackish paste. This was then wrapped in a green leaf and bound to the war-leader's spear. If used correctly during the raid, it was believed able to ward off discovery by either men or beasts.[11]

Enroute

Having received appropriate ritual preparation, the war-leaders would return to their *gaaru* to assemble raiders in numbers sufficient to overwhelm the potential defense. If their own force seemed inadequate, individual *ncamba* would be sent to neighboring *gaaru*, to invite them to join the raiding group. In some instances, single warriors would agree, lured by the hope of loot and glory. In others, entire gaaru would ally themselves, after due consultation with their own elders and ritual specialists. On occasion, a raiding force could number up to 300 men.[12]

In attacks upon neighboring Meru communities, both the selection of routes and march formations were dictated by the unusual nature of the terrain of Mt. Kenya.[13] This is most clearly illustrated by examining a hypothetical raid by a *gaaru* in North Imenti upon the herds of a *mwiriga* in upper Mwimbe.[14]

In this instance, to take their potential target by surprise, the raiders had to travel forty miles from the starting point, without revealing their presence. Intervening *miiriga* between the attackers and their target were all heavily populated, and several were ritually allied to the potential victims. In consequence, the raiding party was forced to ascend the slope within their own area to a point above the (star grass) zone of habitation, then swiftly traverse the bracken belt near the montane forest fringe.

Accordingly, on crossing their own upper boundary, the warriors formed into a rough rectangle, which grew thicker or thinner according to the denseness of the bush. No other effort was made to march in formal units or by age-sets. Instead, the attackers divided themselves into *ngitung'a* (the strong) and *mbutu* (the swift), a division that determined their places on the march.

The oldest, heaviest and most experienced of the *ngitung'a* marched by mutual agreement in the front ranks, with the leading *ncamba* of the expedition in the center. Slightly less experienced *ngitung'a* still known for their bulk and strength, marched on the uphill side of the rectangle, the direction from which a counterattack was most likely. *Mbutu* marched on the downhill side and at the rear, where their speed was most likely to be of use in flanking an enemy counterattack. Finally, those novices who had not yet proven themselves worthy of either status were clustered in the middle, where in case of attack they could be guided by the shouts and movement of the more experienced men.[15]

Lines of command within this formation were based on force of personality rather than rank or position. A single *ncamba* was accepted as the leader of the expedition. Nevertheless, he was considered no more than first among equals by other war-leaders, each of whom commanded a following of his own. Within the ranks, every warrior simply followed the leader of his choice, watching his movements and listening for his commands. If circumstances dictated, a warrior might shift his allegiance to another

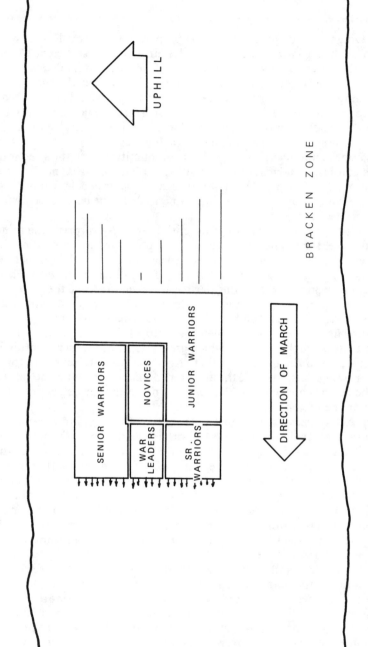

Formation of raiding force

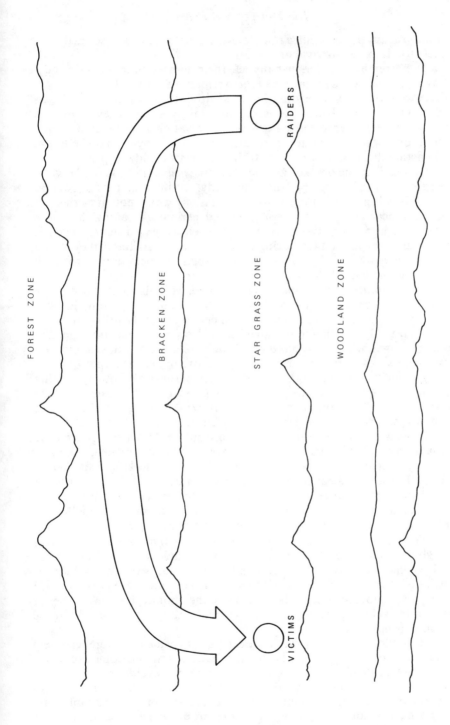

FOREST ZONE

BRACKEN ZONE

STAR GRASS ZONE

WOODLAND ZONE

RAIDERS

VICTIMS

Traditional pattern of attack, Meru, 1890's

ncamba at any point within a raid, following that person who seemed most likely to insure his survival or success.

The assembled raiders usually left their home area in a single body, leaving only a picked group of *mbutu* to remain and guard its herds. Often, these were the sons of leading families within the *mwiriga*, whose cows made up considerable portions of the total livestock. They were thus thought to have the greatest stake in the preservation of the herds, and even when too few to resist attackers, could put their swiftness to good effect in contacting the main force before their opponents could escape.

On reaching the bracken zone, the leading *ncamba* would send several pairs of *mbutu* far ahead of the main body, with instructions to conceal themselves near each of the known paths along which potential enemies might appear. This process was repeated periodically along the entire route, and as many as twenty pairs might eventually be dispatched. Their task was to remain hidden during the entire raid. By so doing, they served as human trip-wires, able to warn the main body of enemy efforts to block the paths and cut off the raiders on their return.

Other *mbutu*, or accompanying *athigaani*, were also sent ahead of the main body to serve as 'tree-scouts.' As the name implies, their function was to climb the highest trees available, then peer through the foliage to make sure that the line of march remained clear. No form of distance signaling was ever used, whether by hand or through imitation of animals. Instead, tree-scouts were sent forward in groups of five or six. At a specified distance from the main body, they would separate from one another, forming a half-circle. Each would then climb the highest tree in his designated sector, descend, then return at a run to report to the leading *ncamba*. Only if the way was clear, would the main body advance.

There were good reasons to avoid long distance signals, especially those which imitated animals. The forest fringes, while uninhabited, were frequently visited by groups of women and children seeking firewood or fruits. The noise of a harmless animal (or any bird) was likely to cause more adventuresome children to search for the source. On the other hand, imitating a dangerous beast, while able to send women and children fleeing, might also bring out local warriors to hunt it down.

The one exception to this rule of silence was the cry of a hyena. This might be used at the end of a march, when the raiders' scouts found themselves unable to advance the final mile or so towards the enemy *gaaru*,[16] without alerting women and children. In such instances, the cry of a single hyena was enought to send them racing to their homes, but the number of warriors likely to appear to hunt it was small enough to be avoided by the scouts themselves.

It should be noted that while the early stages of a march were relatively rapid, fear of discovery might cause the final portion to become excruciatingly slow, extending a trek of little distance over several days. The delay posed a problem of supply, since little food could be either carried or preserved for any length of time. Most war parties solved the problem by carrying meat for the first day, then a mixture of yams and bananas for the second. Thereafter, the raiding force depended on *kimere*, a type of millet which had been soaked in water, then ground to greyish paste. This was then placed in an air-tight gourd carried aross the warrior's chest. During the first two days, it was inedible. Thereafter, fermentation made it palatable for at least a week, permitting a raiding force to march for as long as nine days without resupply.

The Defenses

The outer borders of most *miiriga* were considered a type of 'no man's land' (*kiruiro*: fighting placc), in that they were ridges "on which no man could settle."[17] Most were characterized by a number of static defenses, maintained continuously by members of specified lineages. The most complex of these was a fourteen-mile-long defensive wall which lay along the entire length of the boundary between Muthambe and Cuka, extending the length of the populated areas and four miles upward into the montane forest.

It was created during the final decades of the 1800s in response to increasingly severe raids upon the Cuka by several Meru subdivisions.[18] The former responded to these attacks by creating a wall of trees, felling some in such a manner as to cause them to intermingle with others which were still growing. Gaps were systematically filled in with thornbush. Existing paths were blocked or diverted, especially at traditional river crossings. In their place, the Cuka erected a series of 'gates,' actually lengthy tunnels made of stakes and branches which were interwoven with growing trees. These led to open clearings, where potential raiders could be felled one-by-one with bows and arrows as they emerged. Early European reports mention the barrier as having been anywhere from ten to forty yards in depth, and nearly impassable to raiders unless they were armed with European axes.[19]

Rather than follow the Cuka example, most other Meru *miiriga* chose to defend their border areas with a variety of pits. These had been adopted from *aathi* hunting techniques[20] and took two forms. The more common was oblong, about four feet long, two feet wide and ten to thirteen feet deep. It was placed in the center of a larger path, then lined at the bottom with sharpened bamboo staves. Thereafter, the top was covered with light vegetation.[21] This type of pit was traditionally placed along a major approach at points which were most suitable for ambush. The intent was to stop an enemy's forward motion, then continue the battle with missiles and spears.

The second type of pit approximated the modern one-man fox-hole. Several of these would be dug at irregular intervals alongside a narrow avenue of approach, then carefully screened. If warned of an impending raid, individual warriors of unusual speed would race to these prepared positions, then lie waiting in ambush. Ideally, they would let advance elements of the attacking force pass by unharmed, awaiting the approach of an *ncamba*. As one passed, the defender would discharge an arrow or spear from the prepared position, hoping to kill the war-leader, then escape before those following could overcome their surprise.[22]

Static defenses were supplemented by a number of methods used to provide early warning of impending attack. The most distant of these might come from within the enemy area itself, perhaps from a single lineage with whom the potential victim was ritually allied. During the 1890s, for instance, attacks by the warriors of Rwanderi (Muthambe) upon the *mwiriga* of Kiiunguni (Cuka) were often forestalled by advance warning sent to the Cuka warriors by their *gichiaro*-brothers in the Muthambe *gaaru* of Gaichau.[23]

This type of warning would be carried by a single warrior who would pass directly through the populated zone. Usually, this type of messenger was able to avoid conflict by carrying a 'staff of *kiama*' on one shoulder, indicating that he was on official business and thus immune from attack. In practice, such protection was frequently supplemented by procuring the company of one member of each *gaaru* through whose area he passed. The messenger would travel as far as possible with his companion, then repeat the process for the adjacent area as required.[24]

The second warning of an impending attack usually came from the montane forest area directly above the *mwiriga* concerned. In this instance, the tracks of a raiding party would generally be spotted by individual *aathi* related to lineages in the probable target area, who would hasten to warn their kin.

This form of warning might also come from scattered bands of Ogiek, who either hunted within the forest fringes or herded on the adjacent plains. In certain areas, especially Katheri (North Imenti) and Mwimbe, Ogiek bands had forged ritual alliances (*gichiaro*) with several *miiriga*. In consequence, they had developed traditions of warning their kinsmen against projected attack. In North Imenti, for instance, giving the warning was done by lighting large torches of *miale* wood, which were raised and lowered three times to signal the approach of raiders, then raised and lowered one final time in the direction from which they would come.[25] Other areas used similar systems.

The informal means of early warning were supplemented by a more tightly organized system of lookouts (*lai*), established by each *mwiriga* to guard its major avenues of approach. There were two types. The more important were those set atop hills (*lai ya kilima*: hilltop lookouts) or plateaus with commanding views. The *lai* itself was a miniature *gaaru*, intended to hold between ten to fifteen warriors. It had no stockade, but was usually placed within a large cleared area, to inhibit suprise attacks.

In theory, each *gaaru* had a single hilltop *lai*, always located between itself and a potential enemy. In practice, larger *gaaru* had two or three, while areas with smaller populations might combine to share a single one.

In such cases, two gaaru might pair off, each using the outpost system of the other as protection from attack on its rear.

The second type of lookout was set within the branches of large trees (*lai ya miti*: tree lookouts). It was intended to supplement the larger hilltop outpost and thus was manned by only one or two warriors. Chanler, writing in 1892, described these outposts as "wooden platforms. . . fifteen feet (in height), on which fires were burning . . . around these . . . we could just descry the forms of warriors."[26] He also notes that despite an advance made "as silently as possible," he was able to move less than a quarter mile into the cultivated area of Muthara (Tigania) before the tree-top watchers raised an alarm.[27]

The number of warriors within each type of *lai* varied according to season. In wet periods, when raids were least expected, each outpost was manned by volunteers from clans the military traditions of which included such service. During the dry months, these were supplemented by many of the youngest, swiftest *mbutu*, as well as several more seasoned *ngitung'a*, who assumed command. At this period, a twenty-four-hour watch was maintained, with no fewer than two warriors on the alert at all times.

During such periods, if a warrior who should have been stationed in his *lai* was found near the homesteads (i.e., courting), he was shamed by being driven through the cultivated areas with bells attached to his thighs to attract attention and by bearing bananas on his back in the fashion of a woman. The intention was to display him to the girls of his own territory as a man with whom they must have nothing more to do.[28] To symbolize this, he was labeled with the new name of a *mwiriga* with whom his own group had *gichiaro*. Thus, a Muthambe warrior might have been given the name of a ritually allied *mwiriga* in Imenti (e.g., Mukatheri: man of Katheri), to indicate that he was kin (thus, sexually forbidden) to girls within his own area.

The reason for the preponderance of *mbuti* in the outposts became apparent once an enemy appeared. When appropriate smoke signals or the enemy raiders themselves were sighted, a series of long prepared counteractions was put into effect. In daylight, branches of green wood were bundled together to make a torch which was either raised and lowered in the manner utilized by the Ogiek, or thrown continuously into the air, the resulting smoke column serving as warning. At night, the same practice was followed with the light of other brightly burning branches being used as the required signal.[29]

At the same time, outpost warriors not directly involved with fire-signaling would either ululate or blow the warhorn (*coro, rugoji*),[30] traditionally the horn of a kudu, bongo or buffalo, trimmed at either end with caps of buffalo or cow hide. The pierced narrow end permitted the user to blow a single, monotonous, but far-ranging, note. For this reason, the *coro* was used primarily in time of danger to warn an entire area of potential attack.

There was no variation in the signal. In the daytime, a single, long blast was sufficient to alert the entire *mwiriga*, since the horn was never blown in daylight hours except during enemy attack. At night, the sound could cause possible confusion, since it was also used to signal the rituals used to transfer the status of warriorhood to a younger age-set. Thus, enemy attacks that fell during such transfers might profit greatly from the mistake, as people tended to wait within their homesteads during these periods, and even brief hesitation as to the reason for the signal could preclude effective defense.[31]

Having sounded their alarm with both fire and sound, lookout warriors, unless outnumbering the raiders, would retreat in a body towards their *gaaru*. Selected *mbutu* raced there directly to report details of the raiding force. Others were dispatched to the *gaaru* of neighboring *miiriga* to seek help.

The remaining *mbutu* would initially join the more experienced *ngitung'a*, falling back slowly, but keeping well ahead of the approaching raiders. At each change in their course, or division into additional fighting groups, one of these runners would race for the *gaaru*, thus keeping the main body continuously informed.

The Attack

If undiscovered by the lookouts, however, raiders would ideally reach a position within one mile of the enemy *gaaru* by late afternoon. The entire force would then pause briefly before their final deployment. Scouts were sent forward one more time to observe the size and relative positions of the victim's herds as they returned from the daylight grazing areas. In most *miiriga*, herds were driven onto the cleared area adjacent to the warrior *gaaru*, where they might be watched throughout the night. Having assured themselves of this, and of the number of warriors assigned to guard them, the scouts would return silently to the main body. On their reappearance, all warriors would fall totally silent, to remain so until the moment of attack. The raiding force would then divide into a prearranged number of groups, each containing a rough balance between novices and experienced men.

Each group would approach its final position at a slow, intermittent crawl. The smallest, hereafter referred to as the 'decoys,' would either maintain its place at the original point of deployment or creep as far towards the cattle as available cover permitted. Its eventual task would be to lure the herds as far as possible from the *gaaru*, then silently overpower their guards.

The second group, here designated as the 'herders,' was composed primarily of *mbutu*. It was led by the leading *ncamba* and was slightly larger than the 'decoys.' Its task was to seize control of the livestock after their guards had been disposed of, then herd them off in the direction the attackers had come.

The third group, hereafter referred to as the 'blockers,' was by far the largest. It was composed primarily of *ngitung'a*, and contained the greatest number of *ncamba*. Its task would be to move between the livestock and the enemy *gaaru*, at the moment when the herds began to move away, 'blocking' and thus protecting their 'herder' comrades from counterattack.[32]

Attaining the desired positions might take all three groups the remainder of the day. Thereafter, they had nothing to do but conceal themselves till evening when the defenders would sleep. Attacks occasionally took place in the first hours of darkness, if enemy warriors were believed to be sleeping heavily as the result of a feast. More frequently, they began in the pre-dawn hours (3:00-4:00 A.M.), when the position of the moon made vision possible along the twisting, overgrown paths.[33]

The moment of attack was always preceded by the casting of war-magic against the enemy. This was done by the leading *ncamba* and could be accomplished in several ways. War-leaders of certain areas simply blew the magic, in this instance of powder form, towards the enemy's evening fire. Others bound it carefully to their spear shaft, then moved through the motions of casting it at the opposing *gaaru*, the action having been intended to signal the beginning of the raid, while retaining the element of surprise. In either case the intent was similar to that ascribed to *aathi* hunting magic, to protect the raiders from discovery.[34]

When the magic was judged to have done its work, the 'decoy' group would initiate the second step. This was to lure the guards away from their herds and overcome them. The method most frequently used to achieve this was for a single warrior, usually an *aathi* or Ogiek scout, to creep toward the herd under cover of darkness. On reaching their vicinity, he would scatter handfuls of salt, first near them, then back along the path that he had come. Ideally, a certain number of animals would discover this and drift slowly back towards the waiting reserves. Eventually, one or more of the guards would move after them and could be quietly overcome, the noise of the herd helping to conceal the action. If the ambush had been sufficiently silent, it could be repeated, ideally until every guard had been disposed of.

Members of the 'herder' group, still in concealment, would observe these initial actions in total silence. Since no further verbal communication was possible between attacking units, they had only their eyes with which to judge the success of the 'decoys.' Only after the last of the livestock guards could no longer be seen could the work of the 'herders' begin. Silently, they would advance into the cleared area, then split into two files, both of which formed a half-circle between the defending *gaaru* and the now unguarded herd. At a prearranged hand signal, they would all advance, moving the animals slowly and carefully toward the edge of the clearing, then back up the paths they had come. If this could be achieved in silence, without wak-

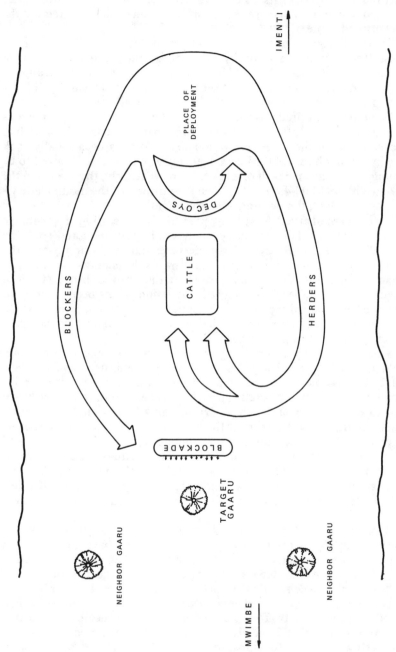

Deployment for attack on enemy *gaaru*

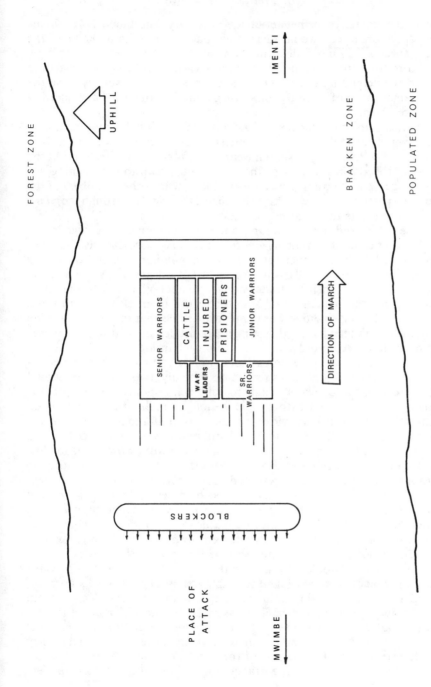

Formation of raiding force on return from raid

ing the defenders, no further action was necessary. The 'blockers,' until this time silent observers, would merely slip back to join the others, and the entire force would move stealthily away.

More frequently, the noise of moving cattle would awaken warriors within the defending *gaaru*. The first of these would instantly raise the traditional shout of warning (*mbu-u-u*), and blow the war-horn, alerting the entire area.

At this point, the 'blockers' would move into action. In some instances, a number of particularly daring *ncamba* might have crept to within yards of the *gaaru* itself, hoping to snatch weapons left lying near the door. At the moment the alarm was raised, these few would leap to the opening, attempting to pin the waking warriors inside it, while other members of the blocking party raced forward to either thrust their spears through the *gaaru* sides, or to set its thatch afire.

One tactic used in such circumstances was to maneuver a large log silently over the roof of an enemy *gaaru*, until it was poised directly above the door frame. If the defenders awoke, raiders holding each end of the log would force it down, collapsing the opening and pinning the defenders inside. Meanwhile, their comrades would attempt both to fire the thatching that covered the structure and stab through it in an effort to kill those inside. An alternate method was to prepare a somewhat shorter, thicker log as a form of battering ram, thrusting it against defenders trying to emerge from the doorway, in order to force them back inside.[35]

In most instances, however, a number of defending warriors would escape the *gaaru* and join ranks for action. Usually, two vague lines would slowly form as the 'blockers' sought to hold their opponents away from the moving cattle, while retreating rapidly enough to inhibit their own envelopment. The pattern of individual combat was similar to that mentioned in warrior training.[36] Raiders would pick out opponents, then lunge forward on one foot and one knee in hope of hooking or beating down their shields. Where possible, *ncamba* would seek out others of like rank, identifiable through differences in headdress, and cut their way toward them by sheer strength. Alternatively, opponents could be deceived by having *ncamba* exchange headdresses with other warriors. Knowing that enemy attention would be focused on others, they were able to inflict great damage.[37]

As the alarm was raised within the enemy *gaaru*, the 'herders' would abandon all efforts at stealth and systematically whip the livestock into a run. Ideally, they would be joined in this by the 'decoys,' racing forward from their place of concealment to help avert an uncontrolled stampede. The decoy group would remain with the herd until it was well away from the enemy *gaaru*, then turn back to assist the 'blockers.' Usually, the raiders' new *ngitung'a* would go with them, as would the leading *ncamba*. This would leave only the swiftest *mbutu* to drive the cattle toward safety. They would attempt this for the rest of the night, forming a loose half-circle around the herd, while beating stragglers with thorn branches to keep them moving.

Meanwhile, the 'blockers,' although reinforced by both 'raider' *ngitung'a* and the entire 'decoy' unit, would fall swiftly back before a steadily increasing number of defenders. Ideally, they would be able to break contact completely, fleeing along paths other than those taken by the livestock, while the enemy was still organizing the pursuit. On rejoining the captured herds, the entire force would form once more into the rectangular formation that marked their outward trip. This time, however, the animals were placed in the center of the rectangle, as were the injured and any captives. The *mbutu* now held the front ranks of the march, as well as the downhill side, where attack was least expected. The *ngitung'a* marched on the uphill side, and at the rear, often dropping well behind the marching body to wait in ambush for pursuers.[38]

The Pursuit

The initial blast of a war-horn would alert not only the warriors of the *gaaru* under attack, but their neighbors as well. In consequence, warriors from adjacent barracks would reply in turn, sounding their own horns to show that the warning had been received. These in turn would be repeated by warriors still farther from the original signal, and the warning would thus spread throughout the area.

In the first moments after an alarm had been sounded, novice-elders still of fighting age would seize their weapons and race for the *gaaru*. Older males, women and children sought concealment. If the attackers could be seen, hiding places were found beneath the fence of thorn-tree branches that surrounded every homestead. Alternately, if there was time for flight, non-combatants fled to the *gakando kwa mwiriga* (small place of the *mwiriga*). This was a portion of every homestead that custom required be left untouched when the land had originally been cleared for cultivation. Usually, it was the place where bush and trees were thickest; consequently it was suitable for concealment of women and children during periods of war.

Once the fighting strength of every *gaaru* had been mobilized, the next step was one of anxious waiting while war-leaders tried desperately to learn the raiders' identity, as well as which neighbor had actually been attacked. No use was made of either fire or sound signals, beyond the rudimentary ones already mentioned. In consequence, potential reinforcers had to await the arrival of runners, first from the lookout that had sighted the raiders, then from the *gaaru* under attack.

Even with this information, reinforcement was not automatic. In rare instances, questions could arise as to whether elements within the raiding force were *gichiaro* with groups among the potential allies, a problem that would call for resolution (thus, discussion and delay) by the appropriate

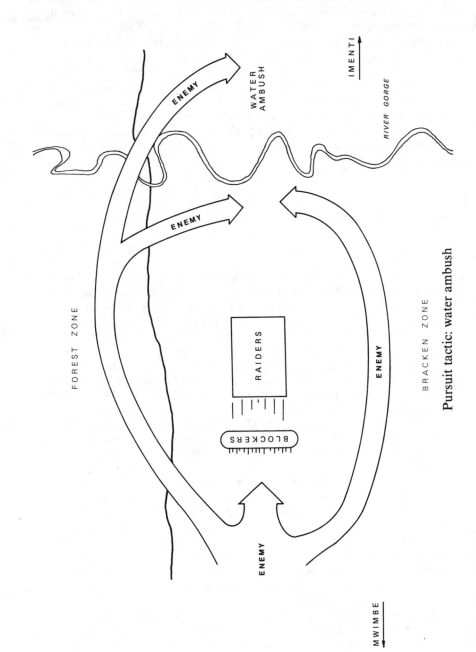

Pursuit tactic: water ambush

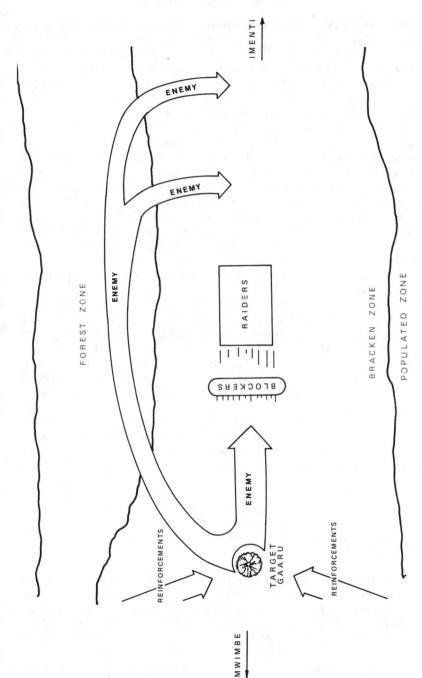

Pursuit tactic: "hammer and anvil"

elders. In other cases, groups of warriors might refuse to help their neighbors if they feared subsequent attack themselves. To race off into the darkness meant leaving one's own livestock relatively unguarded. Therefore, a clever enemy might easily break into two or several raiding parties, sweeping up the herds of those who helped their neighbors, while leaving those of 'stay-at-homers' alone. The Maasai were particularly adept at this tactic. During the 1890s, for instance, a single Maasai raiding force broke into two parties, which simultaneously attacked herds in both lower and upper Mwimbe. The conflicting reports had so confused the *ncamba* of *magaaru* lying between the raided areas that they had refused to leave their own herds, permitting the raiders to pillage undisturbed.[39]

In most instances, however, detachments of neighboring warriors would pour into the raided area, increasing steadily in number as the alarm spread. When sufficient numbers had been assembled, the defenders would set out in pursuit, fully aware that the raiders would be slowed by the presence of their wounded, their prisoners and the captured herds. Since the trail was easily followed, and all possible escape-routes known equally to pursuers and pursued, it would gradually become obvious which paths the raiders hoped to take.

At this point, the pursuers could adopt one of a number of defensive strategies in order to retrieve their lost herds. One of these was known as the 'snare.' It was used in situations where a numerically superior raiding force had put defenders to flight, but had not yet completed the seizure of their herds. If time and terrain were adequate, the neighboring warriors would gather, not at the point where the stolen livestock was collected, but around it, on the hillocks or in the surrounding bush. The intent was to permit the raiders to complete their collection of the animals, then spread their own forces to drive them off. The counter-thrust would come when they were fully burdened with their spoil.[40] Arkell-Hardwick, writing of the mid-1890s, describes the tactic perfectly, when, having collected a quantity of Imenti livestock without encountering opposition, he discovered that[41]

> . . . a shower of poisoned arrows from the surrounding bush winged their destructive way into our midst, killing three of Bei-Munithu's men [his Imenti allies] outright. At the same time, the now familiar war-cry rose on all sides and resounded from hill top to hill top in a manner which showed us we were fully expected.

If the raiding force was small, every possible path leading out of the area would be blocked, at first by only small numbers of warriors from the *magaaru* concerned, but subsequently by reinforcing contingents from neighboring areas. If the raiders proved numerous, however, a second tactic would be used, known as the 'vine.' In this instance, the defenders would block all paths but one. The intent was to force numerically superior attackers to string themselves out (Kimeru: like a vine) along a narrow trail, permitting defenders to harass the returning column (Kimeru: cut off pieces) over its entire length.

Chanler, also writing of the 1890s, has described an effective use of this tactic during a running fight with *miiriga* of Tigania, from which he had stolen cattle:[42]

It seemed, to my great satisfaction, that the Somali and Soudanese appeared . . . accustomed to the cattle punching business and were able to drive the wildest cow along with comparative ease. . . . On both sides of our line of march great numbers of natives followed, at distances varying from 100 to 300 yards.

In instances where the raiding force proved too swift or strong to succumb to such harassment, every effort was made to lead the fleeing column into a 'water-ambush.' This third tactic was always employed at specific water-crossings, whether steep gorges, deep pools or flowing rivers. The intent was to position defending forces on the far side of the water, then launch a concerted attack while the raiders attempted to cross.

Traditions record many successful examples of this tactic. During the early 1890s, for instance, a group of Muthambe raiders became confused while returning with livestock taken from a Cuka *gaaru*, and were driven by their pursuers (herd and all) into a deep pool with subsequent heavy losses.[43] Chanler, during the same decade, was stopped at the edge of a gully by a declaration of peace, then ambushed moments later by a volley of arrows.[44] The same tactic was used against Arkell-Hardwick, who allowed his group to be led by a Tigania warrior (posing as a Maasai) along a narrow, twisted path that ended at a deep ravine. The subsequent ambush came from "every point on the compass,"[45] forcing his party into headlong retreat. Many other examples could be cited.

To set up a successful 'water ambush,' the pursuers would engage in a tactic known as 'hammer and anvil.' The experienced but slower warriors (the 'hammer') would set out along the trail taken by the livestock, hoping to catch, engage and eventually overwhelm the raiders' rear guard. At the same time, large parties of the swiftest *mbutu* would set out at a run, along other, longer trails that led eventually into the raiders' intended route. Their purpose was to bypass the attackers, block their path at a water-crossing (the 'anvil'), then attack as they crossed, hoping to halt their forward momentum until the pursuing 'hammer' could arrive.

If the ambush succeeded in halting the raiders' forward momentum, yet failed to disperse their strength, the way was clear for a pitched battle. Unable to cross the water, the raiders would retain their protective rectangle, and simply reverse direction. With their most experienced warriors now at the front of the formation, they would be ready to retrace their route or seek another. To prevent this, as their numbers increased, groups of pursuers would block one after another of the alternate paths. If unable to break through, the attackers would eventually be forced to a standstill.

The pursuers would then concentrate their striking forces into four identifiable contingents. When assembled, these would charge from four directions simultaneously.[46] Their purpose was not to kill, but merely to penetrate through the defensive screen which protected the stolen live-stock. They then stampeded the cattle, disrupting the defensive formation and reducing combat to the level of individuals and small groups. With their unity shattered and their booty retaken, most raiders simply fled.[47]

Evasion and Return

It must be recalled, however, that defensive tactics of pursuits and interception could conceivably by nullified by the pairs of 'trip wire scouts' left at designated points during the outward march for just this purpose. They were not meant to battle with pursuers, but to slip away and warn the returning raiders that a certain path was blocked. The main body would then shift its direction accordingly and try another route.

Prolonged or unusually determined pursuit of this nature might force the raiders to make numerous changes of direction, to the point where it might take several days to move the livestock to safety. Such delays would so severely lower the raiders' morale that the increasing exhaustion and lack of food might tempt them to abandon their spoils.

To avoid this, the leaders might decide to reverse completely the direction of the group, fleeing for safety into an area with which the raiders were ritually allied. Tradition dictated that such *gichiaro* brothers were required to offer protection to the stolen livestock, usually agreeing to retain them for an unspecified length of time, in exchange for a percentage of the young born therein. It was also permissible for the raiders to negotiate marriage arrangements for their female captives with representatives of the allied clans, with the eventual bride-price going to the respective captors. No refuge, however, was permitted the warriors themselves, who were required to make their way homeward as soon as the required negotiations were complete.[48]

Alternatively, the raiders might simply evade their pursuers and reach their home area unscathed. Their safe arrival was cause for general celebration. The livestock and captives, if any, were driven immediately to the warriors' dancing field, and placed under guard pending their division among the participants of the raid. Thereafter, the entire force toured every homestead in the area, giving the women and girls the chance to sing their praises.[49]

If the raid was a failure, which could be perceived immediately from the lack of livestock or the number of missing warriors, the return was made in silence. In this event, the raiders' tour of the homesteads was intended to be one of mourning, to inform the families and fiancées of each warrior who had been captured or killed.

This was done by pausing in front of the appropriate homesteads to request food in the traditional manner. The food would then be eaten, but the gourd in which it was given would either be returned with the lid upside down or be deliberately dashed to the ground and destroyed. Either action was a sign that a son of that homestead had been lost. Thereafter, no mention might ever be made of the deceased. Instead, he would always be referred to as "the manly one."[50]

Next, each warrior who had knowingly killed an enemy had to remove ritually the *mugiro* (impurity) he had thereby incurred. This was achieved through paying a ram to the *kiama* of elders, and a goat to the curse-remover (*muga*) who performed the rite. Fat from the ram was smeared on the warrior's spear, and the intestines of the goat were first bound round his body, then slashed by the curse-remover's knife. By so doing, the curse-remover symbolically cut the warrior's impurity and restored him to society.[51]

Once the rituals of removal were complete, all warriors gathered once more on the dancing field for division of the spoils. Under ideal conditions, (either at the time of acquisition or during the first resting period during the return march), each would have branded the animals that he alone had taken. The brand was cut with a knife, by slicing either the animal's tail or ear in a manner recognizable to all. In cases of dispute, the conflicting claims were referred to the warriors' council.

Each set of counter-claims (and several warriors might lay claim to a specific animal) was judged and settled on its individual merits, and discussion of a case might go on for many days. However, there were a number of generally recognized principles accepted by all. Chief among these was that the decision of *ramare* was law. No one, not even the leading *ncamba*, would resist its judgment once made. A second principle specified that the man who first laid hands on a cow was considered its future owner. A third held that bravery in battle deserved a rich reward. Thus, those who had sought out enemy war-leaders during the fighting were rewarded for their courage. Those who had battled only with lesser warriors or novices received correspondingly less booty for their efforts.[52]

Occasionally two claims for a single animal would be so nearly equal that the *ramare* would be unable to settle the question of ownership. In such instances, tradition suggested two methods to settle the problem. One was to allow both claimants to fight, fully armed but subject to traditional combat restrictions. The other, more frequently used, was to award the disputed animal to one of the contenders, with the stipulation that he was to give its firstborn to his opponent.[53]

After receiving his portion of the captured livestock, a warrior, particularly if a novice still bound by his military oath, would seek out the person who had served as his sponsor when he first entered the *gaaru*. The latter then took the *muthaka*, still driving his spoils, to the homestead of the latter's father. The livestock would then be formally transferred into the father's hands, to be held for future use as bridewealth. If the transfer sufficed to fulfill the terms of a warrior's public oath, he was released from its obligation and could return to normal existence within the *gaaru*. If not, he would return to the bush to await another chance to raid.

119

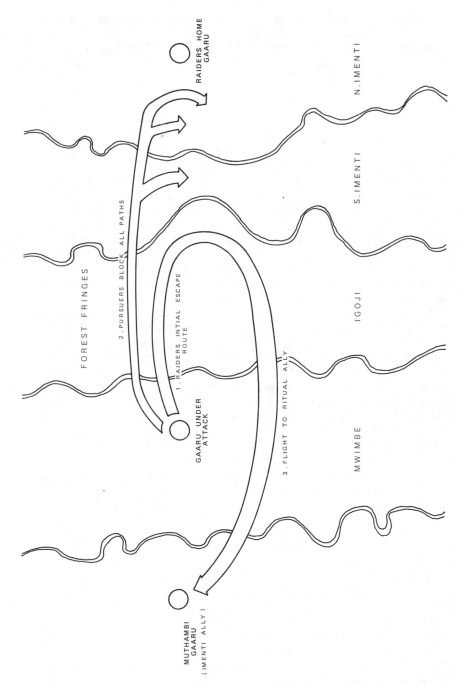

RAIDERS HOME
GAARU

N.IMENTI

S.IMENTI

FOREST FRINGES

2.PURSUERS BLOCK ALL PATHS

1.RAIDERS INTIAL ESCAPE
ROUTE

IGOJI

GAARU UNDER
ATTACK

3.FLIGHT TO RITUAL ALLY

MWIMBE

MUTHAMBI
GAARU
(IMENTI ALLY)

Evasion and flight to sanctuary of ritual ally

The warrior's profit from his labors lay in the praise-name he had earned. This was first given him by his father, in response to the livestock his son had brought. Subsequently, it would be publicly proclaimed at the *authi* dancing that followed. This third type of *authi*, the 'authi of praising' began on the same night. Numbers of the captured livestock were slaughtered for the feasting, and warriors whose animals had been selected were permitted to present the hides to particularly favored girls.

As the feasting ended, the dancing began. At its peak, warriors who had taken trophies would dance one by one into the center of the field, each displaying what he had seized, and describing the moment of its acquisition. His mother would then step forward to strip off his skin cloak, and he would stand armed and naked while girls of his area proclaimed the praise-name by which he would thereafter be known.[54]

The praise-name awarded differed according to the type of livestock, captive or war-trophy that had been taken. Thus warriors who had captured cattle, goats, sheep or donkeys would receive a different name for each type. Others, who had seized a spear, club, sword, clothing, or even a goatskin food bag from a battling opponent would also be named for what each had taken.

Thus a warrior returning with an enemy's sword (*ruchiu*), would be called M'Ruchiu, Ntoruchiu or Mutuaruchiu, each meaning 'son of the sword.' In other instances, the reference would be indirect. The same warrior might also be called M'Ruguti (the tree harvester, from -*gutua* (to harvest from trees). The implication, in this case, would be that the warriors had harvested the sword of a tall opponent.[55]

Praise names were also chosen to reflect behavior during battle. One man might have been named for a decision to bring home the child of a fallen enemy (Mutua Rujiu). Another could have been stigmatized for speaking loudly during a time that required silence (Kirathuku); a third, for momentarily opposing his war-leader (Kibuura). Others, particularly novices, might earn no praise-name at all.

The value of the system, therefore, lay in its impermanence. Unwanted names could be wiped out by boldness during subsequent raids, while those warriors who lacked reputations could try as often as necessary to acquire them. The result was a process that rewarded individual aggressiveness and at the same time insisted on obedience to authority, the very qualities required both to provoke and limit war.

The praise-name most sought by senior warriors was that of 'war-leader.' The highest title awarded only to *ncamba* of exceptional renown, was *ncamba iri iria mbui ya mugongo* (war leader who wears the feather of the back).[56] The physical symbol of this praise-name was a cloak made from the skins of an ox and a goat. It was meticulously decorated with scores of evenly placed cowrie shells and a lower fringe of iron rattles. The cloak itself was worn over the shoulder and hung down over the back and buttocks. In its center, thus on the back of the wearer, rested the *mbui*, a plume of ostrich feathers rising higher than the wearer's head.[57]

121

The title of *mbui* could be presented only at the close of the *authi* of praising. At a previously determined moment, spokesmen for the ruling elders would break into the ranks of dancing warriors in the manner previously described, singing their 'song of *kiama*' and waving green branches to attract their attention. The dancers would fall silent, while the *ncamba* to receive the title stood before them. The cloak was then laid across his shoulders by two youths, neither of whose bodies bore visible scars. The war-leader would then leap up and backwards, shouting out his triumph over the adulation of the crowd. Custom then required him to visit every homestead in the area, accompanied by those who chose to sing his praises, to receive each elder's acknowledgement of his triumph. Only after this tour had been completed could the *authi* of praising end and preparations for the next raiding expedition begin.

On reflection, the actual practice of warfare appears to provide the apparent conflict of a highly militarized society waging a highly chivalrous form of war. It has previously been noted, for example, that military actions throughout Meru were conducted with ample regard for the preservation of life.[58] The aged, pregnant and very young were usually spared the problems of warfare altogether. Captives were rarely mistreated, either returning to their homes in exchange for ransom, or entering their captors' families through adoption. Warriors who spared their opponents in battle by accepting surrender were rewarded with livestock, while those opting to kill their opponents were punished by a *mugiro*, requiring forfeiture of livestock to remove.

Yet, physical combat was not considered a situation to avoid. On the contrary, many circumstances operated to make it virtually inevitable. No effort was ever made, for instance, to conceal the location of potential target herds from the eyes of transient aliens, even though these might have acted as scouts for potential attackers. Nor did any *mwiriga* act to prevent the theft of its animals by enclosing them within a pit or log stockade. Indeed, informants queried on this point would frequently react in anger, exclaiming that with such precautions "there would be no need for warriors."[59] Nor, despite the oral testimony, does existing evidence suggest that raiders were able to 'slip quietly away' with an entire herd while its defenders slept. On the contrary, in most, if not all, instances an active defense was both anticipated and desired, since it formed a primary source of the warriors' subsequent praise-names.

The explanation for the disparity between militarization and chivalry can be found in the Meru perception of military action as part of the process of continuous alternation between conditions of conflict and harmony. Military conflict, however, regulated by convention, was viewed as the essential prerequisite to large-scale acquisition of livestock, particularly cattle. Possession of such livestock, in turn, allowed owners to increase the potential for creating and maintaining harmony within their own immediate society. The defense of this potential, or its restoration in the event of prior loss, was the ultimate reason for waging war.

CHAPTER VI

The End of Warriorhood

Courtship and Marriage

Warriorhood had no established time limit. Each age-set retained military authority until a sufficient number of the following set had matured enough to assume the responsibility. In practice, this occurred when the younger group grew sufficiently numerous to seize control of the *gaaru*. By expelling the senior warriors, they symbolically took the defense of the community upon themselves.

The younger set, of course, would steadily increase in number as more of its members passed through circumcision and into the *gaaru* as novices. The increase, therefore, would inevitably be accompanied by rising feelings of resentment at the authority held by the senior warriors, and increasing eagerness to assume the latters' role.

The impatience of these novice warriors was matched by that of their fathers, now reaching the end of their own period as novice elders. Tradition released from any service to the community males who had attained this rank. Instead, they were supposedly free to establish homesteads and families. In fact, this freedom was sharply circumscribed by members of the age-set above their own, whose status as ruling elders required constant services from their own junior grade.

With their eldest sons passing steadily into the *gaaru*, however, the period of novice elderhood was almost complete. The impending decision of these new warriors to seize physically the symbol of military authority would also signal the promotion of their own set to the rank of ruling elder.

In contrast, senior warriors were caught between two opposing desires.

123

There were many reasons for them to extend their warriorhood indefinitely. They had reached a goal sought since childhood, and attained a role of which society approved. Their age-set, together with that of their fathers, held both military and administrative authority over the community. Their own duties brought material gain for their fathers and status to themselves. In comparison, the role of novice elder which awaited them, despite its promises of sexual fulfillment and children, held no duties of compensating importance and therefore must have seemed relatively empty.

The feelings of senior warriors were often reflected by their fathers. As members of the ruling age-set, they, too, shared the pleasures to be derived from responsibility and power. The deference and respect owed by other sections of society to every member of the ruling set were not lightly put aside. Neither were the material rewards which appeared in the shape of livestock, gifts from persons seeking wisdom or justice at their hands.

For this set, too, the role that awaited its members after termination of their period of authority must have seemed relatively devoid of reward. Their new status would be one of ritual elder, responsible only for appeasing the supernatural by appropriate rites and sacrifices. They would retain a theoretical ability to veto decisions of the age-set that would acquire their secular powers. Nonetheless, their prestige and authority would wane. Thus, like their warrior sons, the group holding secular authority had every reason to extend its period of power.

Among the oldest warriors, however, the desire to retain their military status gradually came into conflict with equally compelling reasons to leave. One of these was the knowledge that men of their age-set were expected by tradition to begin seeking wives. Senior warriors who ignored this injunction were subject to taunts by the novices who would allude (in song, etc.) to the subject in ways that grew gradually less respectful.

A second reason came from each senior warrior's realization that the period required for selection of a suitable prospect, courtship and bride-wealth negotiations could take considerable time. A warrior who delayed the procedure might find it increasingly difficult to locate a satisfactory wife among the women reserved for members of his age-set.[1] The most attractive among them would have been taken by his mates. The fathers of those remaining might react to a warrior's growing impatience by raising the requested bride-price. Seeking brides farther afield might also take time, or could lead to refusal by fathers seeking suitors from areas near their own.

The most compelling reason to begin the search, moreover, came from the fact that no senior warrior knew precisely when his age-set might finally be expelled from their warrior status. Yet, failure to have selected a mate prior to such expulsion meant both humiliation and expense. Seizure of authority by the novice warrior would mean that all remaining women of marriageable age would thereafter be reserved for their own eventual courtship and marriage.

To acquire a wife from this group, an expelled warrior would therefore be required to apply to his juniors for permission, presenting them with appropriate livestock as gifts to assure their acceptance. While tradition required the younger members to grant the request, the procedure was usually accompanied by a torrent of indirect taunts concerning the applicant's lack of ability with the opposite sex.[2]

Thus, however ambivalent his feelings, each senior warrior eventually found himself willing to seek a mate and initiate courtship. There were certain restrictions. No girl was considered mature enough to be courted until her ears had been pierced and her father had publicly proclaimed her "ready to sleep with men."[3]

Completion of these ceremonies permitted the girls (*nkenye*: uncircumcised girls) to attend dances with the warriors. These were sufficiently frequent to give both sexes the opportunity to become mutually attracted and to display their feelings by seeking out partners. They were not allowed to talk, conversation at such a time and place being considered a breach of manners. Nor was fraternization permitted at the end of the evening. The dancing would stop, and the dancers would make their way home alone.[4]

Thereafter, courtship could continue only in daylight, when each girl followed her mother to the fields. Tradition forbade the pair to walk together, lest the mother interfere with such suitors as passed by. A warrior, therefore, needed only to wait for the girl of his choice to appear. Her relative isolation permitted ample opportunity for conversation, and the acquaintance could thus deepen and grow.

Eventually, one warrior could initiate the next stage of courtship by announcing his intention to visit the girl at her family's homestead. If she agreed, tradition required that she approach her mother to beg millet for gruel to offer the suitor. At this point, the mother could ask the warrior's name, and would indicate either her or her husband's disapproval by withholding the requested food. If they approved, the request would be granted.

The warrior traditionally arrived at dusk, announcing his presence by planting his spear before the hut of the girl's mother. The latter greeted him, then retired to her husband's dwelling. The daughter invited the visitor to enter her mother's home and eat. Custom forbade her to eat with him, but conversation was permitted until he had finished the meal. Thereafter, tradition required the suitor to leave.[5]

It should be noted that sexual relations during these early stages of courtship were severely circumscribed. Uncircumcised girls were permitted no sexual expression at all. After circumcision or during the formal courtship that immediately preceded it, girls were allowed limited intercourse with one suitor of their choice. The act was performed in a standing position, with the girl leaning against the wall of her mother's hut. Full penetration of the vagina was permitted, but the suitor was required to withdraw just prior to ejaculation (*coitus interruptus*).[6] Intercourse was forbidden during a girl's menstruation or when her partner had placed himself under military oath.[7]

If no pregnancy occurred, a suitor's visits might continue until the pair began to consider marriage. Thereafter, the warrior's next action was to inform his parents of a wish to create a relationship (*uthoni*: inlawship, relationship) with the prospective bride's family. This was not intended as a proposal of marriage, but a preliminary effort to create bonds of mutual obligation and goodwill between the two families, which might eventually lead to agreement on the girl's betrothal.

The method used to create these bonds involved a continual exchange of gifts of gradually increasing value, intended to involve not only the original suitors but their families. Typically, the pattern of such an exchange began when the warrior presented a small gift of snuff (tobacco) to the girl. She, in turn, passed it on to her mother, who gave it to her husband. The husband traditionally used it for two days, then instructed his wife to give millet to their daughter. Thereafter, the latter ground it to prepare gruel, this time intended for her suitor's father. She would present it, however, to the warrior's mother, receiving in exchange a gift of castor oil and yams to bring to her own mother, who would subsequently divide the gift among her aunts.[8] The exchanges gradually expanded to cover more distant members of both families, until what had originally been an affair between two persons became the concern of all.

In consequence, both the feelings of mutual obligation, and the goodwill fostered by this process supposedly proved strong enough to neutralize the hostilities that inevitably emerged from subsequent bridewealth negotiations. Within the context, even the transfer of traditional marriage gifts would be viewed as part of the larger life-long process of creating relationships between the families, bonds that would expand and deepen until acceptance of the proposed betrothal became inevitable.[9]

At some stage in the courting process, parents of both suitors would confer with elders of their respective clans, to ask whether the proposed match should be permitted. No man might marry a woman from his own clan, nor even one descended from a distant common ancestor whether real or ritually created. Nor could a warrior marry the child of his age-mate. Instead, tradition required him to seek a wife from daughters of the age-set above his own.[10]

This set, novice-elders who had left warriorhood over a decade earlier, would have sired daughters just old enough to begin to consider as possible wives. These would reach sexual maturity at the same time senior warriors began to seek mates. Having married, the warriors, in their turn, would produce a new generation of daughters to be given at puberty to men of the age-set below their own.

In consequence, each age-set gradually formed a pattern of in-law relationships with sets immediately above and below it, thereby supplementing the blood relationships already formed with the set two above (their fathers) and to be created with that two below, their future sons. Viewed within this larger context, the sequence of relationships created by a single decision to marry involved more than the joining of two families or even clans. It was a process intended to link gradually entire age-sets by either blood or ritually created ties of kinship. The intended result was a society within which every social component would be forged into a single, unified whole.

From a warrior perspective, however, the system produced conflicting obligations. As a husband, a senior warrior should spend his nights with his wife; as a warrior, with his *gaaru*. Tradition provided several methods to resolve the conflict. In some areas, senior warriors presented their comrades with livestock at the time of marriage, as "fines" for their subsequent marital absences. In others, fines were extracted from married warriors for each night of absence, a technique not intended to lure seniors back into the *gaaru*, but to force them to leave it completely.[11]

In time, a married warrior's absences from the *gaaru* grew longer and more frequent, until he eventually failed to appear at all. No ritual marked this transition, perhaps since these persons still retained residual military responsibilities. During their first years of marriage, however, married males might periodically sleep at the *gaaru*, particularly during those times when their wives were ritually forbidden to them (e.g., menstruation or pregnancy).[12]

During these periods, they were forbidden to assume positions of leadership within the structure or to take active part in the planning of raids. If approached by younger *ncamba*, however, they were permitted to offer advice on either tactics or terrain and might accompany an exploratory scouting party if requested. Married males might also choose to participate in raids, particularly if enemies or natural catastrophes had decimated their own livestock. In these cases, they were allowed to fight and guide, but never to lead; instead, they must obey the orders of younger *ncamba* despite the disparity in ages. Their efforts during these expeditions could earn them every type of booty, from livestock to human captives. They were forbidden, however, to share in the subsequent rituals of community praise, for the songs and names to be derived from expeditions were reserved for those officially within their warrior years.[13]

The same pattern existed within the *gaaru*. Although permitted to sleep within the structure, they were forbidden to lead or take any part in its internal activities, particularly with regard to the imposition of discipline. In consequence, most married males gradually abandoned the barrack entirely, leaving it under the authority of the declining number of their agemates who remained. It was this remnant which was forced to endure the actual transfer of military power.

The Transfer of Power

In most Meru subdivisions, the act of transferring both military and administrative authority from one age-set to that chronologically beneath it was called *ntuiko*.[14] In Kimeru the word implies the cutting or breaking of existing patterns of authority in order to create a vacuum of power into which a subsequent age-set could move.[15] In Imenti, Miutini and Igoji, this cutting process was symbolized by the previously mentioned physical expulsion of senior warriors from the *gaaru*; in Mwimbe and Muthambe, it was accomplished by the purchase of senior status with traditionally specified amounts of livestock.

In the three northern subdivisions, the actual transfer of authority took place in several stages. Initially, an approaching period of *ntuiko* was expressed only through the steady decline in the ranks of senior warriors, and the corresponding increase in the novices' impatience with the authority wielded by those who still remained. Eventually, leading elements among the junior warriors began to fall back into the patterns of behavior traditionally used to advance the interests of their group. Cautiously, they began to initiate limited forms of conflict with their immediate superiors.

At first, these conflicts were restricted to the daily chores expected of novices, primarily the nightly gathering of wood, food and water. At an earlier period, leading persons among the novices had responded by passing the bulk of these burdens on to their own youngest members. Now, they made common cause with them, encouraging newcomers to express their collective resentment in limited forms of evasion. In consequence, wood and food collections became progressively slower and less reliable, a form of defiance to which the remaining veterans could respond only with fines or beatings.

The novices' resentment was next directed against traditional sexual restrictions. As younger warriors, they were forbidden to express any form of overt sexual behavior, particularly when in the presence of those girls reserved for courtship by senior warriors. Gradually, the older novices evaded this restriction as well, initiating limited forms of courtship in their seniors' absence. At first this was achieved by recourse to songs, sung to or about specific girls, whose words would barely suggest sensuality or courtship. In time, however, the words became progressively rougher and more direct, until everyone in the community became aware that the seniors' prerogative of courtship was being usurped.[16]

Song was also used against those seniors still remaining in the *gaaru* or those who showed reticence in seeking wives. At a safe distance, progressively larger groups of novices would compose songs alluding to nature's growing infertility (" . . . let us sing of clouds which can never bring rain . . .") and to the duty of those whose time to provide such fertility had arrived.[17]

The senior warriors retaliated against these insults in the only ways tradition would permit. Beatings, supplemented with livestock fines, which expanded with each instance of insubordination, were imposed on the entire junior age-set. This retaliation, in turn, invoked the increasing concern of the novices' fathers, from whose flocks and herds the fines were ultimately drawn. Publicly, they complained to other elements of the community of the numbers of animals that were required. Privately, they exhorted their sons to end the drain on their herds once and for all by expelling those that were fining them.

Eventually, unrest within the *gaaru* reached an intensity sufficient to disturb other elements of the community. The novices, deciding that their moment had come, approached their fathers in a unified body to request their permission to seize control. These, in turn, petitioned the ruling elders, requesting consultation with appropriate ritual specialists in order to gain their blessing.[18]

The specialist to be consulted varied among the major subdivisions. Members of *miiriga* from South Imenti, parts of North Imenti, Miutini and Igoji approached the *mugwe* (dispenser of blessings; pl: *agwe*) or *aroria* (foretellers), who performed essentially similar functions.

Traditionally, the delegation approaching the *mugwe* would be composed of twenty-four spokesmen, representing the novice, ruling and ritual elders. No warriors were permitted to attend. On arrival, spokesmen for the two younger age-sets seated themselves in a large circle before the *mugwe* hut, ruling elders forming the right half, and novice elders the left. The ritual elders, joined by the *mugwe*, sat outside the circle as silent observers, prepared to offer advice when asked, or to intervene if tradition was violated.

The two younger age-sets then presented their viewpoints, the novice elders arguing on behalf of their sons for an immediate transfer of military authority, while the ruling set advocated the reasons for its delay. Negotiations centered on each group's interpretation of the internal tranquility and external strength of the *mwiriga*, novice elders insisting that their sons were sufficiently mature to bear the full responsibilities while their seniors disputed it. Ultimately, some form of consensus was reached, and permission for the transfer received the *mugwe's* ritual blessing.[19]

On leaving the *mugwe*, spokesmen for the novice elders informed all other members of their age-set, who in turn passed the news to their warrior sons. Thereafter, both groups, joined by selected spokesmen for the ruling elders, retired to a relatively remote area to feast. Several bulls were usually provided for the feasting, among them one which was pure black and so old as to be considered past the age of possible procreation. This was sacrificed with appropriate ritual. The skin was preserved for eventual presentation to the *mugwe* at the conclusion of the entire *ntuiko* rite.[20] The meat, as well as that taken from other animals, was shared by those present and consumed as a symbol of their agreement to the transfer.

The feasting continued until an hour or so before dawn. At that time, one or more of the more skillful novice warriors would leave the others and attempt to steal the war-horn (*coro*) from its place within the *gaaru*. Theft of the horn was a matter of great significance to everyone. Tradition required that it always remain within the barrack, guarded by the most experienced veterans. As a result, its successful theft by a warrior novice was intended to demonstrate to the entire community the military unfitness of the senior set. In theory, the seniors' continued vigilance should have permanently prevented such a theft, if only by setting out guards. In fact, no waking watch was ever kept, since the posting of sentinels would have betrayed the older warriors' apprehension and reflected adversely on their martial pride.[21]

Tradition also required that the horn rest near the *gaaru* door and that "no hand lie touching it at night."[22] Thus, the actual seizure could be made by a single novice willing to creep through the entrance. If successful, the thief raced instantly for the safety of the distant bush; there he repeatedly blew the *coro* to summon his age-mates.

The repeated blasts of the instrument would waken everyone in the community. At first, hearers were uncertain whether the noise meant *ntuiko* or enemy attack, and would listen anxiously for the songs traditionally chanted at the time of power-transfer. If the war-horn had indeed been seized, the first bugling would draw forth shouted responses, then snatches of song, as the novices drew together in a single band to march in final triumph on the *gaaru.*

Traditionally, the entire junior body approached the structure fully armed. They were met at its entrance by the remaining seniors, angered and shamed by the theft of their war-horn and determined to defend their prerogatives to the last. The ensuing struggle would be brief but violent, with the more numerous juniors inevitably expelling their outnumbered opponents, then seizing the barrack for themselves.

The actual struggle seems to have been more of a brawl than a battle. Informants exaggerate the degree of violence that occurred (". . . a fierce battle . . . ," etc.), while at the same time they note that although many were injured in the moment of *ntuiko,* no one had ever died. The implication was that although weapons were carried, their cutting edges were never used. Such limits would be quite in keeping with the Meru tradition of first provoking conflict, then restricting it to socially tolerated forms. It would also explain the inevitable novice victories. Once negotiations between the novice and ruling elders had been sanctified by the *mugwe,* the transfer of power was inevitable.

This does not imply, however, that the *ntuiko* was carried out without hostility on the part of both victors and vanquished. The novices vented their long repressed anger by destroying the seniors' *gaaru* as soon as they had seized it, then building another for themselves. During this time, custom permitted them to sing of their former tormenters in the most abusive manner possible. The older group was also permitted outlets for its rage. For a limited period after their expulsion, tradition allowed them to band together and scour the countryside, pillaging homesteads, groves and gardens while seeking aliens (non-Meru) on which to blood their spears.[23]

At the end of this lawless period the former warriors were required to return to the site of their former *gaaru* and join in a feast of reconciliation with both the newly appointed set of ruling elders and the warriors by whom they had recently been displaced. Here, for the first time, they were made aware of their own new status, since the victors were required by custom to placate their former opponents with appropriate gifts of livestock (contributed by their fathers, now ruling elders) and, more significantly, by treating them with the deference due novice elders. No further trace of even vocal irony was permitted, even between persons known to have been bitter rivals in their warrior past.[24]

Tradition required that the feast continue until genuine reconciliation had occurred among participants, to the point where the community would be united once again. Recalcitrant ex-warriors could have prolonged it indefinitely, but the daily need for new livestock sacrifices by the participants led those present to exert progressively greater pressure on persons who proved unwilling to reconcile. Inevitably, the will of the majority combined to erode initial feelings of resentment, and the need for conciliation became evident to all.[25]

Thus reunited, the entire community would gather at a place designated by the ruling elders, then proceed as a body to the homestead of the *mugwe* (or a similar ritual specialist) to receive a final blessing for the events that had occurred. In Imenti, representatives from the two new ruling sets presented him with the hide of the aged black bull slaughtered at the beginning of *ntuiko*, thereby symbolically establishing their acceptance of his wisdom. He would respond by blessing the entire assemblage and proclaiming the name by which the newly triumphant warrior age-set would henceforth be known. Thereafter, each set would assume its new position on the social ladder and the *ntuiko* would be complete.[26]

In retrospect, the *ntuiko* process seems once again to reflect the Meru assumptions that both conflict and harmony were essential to social balance. As in earlier instances, social change was permitted only by initiating limited conflict between adjacent age-sets, provoked as always by the younger. Harmony was restored only through intervention of ruling elders, then sanctified by the blessing of ritual specialists and, through them, the ancestors.

At the same time the inevitability of *ntuiko* also shielded Meru from the power-vacuums and succession struggles endured by other societies. Instead, every age set retained a vested interest in preserving the existing structure. Those temporarily removed from positions of authority were assured that their turn (or that of their sons) would come again. Until that time, they felt equally certain that the groups in authority, since they were composed either of actual or potential in-laws, would do nothing to damage their interests.

In sum, although *ntuiko* could be described superficially as a physical struggle between conflicting groups, it was actually an alternative to such conflict. By dividing society into two major groups which alternated every form of authority between them, the Meru created an alternative to battles for either military or political succession. By ritualizing the actual transfer of this authority in a manner which initially provoked, then limited, and finally dissipated the rivalries inevitable among those concerned, they felt protected against the emergence of unlimited rivalry. In so doing, they insurred their own internal continuity and survival.

The Return to Non-Military Status

The return of a former warrior to civilian status must have been traumatic to the person concerned. His new title, *muruau* (pl: *aruau*), signified 'family head' as well as 'novice elder,' but carried with it connotations of insignificance which bordered on contempt. In consequence, it was rarely used in formal greeting as were the titles achieved in earlier periods. Instead, the term of 'elder' (*muthee*) was often substituted as more indicative of respect.[27]

Yet even this more honored title was indicative of the difficulties inherent in his new position. For nearly three decades he had been asked to define all aspects of his existence in terms of a set of military ideals. His community position, feelings of personal worth and very sense of personal identity had been continually evaluated, both by his society and himself, according to the degree to which these standards were achieved.

Suddenly, he had been virtually expelled from that phase of his existence and thrust into a new situation which called for the restructuring of his entire social outlook. As an elder, he found that acceptable behavior was no longer defined in terms of provoking conflict, but resolving it. The skills required were no longer military, but conciliatory, and called for mastering the vast body of ancestral lore by which society lived.

Superficially, the novice elder was simply following the pattern he had traced since childhood, moving from apprenticeship to authority within each stage of the Meru life span. In a larger sense, however, his initial three decades could be regarded as a single major stage, through which he had risen toward adulthood by striving for a single ideal: military mastery. His final three decades could therefore be considered as a second major stage, through which he would rise by striving for a second distinct ideal: the mastery of tradition.

At the beginning of this second stage, however, the former warrior found himself once more considered as a child. In the eyes of the ruling elders he would remain so until he had attained the necessary wisdom.

It could be argued that this second period of childhood was reflected in the paucity of his obligations to society at large. A *muruau* had no administrative or judicial responsibilities and no economic duties other than to establish a homestead and family. Even his residual military duties reflected this condition. Denied all participation in the verbal honors (praise songs, etc.) derived from raids, he was rewarded, by tradition, by being given a portion of the booty, either livestock to sustain a homestead or a captive to enlarge it.[28]

No former warrior could have been expected to learn more than a fragment of the required wisdom during his youth. However, tradition did provide the opportunity to overcome this inexperience. At some time during the period of novice elderhood, each male was expected to apply for admission to the elders' *kiama* of his own *mwiriga*.[29] As had been the case with entrance to the *biama* of the childhood, application was voluntary. However, no one could evade it without exposing himself to the contempt of his age-mates, which would progressively increase as large numbers of them enrolled.[30]

The required application could be made only after establishing a homestead with sufficient economic security to allow payment of the livestock required as prerequisites to entry. In principle, a young *muruau* of exceptional wealth might draw upon his father's herds and begin application immediately after his own marriage. Most novice elders, however, could not hope to apply until near the end of their period of apprenticeship, when their own first-born children were approaching puberty.[31]

At this point, entry into the *kiama* became increasingly urgent, since these children would be forbidden circumcision until their parents had become members. Thus, in time, what had originally been a means of increasing prestige evolved gradually into a matter of embarrassment. In such instances, tradition permitted poorer members of the community to lighten their obligation in a number of ways. In some areas, persons unable to procure the larger livestock (i.e., a bull) required for entry, were permitted to substitute smaller animals (i.e., several goats), payable in installments over indefinite periods of time. In others, poor persons were permitted to borrow the required livestock from wealthier members of their own age-set.[32]

As had also been the case when entering *biama* of childhood, new applicants were required to seek out a sponsor to support them during their periods of initiation and apprenticeship. This person could be chosen only from among the ruling elders. He was petitioned by the novice, plied with the traditionally required gifts, then treated for the balance of his lifetime with the gestures of filial respect due the applicant's own father. In return, the sponsor might provide his 'child' with a portion of the required livestock fees, concern himself particularly with the latter's subsequent education and conciliate all disputes in which his 'son' was involved.[33]

Initiation into the elder *kiama* took place whenever a sufficient number of novices had contributed the traditional fees. Although as elders the applicants were no longer beaten, no effort was spared to impress them with the significance of the step they were about to take. Generally, the initiation began with the construction of a single large hut in a remote, relatively unpopulated area. All applicants were summoned to appear before it, accompanied by their sponsors and bearing specified numbers of livestock. The initiation period lasted four days. From dawn to dusk, candidates were expected to sit motionless and silent while elder *kiama* members instructed them as to the secrets of the organization, the betrayal of which would lead to their deaths. At sunset on the fourth day the novices returned to their homes, each bearing the elders' staff that marked him as a *mukiama* (man of the *kiama*), and singing traditional songs.[34]

The secrets of *kiama* were presented to the applicants in the fashion they had learned since childhood. Much of the instruction dealt with patterns of behavior now expected of them. New forms of demeanor were required when in the presence of women, children and warriors. New attitudes were also demanded towards their own children, particularly sons, to teach them to appreciate and revere the status of elderhood.

The bulk of this knowledge was transmitted to the initiates in the form of maxims as to how they should behave in daily life, coupled with the perpetual threat of supernatural vengeance should they fail to respond as expected:[35]

If you find cattle in another's garden, and fail to seek out the owner . . . let the oath you now take devour you.

If you find a woman in labor along the path and you fail to assist her . . . let the oath you now take devour you.

If your sons speak out to [contradict] you and you fail to whip them . . . let the oath you now take devour you.

Each applicant understood, however, that the wisdom of elderhood was not acquired merely through memorization of a number of oral precepts. Rather, the heart of all instruction was the candidates' realization that the knowledge required could be gained only through years of apprenticeship, spent sitting silently near the ruling elders during their meetings and listening respectfully to the issues in dispute. Only by this behavior could they hope to absorb gradually the oral precedents from which ancestral tradition had been forged, to the point where they might someday themselves interpret the inherent analogies in terms of contemporary affairs.

For former warriors, however, the restrictions inherent in more than a decade of silent apprenticeship must have clashed sharply with their earlier devotion to war. Once again, as the newborn (*ntaani*) of still another kiama, they were compelled to perform its menial tasks. It was this group which was responsible for the nightly supply of firewood, and whose herds and gardens provided food for the ruling elders' feasts. It was they who were assigned to skin and apportion the slaughtered livestock, while accepting only inferior portions of the meat.[36] As in childhood, they were compelled to fall silent in the presence of superiors and accept any discipline the latter might impose. In sum, the new role robbed them of both authority and status, providing only silence and submission in exchange. It was a decade which former warriors of any society would have found difficult to endure; therefore questions are raised as to why they did endure it.

The Military Versus Meru Society

In retrospect, it seems that a system requiring so rapid and thorough a revision of self-image as occurred in Meru must suffer from periodic instability. It can be argued that any community choosing swiftly to downgrade and dismiss its military element after more than a decade of continuous warfare risks (reprisal from those persons involved) which may unsettle the whole society.[37]

Similarly, the Meru practice of periodically ejecting males from a warrior-role toward which they had striven for decades into a position psychologically akin to childhood might well have led those involved to ex-

134

press their discontent. They might even have chosen to resist their expulsion, since those forced into this reduction of status were at a peak of military competence and thus physically able to over-awe the community in any clash of wills.

This possibility seems even more striking if one considers colonial efforts to demilitarize this very same society less than a decade after the period considered in this study. In 1906 and 1907, the peoples of Meru submitted without military resistance to British rule. Within a few months thereafter, the warrior age-set of that period (*murungi*) had been swiftly and totally disarmed. With their raids prohibited, their weapons confiscated, and even their dances subject to British control, they found themselves figuratively ejected from their *gaaru* and sent ("like children")[38] to their homesteads.

The initial impact of this disarmament was to spur several groups of warriors into active resistance. In consequence, a number of barracks from Mwimbe to Tigania defied the new conquerors. The systematic British defeat of these efforts, however, demoralized the warrior age-set to the point where it became an increasingly unstable element within the community. Abandoning military ideals and acting in open defiance of their elders, large numbers of every subdivision turned to drunkenness, brawling, property damage and sexual promiscuity to compensate for the more satisfying role they had been forced to abandon.

On the surface, British efforts at demilitarization seem little different from those practiced in the pre-colonial era. In both instances, a specific, unified, fully armed body of warriors was ejected from its military position while still at a peak of martial prowess. Males were physically disarmed, verbally humiliated, forbidden to wage further war and sent home. Nor, in either instance, did their subsequent roles provide comparable satisfaction.

One would therefore expect both groups to react to demobilization similarly, with the behavior of warriors expelled by *ntuiko* paralleling that of the age-set demilitarized by colonialism. Thus, pre-colonial warriors might well have responded to the revision in their status either by abandoning warrior ideals or by resisting such revision, even if this meant usurping the authority of the elders themselves. There is ample precedent for the most military element of a war-oriented society deciding to strike at the rest, particularly when the alternative was its own demilitarization.

Nevertheless, oral evidence suggests that none of these possibilities occurred. On the contrary, informants insist that senior warriors have passively accepted their reduction of status throughout Meru history, maintaining conditions of relative harmony between themselves and non-military elements of society. No study of Meru military institutions would be complete, therefore, without examination of the factors which permitted such stability to be maintained.

Ultimately, the harmonious balance between military and governmental elements of society was kept by adherence to two fundamental principles. One of these might be characterized as the "principle of division." It has been noted that the Meru divided most aspects of their existence into halves. The universe, for instance, was conceived of in terms of a secular and supernatural sphere. The human life span was similarly envisaged. The first half was devoted to mastering the ability to create limited forms of conflict; the last, to acquiring the wisdom to restore harmony.[39] These halves were in turn each divided into four age-set periods, three of which were expected to contribute productively to society. Each period was once again divided into two roughly equal time spans (apprenticeship, authority), within which persons acted out dual roles (teacher, learner). There are many other examples of such division.[40]

Inevitably, this principle was also reflected within Meru conceptions of political authority. Within the secular sphere, for instance, power was superficially divided into military and governmental spheres. At a deeper level, however, the balance between the two responsible groups was maintained by a division of their corresponding social attitudes as well.

The mental outlook required of a Meru warrior, for example, was a basic factor in maintaining this traditional military/administrative balance. This can be best illustrated by briefly re-examining the basic attitudes required for mastery of the five traditional military ideals, as described earlier in this study.[41] In such a war-oriented society, particularly one in which battle was envisioned in terms of single combat, one might expect the warrior ethic to focus on personal achievement, whether expressed in acts of emotional courage or physical prowess. Instead, the military ideals of Meru emphasize self-regulation, group domination and continuous submission to authority.

It was these qualities that Meru males were taught to revere from their earliest years. The stories taught them throughout their childhood stressed these concepts as embodying the warrior ideal. After they had entered the system of pre-military councils (boys' *biama*), such qualities were continually reinforced by their immediate superiors. Internalization of those qualities proved the only means to advancement, since only by submitting to the demands of the system could they prove their own fitness for future leadership within it.

These attitudes were also internalized by the relative effectiveness of this *biama* system as an agent for the socialization of youth. Ultimately, the basis for this success was the voluntary acceptance of the standards of the system. Unlike contemporary Western cultures, where children are required by written law to attend institutions especially created to transmit the skills and values of adulthood, the youths of Meru were never placed in a formal educational system. Rather, all but a tiny fraction[42] voluntarily sought to learn from their elders in *biama*, simply because they aspired to the proclaimed (military) ideals of the organization. For the same reasons, they submitted freely to its physical and mental restraints, willingly subordinating their personal attitudes to those established by the system, thereby proving their own fitness to mature within it.

The warrior, therefore, willingly adapted his mental outlook to the demands of society. He devoted three decades to internalization of a military ethic based not on self-achievement, but on self-regulation and submission.

Thus, the very act of mastering Meru military standards formed a basis for harmonizing the martial and civilian elements of the society, since a warrior's devotion to his own ideals insured creation of the corresponding mental outlook needed to guarantee domination by his elders.

A second basis for the retention of this balance lay in the contrasting mental outlook required of Meru elders. It has been previously noted that the ultimate source of their authority lay in neither their secular abilities nor their social position, but in the very fact of their advancing years. Those not only gave them increased proximity to the spirits of their ancestors, but also permitted them to seek further into their recollections of the past, in order to recall correctly the ancestral traditions required to guide contemporary affairs.

Since violation of many of these traditions was believed to lead unwittingly to supernatural retaliation, the powers of eldership were ultimately envisaged in terms of the protection they offered against such calamity. The aged used their wisdom to shelter the young against the effects of deviation from ancestral will. In turn, the young submitted willingly to their authority. Within this context, then, the very act of exerting that authority over a warrior age-set was conceived as benevolently protecting them from the consequences of their own youth.

This protection can be most clearly illustrated by examining three of the more formal powers used by elders to enforce this authority. The power of conciliation was restricted by tradition to those of elder status. Warriors attempting to usurp it would find themselves deficient in the knowledge required to resolve those conflicts engendered by their own military activities. Lacking the required mastery of oral precedent, they would inevitably deviate from ancestral guidelines in finding solutions, thereby rendering themselves vulnerable to supernatural wrath. Thereafter, they would have no protection other than that offered by their elders, since only the latters' knowledge would prove sufficient to shelter them from the consequences of their military role.

This protective outlook also dominated a second of the elders' formal powers, that of approval. It has previously been noted that warriors required both secular and supernatural approval for every projected act. This was particularly true of the major milestones of warriorhood (circumcision, *ntuiko*, etc.), as well as the decision to raid. Usurping this power by acting without it, would have placed warriors in the same exposed position, subject to ancestral retribution through the ignorance of their youth. Whether acting in secular capacities (kinsmen, *kiama* members) or as spokesmen for the ancestors (ritual specialists), only elders had the knowledge to guide the young along the track of their warriorhood.

The protective principle can even be found in the elders' formal powers of disapproval. These also took both secular and supernatural forms. Elders acting in *kiama*, for instance, could impose secular punishments (livestock levies, etc.) upon members of younger age-sets who evaded or resisted their authority. In such instances, warriors were compelled by tradition to assist that body by physically enforcing its decisions ('the arm of *kiama'*) even when those involved kinsmen or age-mates. As with the other formal powers, however, the intent was not retributive in the historical Western sense of an 'eye for an eye.' Rather, it was an effort to protect offenders against the supernatural consequences of their acts by reconciling them (through livestock forfeiture, etc.) with those who had been harmed.

The same pattern occurred in supernatural forms of disapproval. If opposed by younger members of society, elders of any age-set could gather in *kiama* to impose a collective curse upon offenders, thereby isolating them from the community by making them ritually impure (*mugiro*). In such an instance, the affronted person would convene his age-mates in *kiama* to appeal for their assistance. They, in turn, would petition the collective spirits of their ancestors to bring ritual impurity (and thus, physical calamity) upon the offenders. The curse of *kirimu* (insult), for instance, was used specifically against warriors believed to have insulted an elder by inadequate response to his commands.[43]

To avoid this, warriors would have little choice but to beg the elders to lift their *mugiro*, repaying them with sufficient livestock to alleviate their collective wrath. Yet, as with secular disapproval, the intent was not punishment, but protection. No elder wished the warriors of his *mwiriga* to sicken, die or suffer similar calamity, thereby diminishing the security of all. Rather, the curse was intended as an instrument to guide offenders back into harmony with their ancestors, by compelling them to make whatever restitution was required to evade the (supernatural) consequences of their own intransigence.

Therefore, as with warriors, the mental outlook of Meru elders served to create a second basis for the tradition of harmony between the two. The very act of exerting their authority over military elements of society was seen as insuring both ancestral approval of their actions and their continued survival.

It seems evident, nonetheless, that the harmony between martial and governmental elements was maintained by more than a simple division of their roles, with warriors learning to accept authority and elders to wield it in the name of tradition. To focus solely upon the Meru pattern of division ignores its interdependent nature, and consequently the second major principle by which a social balance was maintained.

Evidence of this interdependence can be found in many aspects of the Meru social structure, since the artificial divisions which characterized it required the cooperation of their component halves in order to function at all. This was particularly true of the relationship between warriors and elders. In order to carry out its own role, each element required specified gestures by the other which could be obtained only by cultivating the good will of the opposing group.

The interdependent nature of these relationships can best be illustrated by re-examining the pattern by which secular authority (Kimeru: power) was transferred between age-sets. Each age-set was assigned alternately to one of two artificial divisions, Kiruka and Ntiba. Each of these held one-half of the responsibility for administering society. Therefore, age-sets within one division that had reached the grades of warrior and ruling elder (ideally, fathers and sons) were collectively accountable for maintaining secular harmony, while those of the opposing faction (ritual elders), were responsible for relations with the supernatural.

These sections, however, were not merely divisions. Rather the age-sets within them remained mutually dependent. Tradition required both the secular and supernatural responsibilities to alternate regularly between the two divisions at the end of every age-set period, as groups representing first Kiruka and then Ntiba reached the appropriate ranks. The pattern of this alternation, however, depended on the cooperation of both those aspiring to assume authority and those relinquishing it. In turn, the existence of such cooperation created a situation which made alternation inevitable.

It one reconsiders the pattern of power-transfer within a warrior *gaaru*, for example, both the principle of interdependence and the inevitability of alternation become obvious. Ideally, junior and senior warriors within the structure represented opposing divisions as well as different age-sets. In theory, therefore, they had to contend with one another for power. In earliest warriorhood, this conflict was reflected in the tradition which permitted novices to improve their physical position within the *gaaru* only by competing for the sleeping space of their superiors. It must also be recalled, however, that their infringement was invariably preceded by a reduction in the number of seniors able to fill the space; thus their victory was inevitable.

The same pattern appears at the end of warriorhood. The physical conflict between men of opposing divisions which marked the actual moment of power-transfer during the rite of *ntuiko* was also inevitably preceded by a long series of less dramatic rituals (warrior courtship, marriage, etc.), intended to reduce the numbers of one set of combatants to the point where the result of the conflict (and thus, the alternation of power) would never be in doubt.

It can be argued, therefore, that the entire Meru pattern of transferring authority was itself a ritual, within which mandatory elements of both conflict and conciliation were manifested by performers interested only in perpetuating the alternation demanded by tradition. To accept this, however, is to overlook a deeper meaning. A process wherein the efforts of one group to obtain a new position are always matched by those of an opposing group to withdraw from that position implies a high degree of interdependence between the elements involved. In its deepest sense, therefore, this pattern reflects the interdependent nature of the formal divisions of the society, and thereby the unity of its entire social system.

In comparison with the many stabilizing factors within the Meru system, the position of its potential opponents seems weak. I have earlier suggested that the greatest potential for such opposition should have come from the militarized males, whose impending or actual demobilization might have driven them into evasion or resistance. Yet, despite their unity and military competence, opposition by this segment of society appears to have been impossible.

There are several reasons for this. Initially, potential opponents would have to overcome the effects of almost three decades of socialization. To achieve this, they would have to reject the very warrior ideals they had striven to attain, and with these, their entire conception of warriorhood.

Opponents would also have to abandon belief in the supernatural protection offered by the aged, and the traditions they claimed to represent. But having been trained since childhood to accept the inevitability of ancestral retaliation for transgressing such traditions, they could scarcely conceive the idea of abandoning them, especially since to do so would mean revolt against the supernatural itself.[44]

Conversely, potential rebels would also have to set themselves against the controls inherent in the system of cursing. Ostensibly, the primary intent of a formal curse, whether verbally or automatically imposed, was to cause harm to another person. In fact, the intention was to restore an existing condition of harmony by forcing economic restitution.

This becomes evident when one re-examines the actions required by the society of a victim. A person was usually cursed for violating either an ancestral or temporal social norm and thereby injuring another, who responded with a formal curse ('Let him who has . . .'). The very act of cursing would therefore place the person within a condition of *mugiro* (ritual impurity), which was believed to precede calamity.

It must be emphasized, however, that the person thus afflicted was not allowed by society to remain in this state. Psychological compulsions aside, the very creation of ritual impurity prohibited the afflicted person from having both social and sexual intercourse with other members of his community. In consequence, a combination of social pressure and sexual desire assured that no one could permanently ignore the system. Participation, in the sense of formal curse-removal, was universally required.

The processes of curse-removal, however, were economic, with each stage resulting in a specific loss of livestock. In essence, each victim was required to pay punitive damages to the various specialists and *kiama* members who assisted him, as well as eventual compensation to the person he had originally aggrieved. As a result, the disharmony engendered by his original violation of a social norm was restored by a system of fear-induced economic restitution.

Ostensibly, this system applied equally to those in all age-sets. Actually, it discriminated so heavily against younger males, particularly warriors and novice-elders, as to form a crucial element in their continued subordination to the aged. It will be recalled, for example, that neither novice nor veteran warriors were permitted to keep any livestock they acquired. Instead, tradition required that it be given to their fathers, if yet living, and otherwise to other male kinsmen of the same age-set.

For years, therefore, warriors were totally deprived of the potential to ward off such conditions of *mugiro* as they incurred. Yet the very nature of their warrior role called for continuous generation of conflict and the inevitable creation of hostilities and ill will. The result was a relationship of perpetual dependence on their fathers (or kinsmen) who alone could provide them with the means to relieve ritual impurities, a dependence that extended indirectly to every member of their fathers' (ruling) age-set.

Nor did advancement to the position of novice elder alleviate this dependence. Although *aruau* could create an economic base sufficient to permit the production and rearing of children, it was based primarily on the agricultural labors of their wives. While they could acquire livestock (primarily goats) in small numbers, they were denied large-scale acquisition, particularly of cattle, since men acquired their herds primarily through the efforts of warrior sons. Only by rearing children to physical and military maturity could novice elders hope to acquire sufficient livestock to symbolize both social status and emotional security, and that achievement generally coincided with their advancement to ruling eldership. Until that time, however, they remained as poor as warriors and equally dependent upon elder kinsmen to relieve them of such ritual impurities as they incurred.[45]

Finally, opposition to the system would have implied rebellion against the entire network of social relationships on which the Meru community was based. It must be recalled that these relations were envisioned in terms of the mutual obligations and good will that could be created between persons of opposing social units (age-sets, divisions, etc.). The individual relationships thus created were intended to establish a pattern of interdependence indicative of the larger harmony within society as a whole.

When a man married, he was approximately eleven years younger than his father-in-law, who in turn was some eleven years younger than the man's father (twenty-seven, thirty-eight and forty-nine). The males would therefore each be associated with a different age-set and therefore with alternate divisions. Accordingly, the gifts and services preceding such a marriage were a deliberate attempt to link not merely families but larger social units into a web of interdependence, which would leave each side perpetually needful of the other's goodwill. Opposition to the Meru system by males belonging to any one of its formalized components would have placed rebels in the position of opposing groups containing kin, either by blood or marriage. To persist in such action, therefore, would have meant sacrifice of the relationships built up over their lifetimes, and therefore the theoretical destruction of the ties which bound society itself. It would seem, therefore, that any type of opposition by the military element was precluded by these psychological obstructions.

In addition, there were also positive reasons for warriors to accept the Meru system. One was that submission to its restrictions formed the most certain path to power. Within the various *biama*, willingness to accept the authority of chronological seniors virtually guaranteed acquisition of identical prerogatives over juniors. Another was the inevitability of political alternation, which gave every member of the system the assurance that his group would eventually achieve all forms of social status and control.

The chronological basis for this alternation also served to override potential efforts to stop the pattern in order to retain such status as had been achieved. Conceivably, a group of warriors or ruling elders might have wished to retain their prerogatives for a period beyond that which tradition normally allowed. Yet, inevitably, the simple passage of time would have overridden such desires, making them appear steadily less appropriate to men of their age, until they abandoned them entirely in favor of new prerogatives and a status more commensurate with their years.

It seems clear, therefore, that despite both military competence and reasons for resistance, neither warriors nor novice elders could have acted to destroy the traditional balance between civilian and military age-sets. This does not suggest, however, that this relationship was impervious to change. On the contrary, oral evidence suggests another factor within Meru society which, by the 1890s, had begun to undermine relations between both groups and with them the traditional patterns of control.

To understand the disruptive potential of this factor, one must re-examine the evolution of the supernatural curse within Meru society. It will be recalled that cursing was not a stable institution, but had evolved through a number of identifiable stages. Initially, its use was restricted to males who had reached the rank of elder, usually after consultation within their own *kiama*. Such curses were verbally and publicly proclaimed. Their intent was not to harm, but to force an alleged wrong-doer to make restitution for an unjust act by ritually isolating him from society. Within this context, the curse of any elder was widely respected, having been considered an effective form of social control.

Tradition suggests that this form of verbal curse was subsequently practiced in an identical manner by ironsmiths (*aturi*) and hunters (*aathi*), two groups forced by the circumstances of migration to cut themselves partially away from the mainstream of Meru social life. Having developed essentially parallel systems of *biama* and ritual specialists, these fringe groups also utilized a similar pattern of public cursing, intended to punish persons who encroached on their sources of supply.

A serious difficulty in oral cursing, however, was the necessity to learn of each violation before actively seeking the culprit. This may have been possible for the smiths, who needed only to note the depletion of their ore supplies, but it was obviously more problematical for hunters. It was this group, therefore, which upon reaching Mt. Kenya began to supplement the original oral system with one based on physical markers. In this instance, it will be recalled that the various sticks (*ndindi*, etc.) used by *aathi* to mark off their hives and hunting grounds, automatically imposed a condition of ritual impurity upon all who passed them. No longer was it necessary for others to ascertain who was ritually impure. One could now objectively recognize his own impurity.

The advantages inherent in this non-verbal system inevitably proved attractive to the agriculturalists. Within every subdivision, groups of them, primarily those closest to the montane forest, combined into new *biama* in order to apply the new principles to the protection of their fields. The marking sticks, in these instances, were supplemented by vines which could be looped around fields. However, the intent was the same: supernatural protection of the food supply of the group by non-verbal (automatic) sanctions.

The final stage in this evolution emerged through the decision of poorer agriculturalist groups (*biama* of the stomach) to extend the principles of non-verbal cursing from mere protection of food supply to permission of its arbitrary acquisition by a variety of means previously prohibited by tradition. Now some of the younger males (primarily novice elders) had an alternative pathway out of the eleven to twelve years of relative social poverty imposed upon them by tradition, particularly those whose fields were periodically unable to support them. This initial use of the curse for anti-social purposes was followed by others, as the groups involved (*mwaa, kagita*) began to use their cursing powers as a form of supernatural shield to permit the emergence of deviant social and sexual activities.

Thereafter, the societies established for these purposes formed points of refuge within every subdivision for those fringe persons unable to adjust to their required social roles. It will be recalled, for example, that the *kiama* of *kagita* seems to have offered just such a refuge to those demilitarized males (*aruau*) unable to adjust to the restrictions of married life. Its periodic feasting, beer-drinking, dancing and illicit sexual activities provided an alternative in no way different from that turned to on a larger scale by demoralized young males of the colonial period after their demilitarization by the British.

It must also be realized that these deviant groups contained considerable disruptive potential. Unlike either warriors or novice elders, their members had at some point rejected the traditional age-set system of socialization. In so doing, they had grown to maturity without mastering the military ideals on which relationships within the mainstream *miiriga* were based. Nor did they require the supernatural protection afforded by the elders of these *miiriga*, having developed parallel systems of their own.

Certain of these groups could also afford to ignore the network of social relationships which bound other elements of society.[46] All of them were outside the traditional paths of advancement to positions of rank and status. Most important, members of deviant societies could use the tradition of cursing for personal or group gain, secure in the knowledge that the agriculturalist *biama* would tolerate their continued existence, even to the point of refusing their own warriors permission to disperse them.

It must be remembered that the number of persons joining such fringe *biama* in this era was numerically insignificant and the scope of their activities was too modest to threaten actively the far larger mainstream society. Nevertheless, the threat posed by these fringe groups lay in neither their numbers nor their actions, but in the precedent they set for others. The indifference of the original elders' councils to the activities on their fringe, however justified, had permitted the power of cursing to pass from those utilizing it to maintain tradition to others who used it to evade its restrictions. In so doing they allowed the emergence of an alternate form of ritual protection, a means of evading ancestral vengeance which permitted its practitioners to pass outside mainstream control.[47]

By allowing this, the ruling elders tacitly established a limit to their authority. By allowing one segment of the community to disobey, the rulers inevitably set a precedent for others. It was inevitable, therefore, that other elements of the community, particularly among the warrior ranks, would take note and defy the elders' councils in their turn.[48]

One should not exaggerate, however, the impact of these fringe societies on the Meru military system as a whole. Initially, they may even have served to protect its existence, serving on one hand as a means of defining acceptable patterns of male behavior and on the other as a permitted alternative for those unable to adjust to militarization. Even during the decade examined in this study, they sowed no more than the seeds of future discontent. Nevertheless, the very fact of their existence and the evolution of their powers serve to dispel the illusion that warrior-elder relationships were static. Rather, the strands of tradition that had served to create the balance in Meru society throughout the 1890s were beginning to unravel and decay, while forces had begun to emerge that might have led to the restructuring of both witchcraft and warfare, had the Meru not submitted to colonialism.

Meru Methodology:
Collecting Oral History

This research was conducted in 1969. It consisted of over three hundred oral interviews with the most aged and knowledgeable elders in Meru. Within their ranks, oral history may be transmitted in several ways. Formal traditions, where they exist, are passed to successive generations of the aged by means of sacred oaths, taken within the elders' councils. Those receiving the traditions swear never to reveal details to those outside their council. Violating this oath is believed to be followed by death.

The more informal types of oral data, including both historical narration and overt fiction, are passed down through Meru families by grandparents of either sex. These instruct the young in what is regarded as the wisdom of their elderhood, as learned from their own grandparents long ago.

The Meru have no group traditions, in the sense that many elders must agree on what may be transmitted to the young. Instead, when several gather on occasions calling for historical recollection (such as the appearance of an American investigator), they invariably select a single person to act as spokesman for them all. Selection is by consensus, and is based solely on the belief that the man chosen knows most about the incident to be discussed. Thereafter, they will add brief comments to the spokesman's interpretation, but will rarely, if ever, disagree.

Some narratives are told from the perspectives of the person concerned. Most, however, are narrated from the standpoint of the spokesman's *mwiriga*. Meru history, therefore, emerges as a composite of more localized narratives, each adding its fragment to the whole.

Within each *mwiriga*, one elder inevitably emerges as senior spokesman for the past. This may be due to narrative ability, retentive memory, high status, deep interest or simply advanced age. Similarly, certain persons within every *mwiriga* reach a point where their reputation for historic knowledge spreads beyond local boundaries into neighboring areas. In such cases, they are considered spokesmen of spokesmen; to be sought out by anyone—even other elders—who seek knowledge of the past.)

Seekers of history may also choose to inquire ('buy wisdom') of spokesmen who have specialized in some areas of tradition. Supernaturalists predominate within this category, among them men with knowledge of ritual cursing, ritual healing, divination, foretelling and others.

Specialized types of supernatural knowledge have also been retained by three occupational groups: ironsmiths, bee-keepers and descendants of the former forest-hunters. Members of the former feasting and dancing societies (*aathi, kagita*, etc.) can also describe portions of their traditional rites. In addition, there are fewer esoteric specialties such as midwifery and circumcising, each with its cluster of traditions and symbols known only to the practitioners. All these, if properly approached, can be sources for the military past.

Stages in Collection

Initially, the region to be studied was divided into a number of self-designated "interview-areas," at first simply following the administrative sub-divisions (Mwimbe, Muthambe, etc.), then into smaller units as the situation required. Imenti, for example, was divided into three—a southern, a northern and a northeastern section, each of which seemed to have passed through different historic experiences. Each of these was further divided into upper (forest) and lower (plains) units, on the assumption that forest and plains communities might significantly differ in their historical perceptions.

Within each interview area, discussions with respected elders soon produced consensus as to who were believed to be most knowledgeable about each aspect of the past. These, after sharing their knowledge, frequently suggested other, often older, persons from whom they had sought knowledge in the past.

Few interviews were private. Most became public as soon as they began, taking place before an informant's hut and being attended by all who wished to listen. Boys of all ages were actively encouraged to come, having been taught that listening to "elders' wisdom" was a praiseworthy activity. Elders were motivated to share their knowledge by learning of my interest in their age-sets. I introduced myself as a teacher of the history of Africa who had come to Meru to learn of its warrior past. My work was to record in books what they told me so that it "could be read by the children of the Meru yet to come."

That phrase sounds stilted in English. Yet, it proposed a solution to the problem with which Meru elders were most concerned, the unwillingness of younger generations to seek them out as tradition required, and be taught their accumulated wisdom. Instead, most elders believed that the young had been "tricked" into seeking the wisdom of England, to the point of ignoring their own heritage.

My subsequent research substantiates this belief. Meru traditions are recalled only by those in their seventies. Only those in their late eighties add significant detail. Younger generations can no longer narrate the traditions. The very young no longer know that most of them exist. Nor do they wish to take time from their "schooling" to learn.

In consequence, most elders were happy to share what they knew. No formal payment was ever demanded. Rather, small gifts of the type traditionally carried by young men on visits to the aged (snuff, beer, meat) were presented to informants and their age-mates before each interview. These were not intended as an exchange of goods for service, but as expressions of respect for their years and willingness to speak. In response, elders asked women of their homestead to serve us tea. These gestures, however small, created "*uthoni*" (a relationship) between us that formed the social basis of our conversations.

Interviews were based on responses to my questions. A long list of "potential" questions was always at hand, covering every aspect of the proposed topic. No effort was made to follow a script. Rather, each question was open ended, intended to serve as a potential catalyst for either extended narration (as with a tale) or intensive discussion that might open further lines of inquiry. No effort was made to complete question lists within given times. Rather, interviews lasted from one to seven hours and were repeated as often as required.

Questions were asked in either English or Swahili, then translated into the appropriate Meru dialect. Translations were made by one of my research assistants, ideally a man whose family was ritually allied (*gichiaro*) to that of the informant; thus we were assured a welcome. Assistants were not selected for their education, but for their interest in the Meru past. This, in turn, was the result of childhood tutelage by grandparents who themselves retained deep interest in tradition. It was this unflagging interest rather than a formal education which turned these persons into effective seekers of history. Occasionally, variations in Meru dialect would necessitate the employment of a secondary assistant, local to the area, who would be hired for the day.

All conversation was recorded simultaneously by two portable tape recorders. Two more were kept constantly on hand, since the dust endemic to most of Meru assured frequent mechanical breakdowns. Tape recorders were explained to informants as "boxes-that-write," with a pencil set alongside them for illustration. Their use was pointed out as necessary to assure that I (as a younger man) would make no mistake in writing out their words. No replay of the voices recorded was ever permitted, lest elders feel their voices had been captured by the machines.

Ideally, transliteration of the material began within one hour after completion of each interview. It was done by whichever assistant had been present as translator. A second assistant accompanied me to seek other informants. Once on paper, the data were examined for additional lines of inquiry and subsequent interviews were arranged.

Emphasis then shifted to corroborating the initial testimony. All data were labeled "speculative" until corroborated at least once by reliable sources not personally acquainted, thus unable to have learned specific variants from one another. Interviewing then continued within a designated interview-area until it became evident that leading spokesmen had been contacted and no further variants of a specific tradition were likely to emerge.

The work then moved to a second interview area, ideally at considerable distance from the first. Thus, an unusually relevant series of interviews in Upper Northeastern Imenti might be followed by a second series in lower Muthambe. Conflicting testimony would dictate the need for a third series in a third area, and as many more as were required.

After several months of interviewing, it became clear that a number of unusually aged and knowledgeable elders were considered by their age-mates to be "spokesmen of spokesmen" on almost every aspect of history within their respective regions. These specialists lived apart from one another and were therefore personally unacquainted except by reputation. Nonetheless, their testimony was frequently comparable at many points, therefore permitting effective cross-checks on data collected from earlier informants.

The next stage took the form of obtaining corroborative data from outside Meru district. This was done by organizing the initial material into a preliminary paper, entitled "Oral Traditions of the Meru, Mwimbe and Muthambe of Mt. Kenya," which was then made available to scholars working in both those areas adjoining Meru (Embu, Mberre, Kikuyu, Tharaka) and more distant regions (Maasai, Ogiek, Pokomo, Lamu, Miji Kenda) which impinged on some aspect of the more distant Meru past.

Aspects of this data were also made available to interested scholars in other disciplines in the hope of obtaining supportive evidence from their own research. Finally, considerable effort was made to locate persons with detailed ecological knowledge of certain regions remote from Mt. Kenya, though which the ancestral Meru are said to have passed on their migration to Mt. Kenya.

To be meaningful, however, the data collected from oral informants had also to be placed within a system of chronology, to provide a framework within which to relate events to one another. Meru chronology is based on an age-set system, into which all members of society are divided.

Like other peoples, including our own, the Meru categorize people by age. Each category was regarded as having one primary function within the community. Before colonialism, the categories applied to males were as follows:

Table 1

Age	Life Stage	Termination
0-7	Infant/Child	ends with appearance of second teeth
7-15+	Uncircumcised boy	ends with puberty
15-18+	Elder boy (candidate for circumcision)	ends with circumcision
18-29+	Warrior	ends with marriage
29-40+	Family head/novice elder	ends with entry of first son into warriorhood; transfer of military authority to his son's age-set (*ntuicko*)
40-51+	Ruling elder	next *ntuicko*
51-62+	Ritual elder	next *ntuicko*
62-?	The aged	death

In childhood, membership in an age-set was informal, with the time of entry dictated primarily by decisions of the children concerned. Passage into adulthood, however, was formalized by the rituals of circumcision and formation of those completing the operation into a warrior age-set. All initiates passed into the new unit until its ranks were declared full, a process that might stretch over several years. It was given a formal name, then separated from the others by proclamation of a "closed period," during which no further men could be circumcised. Those seeking the operation after termination of the closed period would form the first members of a subsequent set.

Thus, if the formal names of Imenti age-set were applied to Meru males during the last decade before colonial conquest (1896-1906), the following age-set order would appear:

Table 2

Age	Life Stage	Age-Set
0-7+	Infant/Child	Miriti
7-18+	Youth/circumcision candidate	Murungi
18-29+	Warrior	Kiramana
29-40+	Family head/novice elder	Kaburia
40-51+	Ruling elder	Kubai
51-62+	Ritual elder	Nturutimi
62+	Retired elder/the aged	Thamburu

149

Appendix

It is the Meru age-set system that can provide chronological guidelines to the past of the region. Although pre-conquest Meru communities planned economic activities according to seasonal cycles, historic events were recalled by association with whichever age-set were warriors at the time. European chronology, for example, defines the conquest of Meru by England as having occurred in 1906 and 1907. The Meru perceive it as having taken place "soon after *Murungi* (age-set) replaced *Kiramana* (age-set) as warriors."

This association of events and warrior age-sets has significant advantages. It has proved possible, first of all, to acquire lists of all existing Meru age-sets from large numbers of elders, as well as to secure agreement as to the order in which all but the earliest set was formed. It was also possible to obtain a general idea of the time spent by each set in warriorhood by learning the number of agricultural cycles that passed between successive transfers of power.

With this information, it is possible to work backwards from known dates of transfer, such as those occurring after the imposition of colonial rule, and set down theoretical intervals for each set. In Imenti, for instance, the times between age-set transfers average twelve years. In Mwimbe, the average is eleven. These intervals, of course, are only estimates. The actual times of transfer depended on the birth and maturation rate of Meru males, factors beyond the reach of Western measurements. Delays could also occur through famine, drought, dislocation through warfare or simple fluctuation in the Meru birthrate.

Even estimates, however, can cast illumination on the past. By working backwards, investigators can "match" estimated age-set intervals with historic incidents alleged to have occurred when each group served as warriors. When applied in Meru, for example, this approach reveals the following:

Table 3

Set	Date of Transfer	Remembered Events
Miriti	1916 (recorded)	Served, while warriors, in British East African Campaign, World War I
Murungi	1904 (estimated)	New warriors at time of subordination to Great Britain (1906)
Kiramana	1892 (estimated)	(1) Fought several skirmishes with white men— all recorded by European sources, 1890s; (2) Famine, from Igembe to Kikuyu-recorded in Kikuyu, 1899.
Kaburia	1880	First to see, fight white men (first recorded entry into Meru: late 1880s, written sources).
Kubai	1868	Trade with *chomba* (men-of-the-coast: Arabs, Swahili, Somali. Embu traditions record Arabs first entering that area, 1860s, and extending trade northward, early 1870s)

150

Table 3 (continued)

Set	Date of Transfer	Remembered Events
		trade northward, early 1870s)
Nturutimi	1856	(1) Wars against Maasai; (2) Prophecy; "last born children of Nturutimi (i.e., Miriti) will walk unarmed" (i.e., due to peace established in their area by Europeans).
Thamburu	1844	One man still living 1924. (If 90, would have been born 1834, entered warriorhood early 1850s).

The possibility of corroborating these recollections with data drawn from outside Meru is obviously enhanced. Often, the traditions themselves provide little more than scattered verbal clues to past events. Yet without them, investigators would have no idea of where or for what to search.

It is the continued, though precarious, existence of these "living" historical clues that has dictated this inquiry into the Meru past. As in other parts of Africa, the oral history of Meru is dying. Knowledgeable elders from every region have been baffled and enraged by their inability to transmit historical knowledge (elders' wisdom) to members of the younger generations. Traditionally, it was incumbent on the young to solicit knowledge from the old. Acquisition of their wisdom was considered prerequisite to their own entry into elderhood. At the proper times, young men from everywhere in Meru would seek out respected elders, to "buy" their wisdom with the traditional gifts of snuff and meat and beer. In exchange, the old would pass on what they knew, thus allowing the young to become elders in their turn.

Today, however, the oldest men in Meru sit alone, waiting in vain for the young to seek out their wisdom. Once, during my final weeks in Meru, I spent seven hours listening to a single revered elder recount the battle-history of his region. The narration dealt with an unending series of raids and counterraids between Meru and Maasai, that stretched back half a century. The words spilled out across an afternoon, past sunset and into the night. Pots of glowing coals were silently placed around the elder, to keep him warm and thus prevent the interruption of his narration.

Listeners drifted into our circle from every direction. First, the children. Then adults who had finished their work. Finally, the very old appeared, moving slowly and often painfully to hear once more what they recalled so well. Only one age-group was missing, the young men, who once would have been warriors. Now they were off at their schools.

The narrative continued until the moon was high. Finally, the flow of words ended and the elder slumped down in complete exhaustion. Awed, I asked him how often he had completed this narration in its entirety. "Twice," he replied, "and the other one who asked was white like you. Our young men now feel that wisdom lies only within books."

But not even books contain that wisdom. Few studies of pre-colonial warfare have been published, and none for the peoples of Mt. Kenya. After conquest by England, Meru warriorhood was dismantled. Warriors everywhere were disarmed. War-barracks, deserted, fell prey to termites. Warrior dances were turned into caricatures by British administrators. Stripped of their symbolism, they died for lack of those willing to perform them. In short, both the structure of warriorhood and the military ideals that sustained it were obliterated. They now exist only within the minds of those few aged men who actually experienced them—a priceless part of Kenya's ancient heritage, which, if not recorded, may flicker out within the next decade.

This book is intended to record their collective voice. It is meant both as a reconstruction of Meru warriorhood during its final decade and as a tribute to those former warriors—the men of Kiramana, Murungi and Miriti—who wished such traditions to pass on to their descendants yet unborn.

" . . . so they will know the men from whom they are descended, and remember they are Meru."

Imenti Age Sets

The following lists of age-set names have been collected in Imenti between 1924 and 1969. Each list is presented with the name of its collector and the date of collection.

Rev. A.J. Hopkins Methodist Mission 1924	H.L. Laughton Methodist Mission 1931	H.E. Lambert D.C. Meru 1944	J.A. Fadiman Researcher 1969-70
		Kibiringua	Mwangaku
		Mujogo	
		Tangiri (?)	Changiri (Thangiri)
		Mbaini (?)	Mbaini
	Ntangi	Ntangi	Ntangi
	Nkuthuku	Nkuthuku	Nkuthuku
			(1)Mukuruma jwa Koju
Mukuruma	Mukuruma	Mukuruma	(2)Mukuruma jwa Okiugu
Kitharie	Githarie	Githarie	Githarie
Michubu	Michubu	Michubu	Michubu
		(Michugu)	
Latanya	Latanya	Ratanya	Ratanya
Thangiria	Githangiria	Githangiria	Githangiria
Mbaringo	Mbaringo	Mbaringo	Mbaringo
Nkuthugua	Nguthugua	Nguthogua	Nguthugua
Kiruja I	Kiruja	Kiruja	Kiruja Gikuru
			(Old Kiruja)
Thamburu	Thamuru	Thamuru	Thamburu
Nangitia (sub-set of Nturutimi)	Nturutimi	Nturutimi	Nturutimi
Kubai	Kubai	Kubai	Kubai
Mungatia (sub-set of Kaburia)	Kaburia	Kaburia	Kaburia
Memeu (sub-set of Kiramana)	Kiramana	Kiramana	Kiramana
Murungi	Murungi	Murungi	Murungi
Ntarangwi (sub-set of Miriti)	Miriti	Miriti	Miriti
	Kiruja	Kiruja	Kiruja
	Gwantai	Gwantai	Gwantai
			Nangithia

Notes

CHAPTER I

1. Within this study, a "clan" will be defined as the largest social unity within which all members believe themselves descended from a common patrilineal ancestor. A *mwiriga* will be defined as a unit of land-management, government and communal defense, composed of one or more clans.

2. Private papers, S. M'Anampiu, Master of History, Meru Teacher Training College, Meru, Kenya.

3. *Ibid.*

4. This could also occur during the stage of apprenticeship, where a charismatic person became spokesman for the novices.

5. Broadcast talk, "Meru Institutions and Their Place in Modern Government," British Radio (BBC) Broadcast, 1942, H. E. Lambert. Script outline in NTTC/II/II, National Archives. See also Lambert, private papers no. 1, p. 451.

6. The term *njuri* is used here in its general sense. In fact, each 'council of the few' bore a special name. The term *njuri* was used primarily for those councils which represented entire subdivisions, such as the *njuri ya btama* which was composed of spokesmen from all sections of Imenti.

7. The names of the various councils differ slightly from section to section. The pattern of progress through the entire system was the same for all areas.

8. H. E. Lambert, *Kikuyu Social and Political Institutions*, (Oxford University Press, 1956), p. 100.

9. W. H. Laughton, "An Introductory Study of the Meru People," unpublished Master's thesis, Cambridge, U.K., 1938, 1978.

10. Oral Interview 73, North Imenti; 9, South Imenti. See also H. Laughton, "Introductory Study," pp. 76-80.

11. *Ibid.* See also Lambert, *Systems of Land Tenure*, pp. 162-63.

12. Laughton's informants have also suggested that *nkoma* were believed to live underground. "Introductory Study," pp. 76, 90. My own research has failed to substantiate this.

13. Oral Interviews 8 and 10; alleged personal experiences.

14. H. E. Lambert, *Systems of Land Tenure in the Kikuyu Land Unit: Part I: History of the Tribal Occupation of the Land* (Cape Town, 1950). Communication of the School of African Studies, Cape Town University, p. 162.

15. Twathama tweta Rinyuri
    Twatainera Kaurini Urukuni
    Abea, Ukengainga Uthi (Authi)

    English: We are moving to Rinyuri (a location unknown to informant)
              We were cutting (circumcising) in Kauruni (a forest) Ukukuni (a location)
              Priests, don't hurry (hasten) the *authi* (warriors dance)

155

Heard in South Imenti soon after the first European priests appeared in the area. These were particularly shocked by the Meru *authi*, since the warriors dance naked except for their weapons. Heard (as a child) by Oral Interviewee 8.

16. Oral Interviewee 8, South Imenti, and 82, Northeast Imenti. Corroboration: Lambert, private papers no. 9, p. 18.

17. *Ibid.*

18. Oral Interviewee 10, curse-detector, alleged personal experience. Corroboration: Oral Interviewee 9, his older kinsman, at separate interview. Oral Interviewee 13, curse-detector, personal experience. Only male children were visited in this fashion.

19. The fifth: ancestral blood, which could react to certain departures from tradition by wreaking a vengeance of its own.

20. G. St. J. Orde-Browne, *The Vanishing Tribes of Kenya* (London, 1925), p. 183, lists the causes of *mugiro* in Mwimbe. Informants in other areas generally concur.

21. The work of *mugwe* was beyond the scope of individual *miiriga*; thus it is outside the realm of this discussion. For the most detailed study of his function, see B. Bernardi, *The Mugwe: A Failing Prophet*, (Oxford, 1956).

22. Oral Interviewee 9, Foreteller, South Imenti.

23. Oral Interviewees 8, 9, 13, South Imenti; 14, North Imenti.

24. The correct translation is 'poisoner,' since the term for poison and that for bewitching are identical (*urogi*). In English, however, the term carries no supernatural connotations and is therefore misleading. On the other hand, the traditional English terms for this type of supernatural practitioner (witch, witch-man, sorcerer, warlock, etc.) carry with them medieval European connotations which have no bearing on the African experience and thus tend to mislead as well. The most accurate term, in view of the central position of *arogi* within the entire system of specialists, would be 'curse-placer.' Since this is awkward in English, the term 'ritual poisoner' has been chosen to emphasize the fact that his victim sickens as the result of ritual.

25. These may have originated from methods used by hunters as protection from such attack. See subsequent discussion on the origins of war-magic, Chapter V.

26. It proved impossible to identify specific plants, etc. Informants universally protested that knowledge of such details would be tantamount to their own confession of the work.

27. Oral Interviewees 9, Foreteller, South Imenti; 13 and 14, curse-removers, South Imenti; 39, honey-hunter and alleged member of *kagita*, South Imenti; 22, alleged member of *kagita, mwaa*, Muthambe; 59, alleged member of *kagita*, Igoji; and 11, curse-detector (bow-breaker), South Imenti.

28. Note again that in Kimeru the two concepts are identical.

29. Oral Interviewees 13 and 14, South Imenti; 24, Upper Mwimbe, referring to attempt at ritual poisoning made against their father. See footnote 30.

30. Ritual poisoning was duly attempted and failed. The appointee went on to become one of the most powerful chiefs of the Mwimbe sub-division. See note on *interview, interviewee*. Oral Interviewee 24 and two brothers, referring to an attempted ritual poisoning of their father, Mbogori wa Mwendo. Corroboration: Oral Interviewee 25, former employee of Mbogori.

31. It proved impossible to get informants to describe the process by which such reflections appeared. One, irritated by my persistent questioning, replied, "If I dream a wonder and I tell you my dream, you will understand my wonder. But will I have taught you to dream it?" Oral Interview 10, curse-detector, South Imenti.

32. *Ibid.* Corroboration: Oral Interview 13, South Imenti.

33. Oral Interviewee 9, an older relative of #10, describing the reaction of the latter's family and clan to his circumcision by *nkoma*. The parallel drawn was the feeling which occurs when one's dog kills a neighbor's sheep. The dog's owner is only indirectly responsible, yet receives full blame and must pay full damages.

34.　The *aringia* interviewed for this study were of small stature, with slight build, shy personality; in short, poor warrior material. It seems possible, at least, to ask whether such factors may have influenced their decision to become ritual specialists. Available data, however, are inadequate for such conclusions, and additional research will be required.

35.　Oral Interviewee 10, curse-detector (*muringia*); 13, curse-detector (*muringia*); 11, theft-detector (*muni-wa-uta*), all of South Imenti. Corroboration: Oral Interview 36, Northeast Imenti.

36.　Typical questions: "Is there any man whose crop you may have damaged in passing?" "Is there any man whose woman you may have angered in passing?" "Is there any man whose ancestor you may have angered in passing?" etc. Oral Interviewees 10, 11, 13 and 9.

37.　Detection by gourd is only one form of *uringia*. Others include detection by bow and arrow (for theft), and detection by leather, using two strips of leather called 'sandals.' The principles underlying each of these methods are the same. A period of public interrogation permits the detector to suggest a number of possible suspects, drawn partially from spectator reactions to the questioning. The ritual objects are then cast as many times as are required. The order in which they hit the ground and the position in which they fall permit the detector to narrow his choice to one, two or three possible suspects, depending on his skill.

38.　The complete contents of a curse-remover's magic bag (*kiondo*), were collected in southern Meru, 1914, by G. St. J. Orde-Browne, then an Assistant District Commissioner within the area. The bag and its original contents are currently the property of the Ethographic Division, British Museum, London, United Kingdom.

39.　*Aragoli* were often suspected of acting in collusion with *arogi*, the latter deliberately poisoning people in order to gain fees for his confederate. It seems more logical to suggest that each required belief in the existence of the other if both were to survive.

40.　"Let this curse be cut as I cut these strings." In variations of this ritual, the curse would be symbolically brushed from the victim's body by special leaves or squeezed out of his body by squeezing the contents of the intestines. The accompanying ritual was appropriate to the act. Theoretically, the ritual led to a decrease in the victim's mental and emotional anxiety, followed by the eventual disappearance of his physical symptoms. Oral Interviews 14, *muga* and a son of *muraguri*, South Imenti; 15, *muga*, North Imenti; 22, victim, Muthambe.

41.　Mahner, "Insider and Outsider," p. 7.

42.　Kenyatta translates the title of a similar ritual specialist, known among Kikuyu as *moigwithania*, with the term 'unified,' indicative of his primary function of conciliation. J. Kenyatta, *Facing Mt. Kenya* (London, 1961), p. 323.

43.　The basic unit was the goat. Specified numbers of goats would equal a larger animal, such as a cow. Specified units of smaller animals, such as chickens, would equal a goat. Grains, vegetables, chain-iron, millet-beer and honey-wine were also used in transactions, and also accountable at the rate of so many units per goat.

44.　J. Mahner, "The Insider and Outsider in Tigania, Meru," IDS/CD, University of Nairobi, 1970, pp. 1-2.

45.　The Meru concepts of ritual-poisoning, detection, removal, truth-by-oath, etc., have obvious parallels in the secular efforts of our own society to create systems of both conciliation and redress (equity, justice). In the supernatural realm, it can be argued that we, too, expect our own ritual specialists to intercede, both with our Creator and a host of lesser phenomena, either to permit us to avoid catastrophe ("give us this day. . . .") or to smite those who oppose our interests. There are also few of us who do not curse our enemies. Our traditional choice of words ("God damn . . . to Hell") implies, at the very least, the hope of supernatural intervention on our behalf, and the subsequent placement of our opponent in a condition of calamity.

46.　Meru traditions recall their initial point of origin only as Mbwa. For full discussion as to its identification refer to my article "The Early History of the Meru of Mt. Kenya," *Journal of African History*, XIV, I(1973), pp. 9-27. Discussion of the period of Meru migration will be found in my "Origins of the Meru of Mt. Kenya," a chapter in a forthcoming book. *Pre-Colonial Kenya*, ed. B. A. Ogot (University of Nairobi). The term 'ancestors' implies only those that the Meru claim for themselves, and includes groups incorporated into their society at various times within their history.

47. Oral Interviewees 39, 40, honey-hunters, South Imenti; 34, 35, formerly connected with meat-hunters, North Imenti. Curses proclaimed by iron-smiths could also be shouted out from a single point by every male member of that community. In such instances, they were punctuated by strokes of their iron hammers against the anvils. Oral Interviewee 7, South Imenti; Corroboration: 32, South Imenti; personal communication, Mrs. J. Brown, Department of Ethnography, Kenya National Museum, from current research.

48. See G. Adamson, *Bwana Game: The Life Story of George Adamson* (London, 1968), pp. 86-87, for Ogiek use of a system similar to that described subsequently for the *ndindi*. In Kenya, Ogiek are more commonly known as Ndorobo. Bands known to have lived within the Meru region of Mt. Kenya during the pre-colonial period include the Mokogodo, Il Mumunyot, Il Tikirri, and Il Nguesi.

49. *Ndindi* (sing: *rurindi*) were pointed at one end and hollowed at the other. Cursing consisted of pouring a ritual preparation consisting of greyish powder into the hollow space, with appropriate incantation. One feather of a maribou stork (an eater of dead meat) was affixed to the end. Meru Annual Report (1927), National Archives, Nairobi. Typed report by F. M. Lamb, D. C. Mew, 1928. Found in private papers of H. E. Lambert, University of Nairobi. Corroboration: Oral Interviews 34, 35, Northeast Imenti; 39, South Imenti.

50. *Ibid.* The *nguchwa* was a small stick selected from the same tree (local name: *mukenia*) as that used for *ndindi*. It was slowly heated on one side to make it curve into the shape of a claw, then filled with a ritually prepared powder. The tail of a mongoose was then tied to the rear; cord taken from a banana plant was used. Similarities to the preparations required for *ndindi* sticks are obvious.

51. *Ibid.*

52. *Ibid.* The taboo against *aathi* consumption of livestock was surmounted in such cases by renaming the domestic animals after game. Thus, bulls contributed to an *aathi* feast become 'buffalo'; goats became 'bushbuck.'

53. *Kiama kia kagita, kiama kia wathua, kiama kia mwaa, kiama kia gatanga.* Fragmentary data have also been collected for *kiama kia makuiko* and *kiama kia muundo* (*mndio*?), suggesting that their organization and activities were similar to others.

54. Contributors to *aathi* feasts were required to donate meat. Those contributing to the feasts of later *biama* were required to contribute quantities of millet beer and vegetables.

55. Described consistently by current informants as "the poor," "the hungry," "the indolent," etc.

56. These examples and those following are taken primarily from practices attributed to the *biama* of *kagita* and *mwaa*. Branches of both organizations existed in every major section of Meru. *Kagita* informants: 16, Northeast Imenti; 33, North Imenti; 39 (ex-member) South Imenti; 55, 56, 57, 58, 59 (alleged ex-members), Igoji; 52, ex-chief, Igoji (persecution of society); 22, Muthambe. *Mwaa* informants: 6, Northeast Imenti; 22 (ex-member), Muthambe; 54 (alleged ex-member), Muthambe; 52, ex-chief, Igoji (persecution of society). Corroboration: 29 (ex-member), Igembe.

57. Reference is to a disease (elephantiasis?) which causes the feet to swell. All foot diseases were attributed to the curse of *kagita*.

58. See footnote 56.

59. I.e., *kagita, mwaa, wathua, gatanga.*

60. Subsequently, membership prerequisites in *kagita* were still further modified to permit the entry of a limited number of warriors.

61. See footnote 56.

62. Administrative reports of the *kagita* society during the 1920s suggest that women were forced to attend their dances by the threat of a *mugiro*, to be placed on their fathers in the event of refusal. Meru Annual Report (1927). Female informants who admit to having partici-

pated in the dances of that era, however, suggest that force was neither used nor needed, a statement corroborated by J. G. H. Hopkins, writer of the 1927 administrative report in a personal interview. Oral Interview 74, District Officer, Meru District, 1918 and 1927-32, Stellenbosch, South Africa, December, 1970 (interviewed by J. Hewson). Meru informants have emphasized, however, that attendance was limited to 'elder' (i.e., married) women, and that young girls (uncircumcised, unmarried) were forbidden to attend. Oral interviews 56, 57, 58, Igoji; 22, 16, Muthambe.

63. *Mwaa*: To be foolish, stupid, ignorant; (*mu-waa* or *mwaa*: jester, man of the fools). Fr. B. Giorgis, *A Tentative Kimeru Dictionary*, First edition, Catholic Bookshop (Consolata Mission Fathers), Meru, Kenya (1964).

64. See footnote 56.

65. Oral Interviewees 39, 40, honey-hunters, South Imenti.

66. Available evidence suggests that it was very unlikely for *aathi* to become agriculturalists or herders. To do so would have meant infringing social and dietary prohibitions (e.g., no hunter could drink milk; no herder could eat game) intended to keep the two groups apart. Nor is there any evidence to suggest that either hunters or iron-smiths intermarried with agriculturalists. Personal communication, Mrs. E. J. Brown, Head, Department of Ethnology, National Museum of Kenya.

67. Exception: Curse-detector, who would identify the origin of any *mugiro*.

68. This would apply even if the violator was a *muga* himself. He, too, could be aided only by a *muga jwa aathi*. Oral interview 39.

69. Oral Interviewee 6, speaking of occurrences throughout Imenti, Tigania and Igembe. Corroboration: Oral Interviewees 52, for Igoji; 24, Mwimbe, experiences of grandfather, father.

70. *Nkima* is the name of a specific shrub, the branches of which are frequently collected for *aathi* ritual purposes. In South Imenti, the *nkima* was described as an animal horn filled with goat fat. Oral Interviews 34, 35, Northeast Imenti, 39, South Imenti. See Chapter IV for the uses of *nkima* among *aathi* councils of boyhood.

71. Perhaps in unconscious reflection of a world-view that arbitrarily divides its society into two segments, assigning secular responsibilities to one and ritual (supernatural) responsibilities to the other. See the discussion on divisions, Chapter I.

72. These practices continued to evolve after the advent of colonial rule, when *aathi, kagita* and perhaps others began to extort not only food, but social, sexual and economic services from agriculturalist communities—the last named in direct response to British tax-demands. By the mid-1920s the societies had attained influence almost equal to that of the agricultural *biama*, and were competing with these and the Colonial Administration for predominant influence within Meru society. After discovering that several of its appointees (chiefs, headmen, etc.) were members of these societies, the British finally succeeded in breaking their influence (1928-29). See Meru Annual Reports (1927-1930). Kenya National Archives, Nairobi.

CHAPTER II

1. Description from personal experience. See I. Henderson and P. Goodheart, *The Hunt for Kimathi* (London, 1958), p. 23, for description of similar conditions in the Aberdares.

2. This and subsequent ecological descriptions have been drawn from "East of Mt. Kenya: Meru Agriculture in Transition," unpublished Ph.D. dissertation, Dr. F. E. Bernard (Wisconsin, 1968). Subjective impressions of these areas and their implications for military strategy are my own.

3. *Ibid.*, p. 46.

4. A. H. Neumann, *Elephant Hunting in East Equatorial Africa* (London, 1928), p. 128. Clearing was rarely total. Clearings were simply hacked out among the trees, then extended as required. Certain of the remaining forest areas were protected as sacred groves, resting places of the ancestral spirits. Others served as continuous sources of firewood and were gradually nibbled away. Therefore, the most common ecological pattern of the cultivated areas below the forest was one of mixed fields (*shambas*) and patches of forest.

5. Bernard, "East of Mt. Kenya," p. 76.

6. *Ibid.*, *Pennisetum clandestimun*, p. 77.

7. *Ibid.*, *Cynodon dactylon*, pp. 52, 55, 79.

8. *Ibid.*, pp. 18-19.

9. *Ibid.*, p. 28.

10. Tsetse fly: *Glossina spp*; a carrier of sleeping sickness among human beings and of *nagana* (a fatal variant) among livestock.

11. For traditions dealing with the selection of specific targets, see the subsequent discussion on *gichiaro*, p. 105.

12. See Chapter V for full discussion of the *aathi* role in war.

13. Oral Interview 6, former war-leader, Northeast Imenti; 20, former war-leader, South Imenti. Incidents referred to involved pursuit of stock stolen by Maasai.

14. *Nagana*, spread by the bite of the tsetse, is transmitted among animals by reason of their proximity to others already infected. Neither cattle nor man can live in heavily fly-infested areas.

15. For analysis of the tactics used by each side in such situations see Chapter VI: Waging War.

16. H. E. Lambert, private papers No. 1 to 10, University of Nairobi, Kenya. See bibliography for full list (and titles) of manuscripts. Lambert suggests "Nya Mbe ni" or place of the people of Mbe. Other sources corroborate this. Lambert, Private Papers No, pp. 315-317.

17. Lambert, Private Papers no. 1, 263.

18. In Kimwimbe and Kimuthambe, '*kijiaro.*'

19. Lambert, private papers no. 9, pp. 262, 264.

20. Since this chapter will deal with *gichiaro* only within the military context, I will refer to it as 'ritual alliance' rather than 'mutual adoption' from this point on.

21. It must be emphasized that ritually unrelated *miiriga*, although 'potentially' hostile to one another, were not perpetually so. In most instances, certain *miiriga* were preferred as sources of war; others, as sources of wives. In other cases, periods of wife-seeking could alternate with periods of war. Oral Interview 19, North Imenti.

22. E. R. Shackleton, typed report, "Native Tribes and Their Customs," *Native Tribes and Their Customs*, II/II (1930), Kenya National Archives, Nairobi, Kenya; for Igembe (1892), W. A. Chanler, *Through Jungle and Desert* (London, 1896). Oral Corroboration 19, North Imenti; 22, for Muthambe with Tharaka.

23. This type of *gichiaro* was used to establish relationships with *miiriga* in Tharaka and Cuka.

24. Oral Interviewees 22, Muthambe; 83, Mwimbe; 19, North Imenti. See also Lambert, private papers no. 1, pp. 262-71.

25. Oral Interviewee 19, North Imenti.

26. Lambert, private papers no. 1, pp. 278-79. Cuka was included to illustrate the lack of this type of *gichiaro* with the subdivisions of Meru. Miutini was not included.

27. Oral Interviewee 21, formerly of Gaichau *gaaru*, Muthambe.

28. Oral Interviewees 75, Miutini; 65, Miutini. Corroboration: 19 and 76, Katheri, North Imenti.

29. Lambert, private papers no. 1, pp. 269-70.

30. Oral Interviewee 9, South Imenti. Thieves, in turn, were prevented from imitating the actions of *ba-gichiaro* (replacing the lids upside down, etc.) by their fear of the automatic (supernaturally imposed) punishments that could be thereby incurred. See p. 112.

31. *Muruti* is the hard fat at the side of the animal's abdomen. Owners were required by custom to preserve this strip for one day after beginning to consume the meat, in case warriors whose group had *gichiaro* with theirs appeared. Lambert, private papers no. 1, p. 270.

32. For example, he could address them as 'child of an uncircumcised girl' (*mwana mukenye*). Under normal circumstances, this would be a deadly insult. From a *gichiaro* brother, it became the equivalent of our 'son of a bitch' when used in a friendly tone.

33. Lambert, private papers no. 1, p. 270.

34. Lambert, private papers no. 1, p. 270. Corroboration: Oral Interviewee 6, Northeast Imenti; 9, South Imenti.

35. *Ibid.* Lambert cites several individual cases of this type, in each of which persons admitted having done the deed which caused their hands to become diseased. The same principle would apply to persons violating the prohibition against sexual contact with a 'ritual sister,' the diseases, in this instance, attacking the sex organs.

36. *Ibid.* Informant was Kiangi of Antubaita, Tigania, to whom the experience occurred. Interviewed in 1944.

37. Oral Interviewee 77, North Imenti; Lambert private papers no. 1, p. 271. (See tradition of M'Mjibwe.)

38. Oral Interviewee 77, North Imenti. Lambert private papers no. 9, p. 69.

39. See Chapter IV, "Learning Warriorhood," for full discussion of this tactic.

40. *Ibid.*

41. See Chapter V for full discussion of the challenge system and the limitations imposed upon it.

42. Inoti suggests that the Meru calendar year was approximately 354 days, exactly 12 lunar months. Laughton, "Introductory Study," p. 86 (quoting from Inoti).

43. Laughton, "Introductory Study," p. 86. Also, Bernard, "East of Mt. Kenya," p. 172.

44. Bernard, "East of Mt. Kenya," pp. 150-53, for more detail.

45. Laughton, "Introductory Study," p. 84.

46. In this context, the word 'men' refers primarily to junior elders, age 30-42, the age given over to cultivation and raising of families. Warriors had no formal connection with agricultural activities during their period in the *gaaru.* 'Older boys' refers to those below the age of circumcision.

47. Bernard, "East of Mt. Kenya," pp. 225-26.

48. *Ibid.*, p. 243.

49. By the 1890s there were two exceptions to this pattern. Certain *miiriga* in Igembe had begun to trade salt and donkeys to groups in northern Imenti, the latter having been acquired through earlier exchanges with pastoralists. In addition, Kamba, Somali and Swahili traders had begun to visit certain localities in Mwimbe, Imenti and Igembe to exchange coastal trade goods (beads, wire, etc.) for tusks. The general trading pattern, however, was purely local; no system of regional markets existed before the arrival of the British.

50. Bernard, "East of Mt. Kenya," p. 73.

51. Lambert suggests that most circumcisions took place in February, after the conclusion of the millet harvests. There were invariably delays, however, and persons could declare their candidacy for several months thereafter. Lambert, private papers no. 1, p. 443.

52. Oral Interviewee 6, Northeast Imenti; 23, Mwimbe.

53. Oral Interviewee 19, North Imenti; 6, Northeast Imenti. See footnote 49 for trading patterns.

54. Lambert, private papers no. 9, p. 108. Shorter version in private papers no. 1, p. 400.

55. Oral Interviewee 6, Northeast Imenti. Actual incidents cited refer to contacts with both agricultural and pastoral Maasai. This type of agreement frequently led to more permanent settlement, inter-marriage and eventual incorporation into the Meru group. The informant's own clan was originally Maasai and was incorporated in this fashion.

56. This does not apply to war between Meru and non-Meru. In Tigania and Imenti, Meru *miiriga* periodically battled Mwoko (Galla) and Maasai for the rights of access to certain salt licks and grazing areas.

57. Oral Interviewee 7, and private papers. Corroboration: Oral Interview 9, South Imenti; 16, Muthambe.

58. Laughton, "Introductory Study," p. 101.

59. These were the basic items. Additional units of each were negotiable. Other items could be added as 'sweetening,' but could not replace the basic five. Oral Interviews 16, 70, Muthambe. Corroboration: Oral Interview 19, North Imenti.

60. Laughton, "Introductory Study," p. 64. Corroboration: Oral Interviewee 25, Mwimbe.

61. Lambert, private papers no. 9, p. 32.

62. Laughton, "Introductory Study," p. 94.

63. *Ibid.*, p. 101. See also Mahner, "Insider and Outsider," pp. 7-9 for discussion on the implications of this alleged ability. Note also that animal behavior is said to symbolize the creation of disharmony through violation of *gichiaro*; see footnote 34.

64. Mahner, "Insider and Outsider," pp. 7-9.

65. Oral Interviewee 6, Northeast Imenti; 7, South Imenti; 22, Muthambe. Corroboration: Oral Interview 20, South Imenti.

66. Oral Interviewees 7 and 20, South Imenti; 23, Mwimbe; 6, Northeast Imenti. In theory, failure to ransom a captive would lead either to his execution (if he was considered dangerous) or to incorporation into the family of his captor. In practice, every captive had kinsmen willing to pay the required ransom. Lambert, *Systems of Land Tenure*, p. 22, ff. 2.

67. Tradition forbade the seizure of either pregnant women or those carrying infants in arms. Lambert, *Systems of Land Tenure*, p. 22.

68. *Ibid.*

69. Each warrior who killed incurred thereby a condition of ritual impurity (*mugiro*), which could be removed only through sacrifice of livestock. It should be noted that no praise names were awarded specifically for the act of killing.

70. At no time in their lives were young Meru males encouraged (or permitted) to acquire livestock through trade or other non-military means. Their entire education was geared to the concept of raiding. See Chapters IV and V.

CHAPTER III

1. Self control was also considered a prerequisite for success in later life, when, as a ruling elder, the former warrior would be required to conciliate the quarrels of his peers. This role required a maximum of disinterested self-control if the decisions reached were to be acceptable to all.

2. Tale of Kaura Bechau, alleged founder of *njuri* of Meru, as told by Oral Interview 6, ex-senior chief. Mberre are a neighboring people to the southeast of Meru.

3.　North Imenti tradition. Oral Interview 9 and other informants north of Katheri. Variants of this tradition can be found among Bantu peoples from East Africa to the Congo. Personal communication, Professor Jan Vansina, University of Wisconsin. Maasai are a neighboring pastoral people, located to the northwest, southeast and west of Meru, who frequently raided Meru *miiriga* for livestock.

4.　Upper Mwimbe tradition, told to Oral Interviewee 24, Upper Mwimbe, of their father's days as a warrior.

5.　Tradition of North Imenti, Northeast Imenti and Tigania (variant), concerning the period of Tigania-Imenti 'wars,' 1880's. Oral Interviewee 19, North Imenti, 35, Northeast Imenti. Variants (Tigania victorious): Oral Interviewees 46 and 48, Tigania.

6.　Typed report, C. M. Dobbs, District Officer, Meru, 1923-24, found in Lambert private papers. Corroboration: Oral Interviewee 6, Northeast Imenti; 23, Mwimbe.

7.　The names used throughout this chapter will be drawn from boys' *biama* of Imenti.

8.　Mrs. E. J. Brown, Head, Department of Ethnology, National Museum of Kenya, personal communication.

9.　Laughton, "Introductory Study," p. 29. Corroboration: Oral Interviewees 7 and 8, South Imenti; from their own experience in *kiama kia kiigumi.*

10.　In certain *miiriga*, applicants were led through the lines by their sponsors, proceeding through the beaters at a deliberate walk.

11.　Laughton, "Introductory Study," p. 29.

12.　All adult warriors were required to sleep nightly in the warrior-barrack, in order to act in unison against surprise attack. In theory, boys imitated the pattern. In practice, they spent some nights in the hut of their fathers; others in the boys' *gaaru.* The ideal, however, was continuous residence.

13.　Following examples drawn from *kabichu* groups of South Imenti. Patterns in other areas were essentially the same.

14.　Sample: One boy claims the ability to read another's thoughts. He demonstrates this by asking the other to suggest various objects, including one of which he had thought. Depression of the demonstrator's big toe indicates that the correct reply is desired. Depression of the second person's toe indicates that it has been supplied. Demonstrator then guesses the object correctly. Oral Interviewees 7 and 8 from their own initiation.

15.　It will be recalled that in certain instances, the subsequent *mugiro* could be lifted only at the cost of incorporating the violator into the society that had imposed it. See Chapters II and VII.

16.　Oral Interviewees 7 and 9, South Imenti. Corroboration: Oral Interview 39, *mwaathi*, South Imenti.

17.　*Ibid.*

18.　Oral Interviewees 7 and 9, South Imenti. Corroboration: Oral Interview 34, Northeast Imenti.

19.　Oral Interviewees 7 and 9, South Imenti. Also recalled (sung) by 8. Examples are drawn from South Imenti. Pattern in other areas is generally the same.

20.　Informants translate the term *'ncamba'* as 'war hero.' I prefer to use the term 'war leader,' in the sense of one who leads by inspiring others to emulate his actions, rather than through military orders to subordinates.

21.　Except where otherwise mentioned, examples from the following discussion will be drawn from Imenti. Patterns from other areas are similar. Lambert, private papers no. 1, pp. 409-10, suggests that *ndinguri* carries the additional meaning of those who have waited longest (for adulthood). It should also be noted that boys of this age were generally referred to as *biiji* (sing: *mwiiji*), which carried the connotation of 'larger boys.'

22.　Boys were forbidden by tradition to drink this type of beer. Upon receipt, *uringuri* members passed it on to their elders, satisfied that the brewing of it had been adequately performed. Oral Interview 9, South Imenti; 52, Igoji.

23. Oral Interviewees 7 and 9, South Imenti; 21 and 22, Igoji.

24. This and subsequent wrestling songs are taken from Achanku and Gita clans of North Imenti. Songs of other areas are similar in spirit. Oral Interviewee 6, Northeast Imenti.

25. Oral Interviewee 6, Northeast Imenti; 19, North Imenti; 7 and 9, South Imenti.

26. See G. St. J. Orde-Browne, *The Vanishing Tribes of Mount Kenya* (London, 1925), for descriptive detail.

27. Oral Interviewees 7 and 20, Southeast Imenti; 6, Northeast Imenti.

28. Oral Interviewee 6, Northeast Imenti; 7 and 20, South Imenti; 33, North Imenti.

29. *Ibid.*

30. Bands of Ukwavi (Maasai) settled in this area, Tigania and Igembe after the 1880s. Maasai traditionally test the courage of their warriors and warrior-candidates against lions.

31. Oral Interviewees 6 and 34, Northeast Imenti; 33, North Imenti. This applies only to *miiriga* near the plains. Those near the montane forest had no equivalent form of testing.

32. Oral Interviewee 16, Muthambe; 70, Muthambe. Corroboration: 25, Mwimbe. It is due to this restriction that production of children occurred during the period of novice elderhood.

33. Oral Interviewee 77, North Imenti; 7 and 8, South Imenti.

34. Song heard in South Imenti. Oral Interviewee 8.

35. In Mwimbe, three. See Chapter I, age-sets.

36. Lambert, private papers, no. 6 (typed manuscript, "The Meru Yet To Come," dated Christmas, 1944, p. 16). Oral corroboration: 21, Muthambe; 77, North Imenti; 20, South Imenti.

37. Lambert, private papers no. 1, pp. 389 and 471. Each *gaaru* had its own war-horn. See Chapters V and VII for additional detail.

38. Oral Interviewee 21, Muthambe, from his own circumcision.

39. "We sang loudly back at them, but were very fearful inside our stomachs." *Ibid.*

40. The Full title was *muringi wa kirarire akiatha biiji*, which could be translated as 'he who (best) flogs the *kirarire* songs which instruct the eldest youth.'

41. Here, the boy was advised not to insult his mother after circumcision. *Mwano mwari* was the name applied to youngsters who were allowed to maintain a teasing relationship with the intitiate's mother. Thus the core of the *muringia's* advice was that the initiate, once circumcised, should no longer attempt to behave in this fashion, but should become remote and distant from his mother, as befitted a warrior. Oral Interview 9. Song from his own circumcision.

42. *Ibid.*

43. Laughton, "Introductory Study," p. 205.

44. *Ibid.*, p. 36. Corroboration: Oral Interviewee 9, South Imenti.

45. G. St. J. Orde-Browne, "Circumcision Ceremonies Among the Amwimbe," *Man*, Vol. 13, #79 (1913), pp. 137-40. Later versions, such as Laughton's in the 1940s, describe boys as seated, with legs apart.

46. This description is drawn from Imenti. Circumcisers in other areas varied slightly. Oral Interview 77, North Imenti; 9, South Imenti. See J. Adamson, *The Peoples of Kenya* (London, 1969), p. 111 for an artistic reproduction of an Imenti circumciser in full costume.

47. This description is drawn from the earliest European report of this operation, as practiced in Mwimbe in 1913. The cutting varied somewhat among the subdivisions, but the pattern was generally the same. For full description of the Mwimbe version, see Orde-Brown, *Man*, Vol. 13, #79 (1913), p. 138.

48. E. Mbabu, Chief, Igoji location. Untitled, handwritten manuscript dealing with precolonial traditions of Mwimbe, Muthambe and Cuka. Oral corroboration: 22, Muthambe.

49. Laughton, "Introductory Study," p. 205; song to accompany the *ncorobi* dance, North Imenti.

50. Oral Interviewee 20, South Imenti; 22, Muthambe.

CHAPTER IV

1. Rainy seasons in the Meru area are February to April and October to December. Dry seasons are June to September and January to February. Raiding is impossible in rainy periods because of the softness of the earth, when mud impedes movement of both men and livestock.

2. Lambert, private papers no. 1, p. 444. This type of *gaaru* was found in Imenti, Muthambe, Miutini and parts of Igoji. That found in Mwimbe differed in several details but was constructed according to the same principles.

3. Exception: Mwimbe, where a third sub-set could be formed from a surplus of circumcisable males.

4. Names vary slightly among subdivisions. Meanings of 'senior' and 'junior' remain the same. Where three sub-sets coexist within a single gaaru, the respective titles imply 'eldest,' 'second,' and 'youngest.'

5. Lambert private papers no. 1, pp. 445-48.

6. Lambert, private papers no. 10, p. 148. See also private papers no. 10, p. 148. See also private papers no. 1, p. 448 ff. Oral corroboration: 6, former war-leader, northeast Imenti.

7. Alternately, it would refer to the actions of his father's age-set, rather than to the person himself. Laughton, "Introductory Study," pp. 49-50. Corroboration: Oral Interview 20, Southeast Imenti; 21, Muthambe.

8. Laughton, "Introductory Study." '*M*' in Kimeru suggests 'son of . . . .' When fully written out it is spelled *Nto*. Thus, M'Kiambati would actually be translated as 'son of he who took cattle,' etc.

9. Oral Interviewees 7 and 20, South Imenti. Corroboration: 21, Muthambe.

10. Oral Interviewees 7 and 20, South Imenti. Corroboration: 6, Northeast Imenti.

11. Lambert, private papers no. 1, p. 447.

12. Laughton, "Introductory Study," p. 52.

13. See Chapter VI for discussion of the elders' powers of retribution in such instances.

14. Oral Interviewee 78, Miutini. Corroboration: Oral Interviewee 16, Muthambe.

15. Oral Interviewee 78, Miutini; 6, Northeast Imenti.

16. *Ibid.* Also, Oral Interviewees 7 and 20, South Imenti.

17. See Chapter VI for full discussion of practice of creating military alliances through ritual adoption on both sides. The result was ritually created 'kinfolk' who were forbidden to shed one another's blood and thus could serve as allies in war.

18. Oral Interviewee 78, Miutini; 6, Northeast Imenti; 7 and 20, South Imenti.

19. *Ibid.* There were several varieties of this type of training.

20. Oral Interviewee 6, Northeast Imenti. No warrior, novice or veteran was permitted to own livestock. The bulls, required for disciplinary fines, traditional feasts, were thus given the warriors by their fathers. If the herds of a father proved inadequate, the latter could appeal to

more distant, male kin. Failure to provide the animals as required would cause the warrior to lose status among his age-mates.

21. Bulls for *gituuji* were contributed by fathers (or other male kin) of the novices involved. Wealthy families could follow the tradition closely, permitting their sons to proclaim *gituuji* immediately upon their recovery. Those in poorer circumstances were required to delay the proclamation until such time as they could acquire the necessary livestock through war, a fact that would reflect adversely upon their initial status within the group. It appears, therefore, as if initial positions of leadership evolved among the sons of wealthier families, a pattern that could be modified only after sons of the poor had been permitted to attain status (and livestock) through acts of war. See footnote 44 for a second example of this pattern.

22. In Meru, meat was divided in the manner most likely to produce harmony among those persons present. Thus, ideally, all participants had to agree on the disposition of pieces. In practice, differences of opinion were adjusted by division of still smaller pieces of the animal (sinews, strips of hide, etc.) so that all might join in their approval of the procedure. The very nature of the division, of course, served to reflect status differences within the group. Laughton, "Introductory Study," pp. 56-57. Oral Corroboration: 24, Mwimbe.

23. Oral Interviewee 6, Northeast Imenti; 33, North Imenti. Membership in other subdivisions varied slightly.

24. Oral Interviewee 6, Northeast Imenti; 21, Muthambe. See Lambert, *Kikuyu Social and Political Institutions*, pp. 102-6, for description of the same system of leadership selection among the Kikuyu.

25. In North, Central and South Imenti, war-leaders of this type were known as *ncamba*. In Igoji, Mwimbe and Miutini, they were known as *aira*. In Northeast Imenti, they were known as *raing'oni* (from Kimaasai: *ol oing'oni*: the bull).

26. Oral Interviewee 6, Northeast Imenti, from his own experience as *ncamba*. Corroboration: 20, South Imenti.

27. Oral Interviewees 7 and 20, South Imenti; 6, Northeast Imenti.

28. The full title would be *ncamba ya ntaani* (war-leader for the novice warriors). Oral Interviewee 20, South Imenti.

29. *Authi*: a dance restricted to warriors. There are three types, each of which will subsequently be discussed.

30. Oral Interviewee 21, Muthambe.

31. *Nanga* or *nanka*: obtained after the 1860s from Akamba traders.

32. Oral Interviewee 21, Muthambe. Reference is to the penis.

33. Oral Interviewees 7 and 20, South Imenti; 6, Northeast Imenti.

34. *Ibid*.

35. P. M'Inoti, "Asili ya wameru na Tabia Zao" (Origin of the Meru and their customs), unpublished, typed manuscript, Swahili language, 1931, pg. 45.

36. Oral Interviewee 8, song from South Imenti.

37. Oral Interviewees 7 and 20, South Imenti; 6, Northeast Imenti.

38. *Nkurii* or *nkirii*: a leg ornament worn by warrior sons of the wealthy. Oral Interview 6, Northeast Imenti.

39. Oral Interviewees 7 and 20, South Imenti; 6, Northeast Imenti.

40. Oral Interviewees 33, North Imenti; 6, Northeast Imenti.

41. See Chapter VI for details of war planning.

42. Oral Interviewee 6, Northeast Imenti.

43. Under ideal conditions, warriors feasted solely on bulls. If these proved unobtainable in the quantities required, cows or even goats would be devoured. Throughout the feast, these would be referred to as 'bulls.' Oral Interview 21, Muthambe; 33, North Imenti.

44. Orde-Browne, *Vanishing Tribes*, p. 176.

45. Unpublished private papers, Stephen M'Anampio, Vice-Principal and History Master, Meru Teacher Training College, Meru.

46. Oral Interviewee 21, Muthambe; 33, North Imenti.

47. Oral Interviewee 6, Northeast Imenti.

CHAPTER V

1. Oral Interviewees 7 and 20, South Imenti; 33, North Imenti; 6, Northeast Imenti.

2. Oral Interviewees 81, Mwimbe (Father was Ogiek). Corroboration: 6, Northeast Imenti; 20, South Imenti.

3. Oral Interviewees 6, Northeast Imenti; 21 and 41, Muthambe.

4. Oral Interviewees 6, Northeast Imenti; 20, South Imenti.

5. Between 1888 and 1908, Meru tradition contains several accounts of violent disagreement between warriors and elders over the question of whether to attack individual Europeans who had entered their district. It was the elders' eventual re-assertion of their authority which permitted the British to seize control of the area without a single major battle.

6. Oral Interviewees 20, South Imenti; corroboration, 17 and 18, clan and village of *mugwe*. For full discussion of the *mugwe's* traditional functions, see B. Bernardi, *The Mugwe: A Failing Prophet* (London, 1959).

7. Bernardi's data suggest that the institution of 'blessing' (*ugwe*) fragmented after the entry of ancestors of the current Meru into the area they now hold. Thereafter, fragmentation of the original migrant group may have caused claimants to the power of *ugwe* to appear in several of the major subdivisions. During the period of his research (1950s), persons claiming the title of *mugwe* existed in Igembe, Tigania, South Imenti, Tharaka and Cuka. In the remaining areas, the function of 'blessing' was carried out by other ritual specialists. It should be noted that Bernardi often uses the word *muringia* (curse-detector, diviner) to indicate the functions of a *muroria* (foreteller, prophet). Bernardi, *The Mugwe*, Chapter II.

8. Note that one ritualist often has two or more specialties. The pattern followed in the southern sections was similar. The *muroria* used a gourd, rather than a goat, to forecast the future. The order in which seeds within the gourd fell upon his palm determined defeat or victory. Oral Interviewees 41, Muthambe, 23, Mwimbe. Corroboration: 9 (*muroria, muringia*) and 14 (*muga*), South Imenti.

9. Oral Interviewees 19 and 33, North Imenti. Corroboration: 9, South Imenti.

10. Oral Interviewees 34 and 38, Northeast Imenti. Corroboration: 19, North Imenti.

11. Oral Interviewees 34 and 38, Northeast Imenti; 9 and 14, South Imenti. See subsequent pages for discussion of correct use of this magic during a raid.

12. Oral Interviewees 7 and 20, South Imenti; 19, North Imenti. The average number of warriors with a *gaaru* was around fifty, although claims of up to 200 are heard in North Imenti.

13. The patterns of attack and defense discussed here would also apply to attacks on neighboring Mt. Kenya peoples, the Cuka, Embu, Mberre and Kikuyu. It must be recalled, however, that most raiding took place among the Meru themselves.

14. The example is based on discussions with members of the *miirigi* of Katheri (North Imenti), and Kitheruni (North Imenti), whose warriors frequently joined to raid the *mwiriga* of Kabeche (Upper Mwimbe). Additional discussion of march formations, tactics, etc. was

contributed by former warriors of Northeast Imenti, North Imenti, South Imenti and Muthambe.

15. Oral Interviewee 6, Northeast Imenti. Corroboration: 19, North Imenti, and Lambert private papers, no. 10, p. 17. See also the discussion of basic training for the novice warriors (Chapter IV) where 'place' within the *gaaru* also reflects comparative status within the group.

16. When not grazing, cattle herds were kept in a clearing adjacent to the *mwiriga* gaaru. Oral Interview 6, Northeast Imenti; and 22, Muthambe.

17. Oral Interviewee 22, Muthambe.

18. Primarily *magaaru* from North Imenti, South Imenti and Muthambe. *Chuka Political Record Book (1910-1918)*; Appendix: Early History of Chuka-Mwimbe, Nairobi National Archives. Oral Corroboration: 19, 76, 19, North Imenti; 24, Mwimbe.

19. Arkell-Hardwick, writing in 1900, states that it took him an hour to cut through this belt, after marching uphill for two previous hours in a vain attempt to go around. Arkell-Hardwick, *An Ivory Trader in North Kenya*, London, 1903, p. 75. Barricade also referred to in a report by C. R. W. Lane, dated 14 October, 1970, Vol. 533/33, Dispatch 507 of 25 November, 1907, Public Records Office, London.

20. *Aathi* frequently used pits lined with bamboo spikes to trap larger species of wild game.

21. Orde-Browne. *The Vanishing Tribes*, pp. 155-56, for Mwimbe and Muthambe; Chanler, *Through Jungle and Desert*, p. 244; and Arkell-Hardwick, *Ivory Trader*, p. 99ff, referring to 'Embe' (Igembe).

22. See Arkell-Hardwick, *Ivory Trader*, p. 99, for success of this tactic, when 'Embe' (Igembe) succeeded in killing the war-leader of a Somali caravan allied with his own.

23. Oral Interviewee 21, Muthambe. See sketch of the geographical relationships of these *gaaru*, Chapter III.

24. Orde-Browne, Untitled Talk on Native African life, private papers, Oxford Collection. Material drawn from his experience among Cuka, Muthambe and Mwimbe between 1909 and 1912.

25. Oral Interviewees 19, 76, North Imenti.

26. Chanler, *Through Jungle and Desert*, p. 165. Also report by C. R. Lane, 14 October, 1907, in Sadler to Elgon correspondence, Dispatch 507 of 25 November, 1907, 533/33, Public Records Office, London.

27. *Ibid.*, Chanler.

28. Lambert, *Kikuyu Social and Political Institutions*, p. 78. Oral Corroboration: 41, 21, Muthambe.

29. Oral Interviewee 19, North Imenti.

30. Coro could also be made from a cow horn or cut from twisted pieces of wood. Orde Browne, *The Vanishing Tribes*, pp. 169-70.

31. Oral Interviewee 6, Northeast Imenti.

32. Oral Interviewees 6, Northeast Imenti; 19 and 76, North Imenti; 7 and 20, South Imenti.

33. *Ibid.* Also, Arkell-Hardwick, *Ivory Trader*, p. 99, Arkell-Hardwick was attacked by Igembe warriors during these hours.

34. Allegedly, this was to be achieved by permitting the magic to 'push' the enemy warriors more deeply into sleep, to the point where they would neither see nor hear the raiders' subsequent action. Oral Interviews 6, 34, 38, Northeast Imenti; 14, 39, 40, South Imenti. There are several variations to this tradition, but the intent (stealth rather than violence) is always the same.

Notes

35. Unpublished private papers, Alliano M'Mwarania, South Imenti. Unpublished private papers, Chief Ephantus Mbabu, Igoji. Oral Corroboration: 25, Mwimbe, 21, 22, 41, Muthambe. Both tactics were successfully used against the Muthambe *gaaru* of Rwanderi during the 1890s. In consequence, several other Muthambe *Miiriga* began to construct smaller subsidiary barracks adjacent to the main one, in an attempt to neutralize the tactics.

36. See Chapter V.

37. Oral Interviewee 33, North Imenti; 6, Northeast Imenti. Corroboration: Oral Interviewee 79, North Igembe.

38. Oral Interviewee 5, Northeast Imenti. Corroboration: Oral Interview 33, North Imenti; 20, South Imenti.

39. Oral Interviewee 24, Mwimbe.

40. Oral Interviewee 6, Northeast Imenti; 7 and 20, South Imenti.

41. Arkell-Hardwick, *Ivory Trader*, p. 118.

42. Chanler, *Jungle and Desert*, pp. 172-74.

43. Oral Interviewee 21, Muthambe, speaking of Rwanderi *gaaru* (Muthambe), defeated by Kiuuguni *gaaru* (Cuka) and allies.

44. Chanler, *Jungle and Desert*, pp. 175-76.

45. Arkell-Hardwick, *Ivory Trader*, pp. 98-99.

46. Oral Interviewee 6, Northeast Imenti. Corroboration: 79, North Igembe; 19, North Imenti.

47. *Ibid.* Informants: descriptions suggest that all of the reinforcing contingents assembled and charged more or less simultaneously. This action assumes a far greater degree of centralized control than that suggested by available evidence. It seems more likely that individual bands of pursuing warriors (usually from a number of *magaaru*) would reach the ambush site at varying times, depending on the routes they had selected for pursuit. Each group would then simply charge the nearest point in the raiders' defensive formation.

48. *Ibid.* Corroboration: Oral Interview 21, Muthambe. It should be noted that the stolen cattle might remain within the area of sanctuary for years or even generations. Nevertheless, the identity of the original owners of the herd (the raiders) would remain in the minds of both groups for as long as required and could serve as a basis for subsequent negotiations with regard to brides, etc.

49. Oral Interviewee 17, South Imenti; 6, Northeast Imenti.

50. Unsigned report, *Chuka Political Record Book, 1910*, Kenya National Archives. Corroboration: Oral Interview 6, Northeast Imenti.

51. Report by C. M. Dobbs, District Officer, Meru, 1923-24, in Lambert, private papers, University of Nairobi. Corroboration: Interview 14 (*muga*), South Imenti.

52. Oral Interviewees 8, 36, Northeast Imenti; 19, 33, North Imenti; 20 and 9, South Imenti.

53. *Ibid.*

54. Oral Interviewee 33, North Imenti.

55. Oral Interviewee 77, North Imenti.

56. See J. Adamson, *Peoples of Kenya*, (London, 1967), p. 95, for a reconstruction of the costume of *mbui ya mugongo*.

57. The *mbui* was said to symbolize a cock, whose upright feathers give it dignity. Oral Interview 6, Northeast Imenti; Lambert private papers no. 9, p. 42. For convenience, I shall refer to this title as the '*mbui*' from this point on.

58. See Chapter III, "The Economic Setting," for discussion of the conventions of war.

59. Oral Interviewees 20, South Imenti; 6, North Imenti.

CHAPTER VI

1. Girls reaching puberty during the period warriors sought mates were said to be reserved for the warriors of that age-set. Thus men in their late twenties would traditionally be seeking wives among girls in their mid-teens.

2. Oral Interviewees 33, North Imenti; 80, South Imenti.

3. This was done by means of a feast held by the father for his age-mates when the girl attained puberty. Failure to hold the feast, for whatever reason, led to delay in announcing the daughter's new status and thus in her availability for marriage. Oral Interviewees 16 and 21, Muthambe; 78, North Imenti. Lambert, private papers, typed report, A. E. Chamier, District Commissioner (Meru, 1919).

4. Oral Interviewee 16, Muthambe, from her own courtship period. Oral Corroboration: 70, Muthambe; 6, Northeast Imenti.

5. Oral Interviewee 16, Muthambe. Typed report by A. E. Chamier, 1919, now in Lambert private papers. Courtship patterns described apply to Muthambe and Mwimbe. Those in other areas vary slightly.

6. Laughton, "Introductory Study," p. 98, from research by Philipo Inoti.

7. Lambert, private papers no. 9, p. 17. Pregnancy prior to marriage was punished by the humiliation of both partners, combined with efforts to compel the warrior involved to marry the girl. Pregnancy prior to circumcision was punished by death for both partners. In consequence, abortion was frequently practiced, both by the girls themselves and by specialists (*aruthi-mahu*: removers of pregnancy), who used varying combinations of herbal medicines and brute force. See P. Inoti, "Asili ya WaMeru," p. 4. Also, *Embu Political Record Book*, 1927, National Archives, Nairobi. Oral Corroboration: 16, Muthambe; 24, Mwimbe.

8. Oral Interviewee 16, Muthambe. Corroboration: 70, Muthambe; 6, Northeast Imenti. The pattern described is from Muthambe. Other areas show slight variation in the pattern of giving and gifts given.

9. The entire process, including transferral of bridewealth, was called *uthoni wa mukenye*, the relationship (inlawship) created out of an uncircumcised girl. Oral Interview 16, Muthambe. Corroboration: 70, Muthambe.

10. Mahner, "Insider and Outsider," pp. 5-6.

11. Oral Interviewee 6, Northeast Imenti; 81, South Imenti.

12. See Chapter IV, "Learning Warriorhood."

13. Oral Interviewee 6, Northeast Imenti.

14. This statement applies to Imenti, Miutini, and most of Igoji. In Mwimbe and Muthambe, the process was called *rukunjix* and took place without the physical violence to be subsequently described.

15. See tuika, 'to cut,' in *A Tentative Kimeru Dictionary*, Father B. Giorgis, Consolata Mission, Meru Catholic Bookshop, Meru, Kenya.

16. It should be noted that novices made no attempt to court these girls physically. Their intention was not to seek wives, but to assume systematically the roles of the senior warrior. For this, the very act of courting (in song, etc.) was sufficient. Oral Interview 16, Muthambe; 20, South Imenti; 8, South Imenti.

17. Song: Oral Interviewee 8, South Imenti.

18. The ritual specialists to be consulted in these instances functioned in the capacity of ritual leaders (*ntindiri*) regardless of their actual age. Thus, in the subsequent example, it should be noted that the *mugwe*, although present at all negotiations, did not function as a judge, nor resolve in any way the issue under discussion. His only function was to sanctify (bless) ritually the decision that was made. The same would apply to other ritual specialists consulted in this manner. Oral Interviewee 17, South Imenti; Omo clan (clan of *mugwe*), South Imenti.

Notes

19. Oral Interviewees 17, 18, Omo clan (clan of *mugwe*), South Imenti. See also Lambert private papers no. 1, pp. 284-86, for description of this process as it takes place in Igembe.

20. Bernardi, *The Mugwe*, pp. 91-92.

21. Oral Interviewee 6, Northeast Imenti.

22. *Ibid.*

23. Oral Interviewees 7, 20, Southeast Imenti; 33, North Imenti, Bernardi refers to this period as one in which lawlessness was practiced by the incoming set of warriors and consisted of attacks on women as well as property. Bernardi, *The Mugwe*, p. 92. Neither statement has been corroborated by oral testimony.

24. Oral Interviewee 6, Northeast Imenti; 20, South Imenti.

25. Oral Interviewee 20, South Imenti. Note that pressure to conform could be exerted on a recalicitrant ex-warrior merely by drawing from the herds of his father the animals required for further feasting.

26. Oral Interviewees 17, 18, South Imenti, Omo clan (clan of *mugwe*).

27. Oral Interviewees 9, South Imenti; 6, Northeast Imenti.

28. See Chapter VI, "Waging War," for discussion as to utilization of captives.

29. Names for these varied among areas. In Imenti, *kiama kia nkomango* (council of the throwing stone). In Miutini and Igoji, *Kiama kia njuguma* (council of the throwing club). In Mwimbe and Muthambi, *kiama kia kibogo* (council of the buffalo). It should be recalled that a higher council composed of representatives of these *mwiriga* councils would be called an *njuri*.

30. Laughton, "Introductory Study," p. 29.

31. Lambert, private papers, p. 442. Corroboration: unpublished handwritten manuscript, English language, "Traditions and Customs of the / Imenti/ Meru of Long Ago." Anderson's Archives, 1.

32. C. F. Atkins, "Igembe Customs: Kiama," miscellaneous report, 1938, in Lambert private papers, University of Nairobi. Corroboration for Imenti: Oral Interviewee 19, North Imenti.

33. Diary of Father A. Bellani, "Ntuara ya Igoji (Bell of Igoji)," 1923-1926, Archives, Consolata Mission Order, Italy, p. 16.

34. Bellani, "Bell of Igoji," p. 23, contains many details of the initiation, as watched from afar by a disapproving European observer. It is, nonetheless, the earliest description found to date. Meru informants uniformly refuse to reveal details of the initiation lest violation of the oath of secrecy lead to their deaths.

35. Oral Interviewee 21, Muthambe. Similar examples found in Laughton, "Introductory Study," p. 130, as drawn from Inoti, "Asili ya Wameru." See Chapter 1, footnote 6, for discussion of the problem of deducing information withheld from an investigator by formal oath.

36. Lambert private papers no. 2, "The Constitution and Personnel of Statutory Institutions in the Meru Native Reserve," p. 8. Corroboration: Oral Interviews 23, Mwimbe; 33, North Imenti.

37. Consider, for example, the condition of post World War I Germany after demobilization of its Landwehr, or the unsettled condition of Vietnam veterans in the United States today. Contemporary Africa also provides several examples of this problem, including at least one (Togo, 1963) where frustration over his demobilization brought an ex-army sergeant to assassinate the president of that country, and seize the government for himself. See R. First, *Power in Africa: Political Power in Africa and the Coup d'Etat*, 1971, pp. 209-309.

38. Oral Interviewee 6, Northeast Imenti; 21, 22, Muthambe. Corroborated by members of Murungi age-set in every area of Meru. The most frequently repeated phrase: "After taking our weapons and stopping our *authi* (dance), the white men sent us like small children to our

171

homes." The impact of this disarmament upon Meru society will be more fully examined in a subsequent publication.

39.   Note that human relations were also conceived of in dual forms. People were in a condition of either conflict or harmony.

40.   This dualism can be found throughout Meru society. Needham has suggested its existence within geographic and spatial relationships assigning supernatural associations to the left and secular to the right. R. Needham, "Left Hand of the Mugwe: An Analytical Note of the *Structure* of Meru Symbolism," *Africa*, Vol. 30, No. 1. Mahner, "Insider and Outsider" has cited similar examples.

41.   Self-development, self-regulation, subordination to group, age and ancestral tradition. See Chapter III, "Learning Warriorhood," for full discussion.

42.   No reliable data are available as to the percentage of Meru joining either the earlier or later supernatural societies during pre-colonial times. Colonial sources from the 1920s record only that they were strong and had gained great influence over certain subdivisions, particularly in the North. Oral informants, when asked to evaluate their position within the pre-colonial era, concur only in the fact that they existed within every major area of Meru, and that very few persons concerned themselves with such activities. My own estimate for the subdivisions considered in this study would be less than three percent of the total adult population.

43.   Untitled typed list of elders' curses, collected by a colonial administrative officer (J. G. Hopkins?) in the 1920s. Lambert private papers, University of Nairobi. Corroborated for *biama* of Imenti by Oral Interview 19, *njuri* member, North Imenti.

44.   This would not apply to persons who had acquired alternate means of supernatural protection, such as Meru, who subsequently accepted Christianity. See also the discussion of fringe *biama* in Chapter I and on subsequent pages.

45.   Many of the ideas contained in this and the following sections have evolved through discussion with my research assistant, Mr. Frank Duff, a student at Eastern Michigan University.

46.   Intermarriage, for example, was not practiced between agriculturalists and iron-smiths, and only infrequently between the former and hunters. Personal communication, Mrs. E. J. Brown, Head, Department of Ethnology, Kenya National Museum, Nairobi. Oral Interviews 39 and 40 (honey-hunters), South Imenti.

47.   It is interesting to note, for instance, that the first converts to Christianity within the Mwimbe-Muthambe area included the entire membership of *mwaa*. Evidently, the European deviation proved more effective than the Meru one in allowing its adherents to escape traditional social controls. Benjamin Karaya was Njara, former *mwaa* member, now a Christian.

48.   In the final years before colonialism, the impact of this precedent began to take effect. The Muthambe, Mwimbe and North Imenti, individual *ncamba* began to defy the elders' councils in the interests of military efficiency. Oral Interviewees 24, Mwimbe; 33, North Imenti; 21, Muthambe.

Bibliography

Published Sources

Adamson, J. *The Peoples of Kenya*. London, 1967.

Adamson, G. *Bwana Game: The Life Story of George Adamson*, London, 1968. (American Title: *A Lifetime With Lions*, New York, 1968).

Ademuwagun, Z. A., Ayoade, J. A., Harrison, I. E., Warren, D. M. *African Therapeutic Systems*, Crossroads Press, 1979.

Arkell-Hardwick, A. *An Ivory Trader in North Kenia*. London, 1903.

Bernard, F. E. *East of Mt. Kenya: Meru Agriculture in Transition*. Weltforum Verlag, Munich, Germany, 1972.

_____. *Recent Agricultural Change East of Mt. Kenya*. Ohio University, Africa Series, 1973.

_____. "Recent Agricultural Change among the Meru of Mt. Kenya," in *Readings on Spacial Structure in Kenya*, ed. R. Obduho and F. Taylor, Colorado: West View Press, 1980.

Bernardi, B. *The Mugwe: A Failing Prophet*. London: Oxford Press, 1959.

Broun, W. H. "A Journey to the Lorian Swamp, British East Africa," *Geographical Journal*, Vol. 27 (1906), pp. 533-34.

Champion, A. H. "The Atharaka," *Journal of the Royal Anthropological Institute* (JRAI), Vol. 42 (1912), pp. 68-90.

Chanler, W. A. "Mr. Astor Chanler's Expedition to East Africa," *Geographical Journal*, Vol. I (1893), pp. 533-34.

_____. *Through Jungle and Desert*. London, 1896.

Dundas, C. "The History of Kitui," *JRAI*, Vol. 43 (1913).

Dutton, E. A. T. *Kenya Mountain*. London, 1929.

Fadiman, J. A. "Early History of the Meru of Mt. Kenya," *Journal of African History*, XIU, I, 1973, London.

_____. "Mountain Warriors: Traditional Warfare Among the Meru of Mt. Kenya," Ohio University, Africa Series, (Monograph) 1975.

_____. "The Meru Peoples," in *Kenya Before 1900*, B. A. Ogot, ed., Nairobi: East Africa Publishing House, 1976.

_____. "Mountain Witchcraft: Supernatural Practices and Practitioners among the Meru of Mt. Kenya," *African Studies Review*, Vol. XX, No. 1, University of Syracuse, 1977.

_____. "The Moment of Conquest: Meru, Kenya, 1907," Ohio University, Africa Series, (Monograph) 1979.

173

Bibliography

First, R. *Power in Africa: Political Power and the Coup d'Etat*, Penguin, 1971.

Freeman-Grenville, G. S. P. "The Coast, 1498-1840," *History of East Africa*, Vol. I, ed. R. Oliver and G. Mathew, Oxford (1968), pp. 128-68.

Gedge, E. "A Recent Exploration under Captain F. G. Dundas, R. N., up the River Tana to Mt. Kenya," *Proceedings of the Royal Geographical Society*, Vol. 14 (1892), pp. 513-33.

Giorgis, B. Fr. *A Tentative Kimeru Dictionary*. First Edition, Catholic Book Shop (Consolata Mission Fathers), Meru, Kenya, 1964.

Gurney, H. L. G. "The Mwimbi," Appendix VI, in E. A. T. Dutton, *Kenya Mountain*, London, 1929, pp. 203-207.

Henderson, I. and Goodheart P. *The Hunt for Kimathi*, London, 1958.

Hobley, C. W. *Ethnology of the A-Kamba and Other East African Tribes*. Cambridge, 1910, pp. 156. (Notes on the Mogogodo.)

Holding, E. M. "Some Preliminary Notes on Meru Age Grades," *Man*, Vol. 42, (1942), pp. 58-65.

Hopkins, A. J. *Trail Blazers and Road Makers: A Brief History of the East African Mission of the United Methodist Church*. London, Henry Hooks, 1928.

Huxley, E. *A New Earth*. New York, 1969, pp. 217-30.

———. *White Man's Country: Lord Delamere and the Making of Kenya*. Vol. I, 1870-1914, London, 1953.

Jacobs, A. H. "The Chronology of the Pastoral Maasai," *Hadithi*, Vol. I, University of Nairobi, Department of History, 1968.

———. "Maasai Pastoralism in Historical Perspective," in *Pastoralism in Tropical Africa*, Ed. T. Monod, International African Institute, London, 1975.

———. "Maasai Inter-Tribal Relations: Belligeraot Herdsmen or Peaceful Pastoralists?" in *Warfare among East African Herders*, Ed. K. Fukui and D. Turton, Senri Ethnological Studies, 3, 1979, National Museum of Ethnology, Senri, Osaka, Japan.

Kenyatta, Jomo. *Facing Mount Kenya*. London, 1961.

Kolb, G. "Vom Mombasa Durch Ukambani Zum Kenia," *Petermanns Mitteilungen*, Vol. 42 (1896), pp. 221-31.

Lambert, H. E. *The Systems of Land Tenure in the Kikuyu Land Unit: Part 1; History of the Tribal Occupation of the Land*. Cape Town University, Communication of the School of African Studies, No. 22, Cape Town, South Africa, 1950.

———. *The Use of Indigenous Authorities in Tribal Administration: Studies of the Meru of Kenya Colony*. Cape Town University, Communication of the School of African Studies, No. 16, Cape Town, South Africa, 1947.

———. *Kikuyu Social and Political Institutions*. Oxford, University Press, 1956.

Laughton, W. H. "A Meru Text," *Man*, Vol. 64, No. 9 (1964), pp. 17-18.

———. *The Meru*. Peoples of Kenya Series, No. 10, Nairobi: Ndia Kuu Press, 1944.

Mathew, G. "The East African Coast until the Coming of the Portuguese," *History of East Africa*, Vol. I, ed. R. Oliver and G. Mathew, pp. 94-129.

Middleton, J. and Kershaw, G. *The Central Tribes of the Northeastern Bantu*. Ethnographic Survey of Africa, Part V, ed. D. Ford, London, 1965.

Miracle, Marvin. "The Kikuyu Economy at the Beginning of the Colonial Period," *Cultures et Developement*, Belgium, 1977, pp. 3-31.

Moyse-Bartlett, H. *The King's African Rifles: A Study of the Military History of East and Central Africa*. Aldershot, 1956.

Mungeam, G. H. *British Rule in Kenya, 1895-1912: The Establishment of Administration in the East African Protectorate*. Oxford, 1966.

Munro, J. F. "Migrations of the Bantu-Speaking Peoples of the Eastern Kenya Highlands: A Reappraisal," *Journal of African History*, Vol. 7, No. 1 (1967), pp. 25-28.

Muriuki, G. "Kikuyu Reaction to Traders and British Administration, 1850-1904," *Hadithi*, Vol. I, University of Nairobi, Department of History, 1968, p. 101.

———. *A History of the Kikuyu, 1500-1900*, Oxford University Press, 1974.

Bibliography

Mwaniki, H. S. K. *The Living History of Embu and Mbeere*, East African Literature Bureau, Nairobi, 1973.

Needham, R. "The Left Hand of the Mugwe: An Analytical Note on the Structure of Meru Symbolism," *Africa*, Vol. 30, No. 1 (1960), pp. 20-33.

Neumann, A. H. *Elephant Hunting in East Equatorial Africa*. London, 1898.

Ogot, B. A., ed. *War and Society in Africa*, Nairobi: East African Publishing House, 1972.

Orde-Brown, G. St. J. *The Vanishing Tribes of Kenya*. London, 1925.

————. "Circumcision Ceremonies among the Amwimbe," *Man*, Vol. 13, No. 79 (1913), pp. 137-40.

————. "The Circumcision Ceremony in Chuka," *Man*, Vol. 15, No. 5 (1915), pp. 65-68.

————. "Mount Kenya and Its People: Some Notes on the Chuka Tribe," *Journal of the African Society*, Vol. 15 (1916), pp. 225-233.

————. "The Southeast Face of Mt. Kenya," *Geographical Journal*, Vol. 51 (1918), pp. 389-92.

Peters, K. "From the Mouth of the Tana to the Source Region of the Nile," *Scottish Geographical Magazine*, Vol. 7 (1891).

Piggot, J. R. W. "Journey to the Upper Tana," *Proceedings of the Royal Geographic Society*, Vol. 12 (1890), pp. 129-36.

Prins, A. J. H. *The Coastal Tribes of the Northeast Bantu*. Ethnographic Survey of Africa: East Central Africa, Part III, London, 1952.

Shackleton, E. R. "The Njuwe," *Man*, Vol. 30, No. 143 (1930), pp. 201-202.

Sorrenson, M. P. K. *Origins of European Settlement in Kenya*. Nairobi, 1968.

Tate, H. R. "Journey to the Rendile Country, British East Africa," *Geographical Journal*, Vol. 23 (1904), pp. 220-28.

Thompson, J. *Through Masailand*. London, 1885.

Tignor, R. L. *The Colonial Transformation of Kenya: The Kamba, Kikuyu and Maasai from 1900-1934*, Princeton University Press, 1976.

Vansina, J. *Oral Tradition: A Study in Historical Methodology*. Translated by H. M. Wright, Chicago, 1965.

Wisner, B. and O'Keefe P. *Land Use and Development*, International African Institute, London, 1977.

Unpublished Research

Almy, S. W. "Rural Development in Meru, Kenya: Economic and Social Factors in Accelerating Change." Unpublished Ph.D. thesis, Stanford University, 1974.

Bernard, F. E. "East of Mt. Kenya: Meru Agriculture in Transition." Unpublished Ph.D. thesis, University of Wisconsin, 1968.

Jacobs, A. H. "The Traditional Political Organization of the Pastoral Maasai." Unpublished Ph.D. thesis, Oxford University, 1965.

Kamunchululu, J. S. T., "Meru Participation in Mau-Mau." Unpublished research paper, University of Nairobi, 1975.

Laughton, W. H. "An Introductory Study of the Meru People." Unpublished M.A. thesis, Cambridge University, 1938.

Lowenthal, R. A. "Tharaka Age-Organization and the Theory of Age-Set Systems." Unpublished Ph.D. dissertation, University of Illinois at Urbana-Champaign, 1973.

Mahassin, A. Gh. El-Safi. "Some Contributions of Swahili Poetry to the Understanding of the History of the Northern Coast of Kenya." Unpublished research paper, Institute of Development Studies, Cultural Division, University of Nairobi, 1970.

Bibliography

Mahner, J. "The Insider and the Outsider in Tigania, Meru." Unpublished preliminary research paper, Institute of Development Studies, Cultural Division, University of Nairobi, May, 1970.

McKim, W. L. "The Role of Interaction in Spacial Economic Development Planning: A Case Study from Kenya.

Mwaniki, H. S. K. "The British Impact on Embu, 1906-1919." Unpublished preliminary research paper, Department of History, University of Nairobi, 1970.

Temu, A. J. "British Protestant Missions in Kenya, 1873-1929." Unpublished Ph.D. thesis, University of Alberta, 1967.

Archival Collections

Kenya National Archive, Nairobi, Kenya.

    The Kenya National Archives contain voluminous records of the colonial period, the earliest years of which are relevant to this study. It should be noted that Mwimbe and Muthambi were originally designated as part of Cuka sub-district, which in turn was administered from Embu. Insight as to the initial British impact on Meru-Mwimbe social institutions can be gained from examination of the following:

    a.   Chuka [sic] Sub-District Political Record Book, 1907-1918. See "Early History of Chuka and Mwimbe," unsigned typewritten manuscript.

    b.   Meru District Record Book, 1908-1921.

    c.   Marsabit Political Record Book, 1908-1914. See Appendix D (Meru), "Safari Record," Bois, Captain J.: one of the earliest European accounts of conditions in Meru at the time of its submission to Britain.

    d.   Meru District Annual Reports, 1911-1926.

Consolata Mission Archives. Consolata Roman Catholic Mission Order, Torino, Italy.

    The archives contain several diaries written by the first Roman Catholic priests to enter Meru after 1912-1913. There are several detailed descriptions of Meru customs as observed up to the 1920s. All diaries are in Italian. The most significant are the following:

    a.   Father R. P. Balbo. Personal diary, 1914-1926.

    b.   Father P. A. Bellani. Personal diary entitled "Ntuara ca Egoji (The Bell of Igoji), 1923-1926.

    c.   Father P. S. Bellani. Handwritten travel diary entitled "Da Nyeri al Paese di Meru," dated February, 1915.

    d.   Father P. A. Bellani. Handwritten notebook entitled "Costumi dei Bameru," 1920.

    Note: Photocopies of the Balbo papers and certain of those by Bellani are in this writer's possession.

Consolata Mission Archives, Mujwa Village, South Imenti, Meru.

    a.   "Note di etnologia sulla tribu Meru." Typewritten manuscript, unsigned, undated.

    b.   "Mezzo soculo di attiva dei missionaria Consolata (Meru)." Typewritten manuscript, unsigned, undated.

Rhodes House, Oxford, England.

    The collections at Rhodes House hold the private papers of those working in British Africa during the colonial period. Investigators dealing with the history of Meru will find the following of interest:

    a.   Orde-Browne, G. St. J. District Commissioner, Cuka subdistrict, 1912.

    b.   Platts, Mrs. Laverne. Diary extract, November 1912 through May 1913, while residing in Meru as wife of W. F. Platts, Acting District Commissioner.

Historical Archives, St. Paul's Theological Seminary, Limuru, Kenya (Anderson's Archives).

    Rev. William B. Anderson, Master of History, has supervised the collection of oral history by students of the seminary since 1961. Emphasis was on pre-colonial customs and initial experiences with European missionaries. The data were not always systematically collected and should be considered reliable only if corroborated by additional oral testimony. It has, however, proven valuable in identifying historically reliable informants and as corroborative material. When cited in the text of this study, it has been labeled as "Anderson's Archives," with the appropriate document number. The documents are numbered as follows:

    a.   "Traditions and Customs of Meru Long Ago." Handwritten manuscript, unsigned, undated. Marked Anderson's Archives #1.

    b.   "Traditions and Customs of Nyambene Division, Igembe." Handwritten manuscript, Igembe, North Meru, unsigned, undated. Marked Anderson's Archives #3.

    c.   "Traditions and Customs of Mwimbe." Handwritten manuscript, unsigned, undated. Marked Anderson's Archives #8.

    d.   "The History of Communications in Meru District." Deals with pre-colonial obligations for communal labor with regard to construction and maintenance of paths, bridges, etc. Collected by Justus Thambu, Imenti, 1962. Marked Anderson's Archives #9.

    e.   "Customs and Traditions of the Meru People of Thaichu, Tigania." Handwritten manuscript, collected by Festus Ringeera, 1961. Marked Anderson's Archives #10.

Private Papers

H. E. Lambert.

    H. E. Lambert was District Commissioner of Meru between 1933 and 1935, as well as in 1940 and 1941. During these periods he spent considerable time investigating Meru history and social structure. After his death in the late 1960s, his private papers were donated by his widow to the University of Nairobi. As of this writing, they have not been catalogued, but are accessible to scholars. Only a small portion of Lambert's writings was devoted to the Meru, chiefly a series of essays appended to the annual reports of the District. In addition, he had begun to organize a number of larger manuscripts, including one of almost 500 pages, for eventual publication. A partial listing of the documents most relevant to the study of Meru appears below.

    a.   "The Social and Political Institutions of the Tribes of the Kikuyu Land Unit." Typewritten manuscript, 479 pages. Used as the basis for his book *Kikuyu Social and Political Institutions*, London, 1956. Referred to as Lambert private papers, no. 1.

    b.   "The Constitution and Personnel of Statutory Institutions in the Meru Native Reserve." Typewritten manuscripts, 47 pages, dated December 6, 1939. Referred to as Lambert private papers no. 2.

    c.   "The Place of Stock in the Native Social System." Typewritten manuscript, 16 pages, dated 1938. Referred to as Lambert private papers no. 3.

    d.   "Disintegration and Reintegration in the Meru Tribe." Typed manuscript, 22 pages, dated January 9, 1940. Referred to as Lambert private papers no. 4.

    e.   "Administrative Use of the Indigenous Institutions of the Meru." Typewritten manuscript, 18 pages, dated October 8, 1939. A revised version of this appeared as *The Use of Indigenous Authorities in Tribal Administration: Studies of the Meru in Kenya Colony*. Cape Town, 1946. Referred to as Lambert private papers no. 5.

    f.   "The Meru Yet to Come." Typewritten manuscript, 38 pages, dated Christmas, 1941. Referred to as Lambert private papers no. 6.

    g.   "Meru District: Notes for Chiefs." Typewritten manuscript, 14 pages, dated January 11, 1941. Referred to as Lambert private papers no. 7.

    h.   "Female Circumcision and Early Initiation." Typewritten manuscript, 13 pages, dated November 3, 1934. Referred to as Lambert private papers no. 8.

   i.   Long, bound notebook, marked "Native customs." Filled with handwritten notations. Referred to as Lambert private papers no. 9.

   j.   Short, thick bound notebook, marked "Native customs." Filled with handwritten notations. Referred to as Lambert private papers no. 10.

H. L. Laughton

These are in the owner's possession and are as yet uncatalogued. Laughton was an educational missionary in Meru between 1931 and 1957. His papers deal primarily with his work for the United Methodist Mission during the 1930s and 1940s, as well as with anthropological research conducted in Imenti.

Filipo M'Inoti. Ex-chief, Miiga Mieru, M. Imenti, Meru.

"Asili ya Wameru na Tabia Zao" (The Origin of the Meru and Their Customs). Typewritten manuscript, 49 pages, Swahili language, Meru United Methodist Mission, North Imenti.

Stephan M'Anamtiu. Master of History, Government Teacher Training College, Meru Town, Imenti.

Several handwritten manuscripts, English language, dealing with the origins and precolonial history of selected clans of North Imenti.

Alliano M'Mwarania. Housepainter, South Imenti.

Several handwritten manuscripts, Meru language, dealing with pre-colonial law, military training, spirit worship and cursing (iron-smiths). Written data subsequently corroborated by oral interviews with original informants.

Rufus Kirera. Farmer and storekeeper, Nkubu, South Imenti.

"Murombere jwa tene jwa Imenti; Murombere jwa ntire" (Imenti prayers of long ago; prayers of sacrifice). Handwritten manuscript, Meru language.

Ephantus Mbabu. Chief, Igoji subdivision, Meru.

Handwritten manuscript, untitled, Meru language, dealing with origins and precolonial methods of war among the Mwimbe, Muthambe and Cuka.

Mukungu wa Mbogore. Chogoria, Mwimbe.

Handwritten notebook, Meru language, untitled, dealing with family affairs, geneology and property of his father, Mbogore wa Mwendo, first Chief of Upper Mwimbe under the colonial regime.

Oral Interviews

The following is a partial list of persons interviewed during the fieldwork period of this study. Interviews with Europeans were in English. Interviews with Africans were in Swahili or Meru, with subsequent translation into English. All interviews were tape recorded and subsequently transliterated into manuscript form. Copies of these manuscripts have been deposited with the Department of History, University of Nairobi, Nairobi, Kenya, where they are currently available to scholars.

Within this dissertation, footnotes attributed to oral informants have been listed by number. Each number on the list below will contain the following supplementary information:

   a.   Full name of informant, place and dates of interview(s).

   b.   Name of Meru age-set (e.g., Murungi), and estimated age.

   c.   Status within Meru social structure (e.g., warrior, farmer).

   d.   Additional relevant data.

   e.   Purpose of interview(s); e.g., duties of warriorhood.

*Note: Within Imenti, the age-set Murungi has two sub-sets, Riungu (the older) and Kirianki (the younger). In Muthambe, the two sub-sets of Murungi are Kiraithe (older) and Riungu (younger). In Mwimbe the equivalent age-set would be Kirianki, with three sub-sets consisting

Bibliography

of Riungu, Marangu and Kirianki. All men of these sets would be in their eighties. See Appendix I for complete listing of sets and sub-sets.

1. H. L. Laughton. Six interviews, May 1969, Hull, England. Educational missionary, United Methodist Mission (UMM, 1931-1957). Carried out anthropological research in North Imenti, Tigania, 1930s. Purpose: identification of potential informants, anthropological and historical orientation.

2. H. Brassington, M. D. One interview, May 1969, Bristol, England. Medical missionary, UMM, late 1920s-early 1930s. Founded Maua Hospital, Igembe, Meru. Purpose: supernatural forms of resistance ('witchcraft') used by local population to stop construction of hospital, 1930-1931.

3. B. Bernardi. One interview, June 1969, Consolata Roman Catholic Mission Headquarters (IMC), Torino, Italy. Missionary in Meru, 1950s, author of *The Mugwe: A Failing Prophet*. London, 1956. Purpose: traditional position of Mugwe; impact of colonial occupation upon the institution.

4. C. Irvine, Rev. Dr. Four interviews, August 1969, Nairobi, Kenya. Medical missionary, Presbyterian Church of East Africa (PCEA). Founded Chogoria Mission, Mwimbe, 1923. Forty years of mission work in Mwimbe area. Purpose: reaction of Mwimbe to early mission contact; supernatural forms of resistance.

5. Mrs. G. Lambert. One interview, Nairobi, August 1969. Wife of H. E. Lambert, former District Commissioner, Meru. Residence in Meru, 1935-37, 1940-41. Purpose: to locate husband's private papers; identification of potential informants; discussion of husband's methods of oral research.

6. M'Muraa wa Kairanyi. Six interviews, September-October 1969, Kirua village, Northeast Imenti. Murungi (Riungu) age-set; estimated age, eighty-five years. Status: warrior (claims to have been a war-leader); translator (for H. E. Lambert); Chief; Senior Chief; Chairman of Njuri Nceke (highest elders' council). Considered by community as expert on historical subjects, especially those related to military affairs. Purpose: traditional war; history and functions of councils of elders, warriors. Frequently corroborated data from other areas.

7. Alliano M'Marania. Five interviews, September-October 1969, Nkubu, South Imenti. Kiruja age-set; estimated age, fifty years. Member of Omo clan (clan of Mugwe), thus unusually interested in retention of pre-colonial customs. Has spent leisure time in learning from elders of Imenti, Igoji. Current occupation: housepainter. Purpose: identification of potential informants (his original sources); *biamas* of boyhood; traditional spirit worship; traditional war; cursing; iron-smiths.

8. Gerrard M'Ikaria. Two interviews, September-October 1969, Nkubu, South Imenti. Kiruja age-set; estimated age, fifties. Status: farmer; housepainter. Member of Omo clan; father a prophet (*muroria*); claims also to have dealt with spirits (*nkoma*) in childhood. Unusual interest in singing of traditional (pre-colonial) songs, particularly those concerned with male circumcision, warriorhood. Purpose: to record these; traditional spirit worship; relations between spirits and men.

9. M'Anyoni wa Ntangi. Four interviews, October 1969, Nkubu, South Imenti. Murungi age-set; estimated age, late seventies. Status: *muroria* (prophet); also functions as curse-detector (*muringia*). Purpose: functions of *muroria* and related ritual specialists; types of contact between ancestral spirits (*nkoma*) and man.

10. M'Rinkanya M'Ringui. Two interviews, October 1969, Nkubu, South Imenti. Kiruja age-set; estimated age, late fifties. Status: curse-remover (*muringia*) and son of a curse-remover. Allegedly circumcised by ancestral spirits (*nkoma*) as a child. Purpose: work of *muringia* and related ritual specialists; types of contact; relationships between ancestral spirits and men.

11. M'Mwiriria M'Murungi. One interview, October 1969, Kirea village, South Imenti. Murungi age-set; estimated age, eighties. Status: curse-detector (*muni wa uta*: breaker of the bow). Purpose: functions of *muni wa uta* and related ritual specialists.

12. Ngaruro M'Munyiri. One interview, October 1969. Kirea village, South Imenti. Murungi (Kirianki) age-set; estimated age, low eighties. Status: truth-seeker (*mugwatithania*

179

Bibliography

gikama: administrator of the oath of the [hot] iron). Purpose: functions of *mugwatitha-nia* and related ritual specialists.

13. M'Mukwea wa Kinugu. One interview, October 1969, near Kirea village, South Imenti. Murungi age-set; estimated age, eighties. Status: curse-detector (*muringia*); allegedly circumcised by ancestral spirits (*nkoma*) as a child; still practicing today. Purpose: functions of *muringia* and related ritual specialists.

14. Mwembu wa Kiringuri. Two interviews, December 1969-January 1970, U. Chure village, South Imenti. Murungi age-set; estimated age, eighties. Status; curse-remover (*muga*) and son of a curse-remover (*muraguri*). Purpose: functions of *muga* and related ritual specialists; traditional spirit worship; persecution of ritual specialists by the colonial regime.

15. M'Mukira Gacoro. One interview, December 1969, Miiriga Mieru, North Imenti. Murungi age-set; estimated age, eighties. Status: curse-remover (*muga*). Purpose: work of a *muga* and related ritual specialists; traditional spirit worship; persecution of ritual specialists by colonial regime; supernatural societies (Mwaa, Wathua) in North Imenti.

16. Ms. Mwamucheke wa Gakuru. Twelve interviews. December 1969-June 1970, Gaichau village, Muthambe. Refused to reveal name of age-set; estimated age, eighties. Nearly blind, thus takes unusual pleasure in recounting events of the past. Purpose: traditional death and hereafter; traditional religion (spirit worship); supernatural societies, with particular focus on role of women therein; traditional courtship and marriage in Muthambe. Frequently corroborated data gathered from or about women in other areas.

17. M'Muthanya M'Kieberia Muiri. Two interviews, April 1970, Kirirwa village, South Imenti. Murungi (Riungu) age-set; estimated age, eighties. Member of Omo clan (clan of Mugwe). Status: farmer. Purpose: traditional functions of Mugwe and related ritual specialists; initial reactions to colonialism; decline and disappearance of the institution (Ugwe).

18. M'Munyugi M'Imotho. Two interviews, April 1970, near Kirirwa village, South Imenti. Murungi (Riungu) age-set; estimated age, eighties. Member of Omo clan. Status: farmer. Purpose: traditional functions of Mugwe and related ritual specialists; initial reactions to colonialism.

19. Hezikiah M'Mukiri. Nine interviews, December 1969-July 1970, Katheri village, North Imenti. Murungi (Riungu) age-set; estimated age, eighties. Status: former member of Njuri Nceke, present member of *kiama kia mbiti* (council of oldest living age-set). Highly intelligent, deeply aware of the Meru past and his own role in transmitting it to the young. When younger, actively sought out knowledgeable elders in order to learn historical traditions. Now considered by contemporaries as the most historically learned man of his area (North Imenti). Purpose: origins of Imenti people; migration onto Mt. Kenya; relations with Maasai; Tigania-Katheri wars; history of Njuri Nceke, witchcraft societies (*aathi*); traditional warfare, etc. Frequently corroborated data from other areas.

20. Gituuru wa Gikamata. Five interviews, December 1969-June 1970, Kionyo village, South Imenti. Kiramana (Kiriambobua) age-set; estimated age, mid nineties. Status: war-leader (*ncamba*). Purpose: origins of Meru; pre-Meru occupants of Mt. Kenya; traditional military tactics, training; persecution of ritual specialists under colonialism. Considered by contemporaries as most historically reliable man in his area (South Imenti). Consistently refused to deviate from original wording of traditions, even when logically flawed. Frequently corroborated data gathered from other areas.

21. M'Thaara M'Mutani. Fifteen interviews, December 1969-July 1970, Kauuni village, Muthambe. Murungi (Riungu) age-set; estimated age, early eighties. Status: warrior; later, chief of warriors, U. Muthambe, under early colonial administration. Extraordinary command of the past. Purpose: traditional warfare; impact of colonialism on (Muthambe) warriorhood; origins of Muthambe; supernatural societies; elders' council of Muthambe (*kiama kia kibogo*).

22. Matiri wa Kirongoro ('Paul'). Twelve interviews, December 1969-July 1970, Muthambe Chiefs' Camp, Muthambe. Miriti age-set; estimated age, seventies. Status: farmer; former member, supernatural societies. Unusual interest in Meru past, specifically tradi-

180

tional forms of war and religion. Purpose: traditional spirit worship; cursing; supernatural societies; traditional warfare.

23. Rwito wa Ruganda. Eight interviews, January-March 1970, Thigaa village, Mwimbe. Kiramana (Kabaya) age-set (only one remaining in Mwimbe-Muthambe); estimated age, nineties. Status: warrior, farmer. Considered most knowledgeable in area. Purpose: origins of Mwimbe; migration to Mt. Kenya; earlier occupants; traditional war, cursing; supernatural societies in Mwimbe; etc.

24. M'Rutere M'Mbogore, Mukungu M'Mbogore, M'Iniu M'Mbogore. Three brothers, all sons of Mbogore M'Mwendo, former warleader (*ncamba wa mbui ya mugongo*) for Mwimbe, and first chief of U. Mwimbe under colonial administration. Three interviews, January-March 1970, Chogoria, U. Mwimbe. Age-sets: Miriti and Kiruja. M'Rutere served as spokesman for all three, the others commenting as required. Purpose: traditions of their family, which go back to initial occupation of Mwimbe area; struggles between Mbogore M'Mwendo and ritual specialists before and after coming of Europeans; military exploits of Mbogore M'Mwendo; etc.

25. Muriuki M'Muriithi. Seven interviews, January-April 1970, Kyeni village, Mwimbe. Murungi (Riungu) age-set; estimated age, low eighties. Status: warrior; thereafter, subordinate of M'Mbogore wa Mwendo; respected by contemporaries as knowledgeable of past. Purpose: origins of Mwimbe; earlier occupants of Mwimbe region; traditional warfare; Mwimbe council of elders; military role of M'Mbogore wa Mwendo; expulsion of Cuka.

26. Kiringo M'Munyari. Five interviews, April 1970, Itura village, Igembe, North Meru. Gichunge age-set (Igembe equivalent of Kiramana), only one remaining in Igembe; estimated age, nineties. Considered most knowledgeable in area. Status: warrior. Purpose: origin of people of Igembe (Mbe); migration to Mt. Kenya; earlier occupants; traditional warfare; origins of warrior-councils (*kiama kia ramare*); supernatural societies.

27. Gichungu Baibuatho M'Barui. Five interviews, April 1970, Kithetu village, Igembe. Kilamunya age-set (equivalent of Murungi); estimated age, eighties. Status: warrior. Purpose: traditional war; origins of Igembe; supernatural societies.

28. Ikuciambuu Nguciala. Three interviews, April 1970, Luluma village, Igembe. Kilamunya age-set (equivalent to Murungi); estimated age, eighties. Status: warrior, farmer. Purpose: supernatural societies in Igembe; origins of warriors' council (*kiama kia lamale*) in Igembe.

29. M'Ngaruni M'Mutiga. One interview, April 1970, near Luluma village, Igembe. Kilamunya age-set (equivalent to Murungi); estimated age, eighties. Status: farmer; allegedly former member of supernatural society. Purpose: *Mwaa* society in Igembe.

30. M'Ikirima wa Gichoro. One interview, January 1970, Kigane village, South Imenti. Murungi (Riunga) age-set; estimated age, late eighties. Respected by contemporaries as knowledgeable of past. Status: warrior. Purpose: traditional war; council of elders for South Imenti (*njuri ya kiama*).

31. M'Mwongera M'Mungania. One interview, January 1970, Menwe village, South Imenti. Murungi (Riungu) age-set; estimated age, eighties. Status: allegedly a member of supernatural society. Purpose: secret societies; ritual and magic.

32. M'Mukindia wa Nkurunge. One interview, January 1970. Menwe village, South Imenti. Murungi (Riungu) age-set; estimated age, early eighties. Status: warrior, herder, farmer. Allegedly knowledgeable of 'magic' used by iron-smiths. Purpose: iron-smiths; relations agricultural community.

33. M'Ikieni M'Irimbere ('M'Iniu'). Two interviews, February 1970, Thimangari Market (Thuura), North Imenti. Murungi (Riungu) age-set; estimated age, eighties. Status: warrior (allegedly war-leader), farmer. Purpose: traditional warfare; origins of peoples of North Imenti; previous occupants of Imenti area; impact of Europeans on warriors of Thuura.

34. M'Mwongera wa Kabutai. Two interviews, February 1970, Kibirichia Market and Ntugi village, Northeast Imenti. Miriti age-set; estimated age, seventies. Status: warrior, farmer, Allegedly connected with *aathi* (hunters). Purpose: 'magic' of *aathi* ('bite and blow'); traditional warfare against Maasai.

Bibliography

35. Mathiu wa Gacece. Two interviews, February, 1970, Kiamogo village (Kibirichia), Northeast Imenti. Miriti age-set; estimated age, early 80's. Status: forest hunter, farmer. Former member of *kiama kia aathi*. Purpose: functions of *kiama kia aathi*; protective magic ('bite and blow'); cursing; relations of *aathi* to agricultural Meru.

36. Thangara wa Kairanya. Two interviews, near Kibirichia Market, Northeast Imenti. Miriti age-set; estimated age, 70's. Status: cattle herder. Reputed by contemporaries to be knowledgeable of past. Purpose: traditional warfare, weaponry; Meru and Maasai post-raid rituals.

37. Majogu wa Mathiu. One interview, February, 1970, Kitheruni village, Northeast Imenti. Miriti age-set; estimated age, 70's. Status: cattle herder. Alleged to be knowledgeable of *aathi*. Purpose: occupation of Northeast Imenti by present inhabitants; warfare with Maasai, Umpua (Ogiek); hunter, herder groups (*aathi*?) within Northeast Imenti.

38. Kibere wa Mbagine. Two interviews, February, 1970, Kiamogo village, Northeast Imenti. Miriti age-set; estimated age, 70's. Status: cattle herder. Purpose: cattle raiding by Maasai (defensive tactics).

39. M'Nkanata M'Mkatemia ('Kibunja': the destroyer). Three interviews, February, 1970, near Menwe village, South Imenti. Miriti age-set; estimated age, 70's. Status: honey-hunter; council of *aathi* (*kiama kia aathi*); magic, rituals of *aathi*.

40. Daudi M'Mungaria. Two interviews, February, 1970, U. Chure area (near forest edge), South Imenti. Miriti age-set; estimated age, 70's. Status: honey-hunter. Purpose: work of honey-hunters; council of *aathi*; magic, rituals of *aathi*; cursing (*urogi*).

41. M'Thaara wa Kathugu. Two interviews, February, 1970, Ruguta village, Muthambe. Murungi (Riungu) age-set; estimated age, 80's. Status: warrior, farmer. Purpose: traditional warfare; origins of Muthambe.

42. M'Ndegwa Kiithithira. Two interviews, February, 1970, Iriene village, Kibirichia, Northeast Imenti. Miriti age-set; estimated age, early 80's. Eldest living member of Ncuunca clan, a Maasai group that assimilated into Northeast Meru during the 1870s and 1880s. Status: warrior, farmer. Purpose: clan history; Maasai-Meru non-military relationships.

43. M'Kiambati wa Kirenga. One interview, February 1970, Katheri village. North Imenti. Murungi age-set; estimated age, eighties. Status: warrior, farmer. Purpose: history of Katheri area; the Maasai of Katheri; Katheri-Tigania wars.

44. M'Murithi Kainyuru. One interview, February 1970, near Katheri village, North Imenti. Murungi age-set; estimated age, eighties. Status: warrior, farmer, herder. Purpose: Maasai of Katheri; Katheri-Tigania wars.

45. M'Kirera M'Rinyiru. One interview, February 1970, Mpuri village (Katheri location), North Imenti. Murungi (Riungu) age-set; estimated age, eighties. Status: warrior, herdsman. Allegedly descended from Maasai. Purpose: Maasai assimilation into Katheri (rituals of mutual adoption); Tigania-Katheri wars.

46. Nguluu M'Mungaine. Two interviews, March-June 1970, Kanjalu village (Kianjai), Tigania. Kiramunya age-set (equivalent to Murungi in Central Meru); estimated age, eighties. Status: herder, farmer. Purpose: history of Kianjai area; assimilation of Maasai; Tigania-Katheri (Kianjai) wars.

47. M'Mucheke Likira. Two interviews, March-June 1970, Nkui village (Akithii), Tigania, North Meru. Kiramunya age-sets; estimated age, eighties. Status: warrior, herder. Purpose: history of Akithii area; assimilation of Maasai; Tigania (Akithii)-Katheri wars; raiding tactics against Northeast Imenti.

48. M'Arusha M'Amuru. Two interviews, April-June 1970, Amatu village (Mikinduri), Tigania, North Meru. Kiramunya age-set; estimated age, eighties. Status: warrior, herdsman, farmer. Purpose: history of Mikinduri area; assimilation of Maasai; Tigania (Mikinduri) raids against Katheri, Northeast Imenti, Igembe.

49. M'Ncurai wa Kabuthu. One interview, May 1970, near Tigania Mission Station (Muthara area), Tigania, North Meru. Kiramunya age-set; estimated age, late eighties. Status: warrior, herdsman, farmer. Purpose: history of Muthara area; assimilation of Maasai; raids against North and Northeast Imenti; elders' council of Tigania-Igembe (*njuri nceke*).

50. M'Muambe M'Mbuthu. One interview, May 1970, Muthara, Tigania. Kilamunya age-

set; estimated age, eighties. Status: warrior, policeman for colonial administration, farmer. Purpose: impact of colonialism on military and judicial councils of Muthara; history of elders' council of Tigania-Igembe.

51. Kairu Baimwera. Two interviews, March 1970, Mugaani village, Mwimbe. Miriti age-set; estimated age, early seventies. Status: farmer. Alleged former member of supernatural society. Purpose: supernatural societies of Mwimbe.

52. M'Ruiga M'Mbatau. Three interviews, March 1970, Igoji Township, Igoji. Murungi age-set; estimated age, eighties. Status: warrior, farmer. Former member of supernatural society. Purpose: supernatural societies of Igoji; traditional raiding; military resistance to colonial rule by Miutini; persecution of supernatural specialists, societies, under colonialism.

53. M'Mungori wa Baikare. Two interviews, April 1970, Magundu village, Muthambe (near Cuka boundary). Murungi (Riungu) age-set; estimated age, eighties. Status: warrior, farmer. Purpose: origins and migration route of Muthambe; military expulsion of Cuka, 1880s.

54. Karaya wa Njara ('Benjamin'). Two interviews, April 1970, Kauri village, Muthambe. Kabuuru age-set (equivalent of Kiruja); estimated age, sixty. Status: farmer; former member of supernatural society. Purpose: Mwaa society (*kiama kia nkoma*) in Muthambe.

55. Ms. (Informant withheld name). One interview, May 1970, Geto village, Igoji. Regeria age-set (married Murungi); estimated age, early seventies. Status: alleged member of supernatural society. Purpose: supernatural societies in Igoji; role of women within *kagita*; *chigiira*, a supernatural society of unmarried girls.

56. Ms. Kainyu Murungi. One interview, May 1970, Murerʉ village, Igoji. Regeria age-set (married Murungi); estimated age, late sixties. Status: alleged member of *kagita*. Purpose: women's role in supernatural societies; relations of *kagita, aathi* to agriculturalists.

57. Ms. Mwakireu Gikabu. One interview, May 1970, Karia village, Igoji. Regeria age-set (married Murungi); estimated age, late sixties. Status: alleged member of *kagita*. Purpose: women's roles in supernatural societies; cursing and curse-removal by supernatural societies.

58. Ms. Gacaba Murungi. One interview, May 1970, near Murerʉ village, Igoji. Refused to reveal age-set; estimated age, late sixties. Status: allegedly a member of *kagita* (refused to 'break oath' on this topic). Purpose: women's role within supernatural societies; *chigiira*, women's supernatural society.

59. Mburunga M'Muguongo. One interview, May 1970, Murerʉ village, Igoji. Murungi age-set; estimated age, early eighties. Status: alleged member of *kagita*. Purpose: roles of men, women within supernatural societies; cursing and curse removal by supernatural societies.

60. Ms. Jwanina Murungi. One interview, May 1970, Mwira jwa Ngondu village, Igoji. Refused to reveal age-set (married to Murungi). Status: allegedly member of supernatural society. Purpose: *chigiira*, an *aathi kiama* for unmarried girls.

61. Nciru M'Ngentu. One interview, March 1970, Mugaami village, Mwimbe. Riungu age-set; estimated age, eighties. Status: warrior, farmer. Purpose: origins of Mwimbe, secret societies in U. Mwimbe.

62. M'Raria M'Mugambe. One interview, June 1970, Mathagwe village, Igoji. Murungi age-set; estimated age, eighties. Status: warrior, farmer. Purpose: origins of Igoji.

63. M'Muga M'Muga. One interview, June 1970, Kathigiri village, Igoji. Miriti age-set; estimated age, late seventies. Status: farmer. Purpose: origins of Igoji; curse-removal in Igoji.

64. M'Matiri Kiruguru. One interview, June 1970, Rugomo village, Miutini. Murungi (Riungu) age-set; estimated age, early eighties. Status: warrior, farmer. Purpose: origins of Miutini; military resistance to colonialism.

65. Kibuja Nkarami. One interview, June 1970, Kiamwere village, Miutini. Murungi (Riungu) age-set; estimated age, early eighties. Status: warrior, farmer. Purpose: origins of Miutini; initial resistance to colonialism.

66. Matiiri wa Njogu. One interview, June 1970, Kioni village, Miutini. Murungi age-set;

estimated age, late eighties. Status: warrior, farmer. Purpose: origins of Miutini; resistance of Miutini to people of Kangangi (E. B. Horne, First British Administrator).

67. M'Muga M'Murithi. One interview, June 1970, Ithitu village, Igoji. Murungi age-set; estimated age, eighties. Status: warrior, cattle herder. Accepted by contemporaries as most knowledgeable of the past. Purpose: origins of Miutini, Igoji; supernatural societies (*aathi*) in Miutini, Igoji; military resistance of Miutini to colonialism.

68. Muthongomia M'Mucomba and Ms. Kirumu Muthongomia. One interview, June 1970, Geto village, Igoji. Man is in Murungi age-set; estimated age, nineties. Spouse in late seventies. Man's memory is failing; when prodded by wife, he recalls. Status of man: warrior, farmer. Allegedly a member of supernatural society. Status of women: allegedly member of supernatural society. Purpose: men's and women's role within *kagita, aathi*; cursing and curse-removal by secret societies; *chigiira,* a *kiama* for girls.

69. M'Muthara M'Mwebia. One interview, June 1970, Kuiri village, Igoji. Murungi age-set; estimated age, low eighties. Status: warrior, farmer. Mother was a *mwathi*, although he himself was not. Purpose: childhood of *mwathi; aathi* boys' *biama.*

70. Mukangu M'Njage and Miemba wa Njeru. One interview, June 1970, Muthambe Chief's Camp, Muthambe. Miriti age-set; estimated age, seventies. Mukangu is older, thus served as spokesman for both. Miemba commented and corrected. Status: farmers. Purpose: *aathi* in Muthambe; traditional courtship; cow-in-lawship (*uthoni wa ngombe*); girl-in-lawship (*uthoni wa nkenye*).

71. Karuke Rwito. One interview, June 1970, Kianjage village, L. Mwimbe. Murungi (Riungu) age-set; estimated age, early nineties. Status: warrior, farmer. Purpose: traditional raiding; resistance of Kanyoro's village (L. Mwimbe) to British control.

72. Stephan M'Anampiu. Five interviews, December 1969-April 1970, Meru Teacher Training College, North Imenti. Age-set not given. Status: History Master and Vice-Principal, Meru Teacher Training College. Purpose: research into origins, history of major clans of North Imenti.

73. M'Mugambe M'Mburu. One interview, December 1969, Katheri village, North Imenti. Murungi age-set; estimated age, eighties. Status: warrior, farmer. Purpose: Meru traditional religion.

74. J. G. H. Hopkins. One interview, December 1970, Stellenbosch, South Africa. (Interviewer: J. Hewson). Former Colonial Officer, Meru District, 1917-18, 1927-1932. Instrumental in breaking the influence of two supernatural societies (*aathi, kagita*) over large sections of Meru district. Purpose: supernatural societies in Meru; impact on nonmembers; stages of elimination.

75. Mwoga M'Mangania. One interview, June 1970, near Kiamwere village, Muitini. Murungi age-set; estimated age, eighties. Status: warrior, farmer. Purpose: origins of Miutini; Miutini raiding patterns; military alliance.

76. M'Rimberia M'Iroga (Henry). Two interviews, April-June 1970, near Katheri village, North Imenti. Murungi age-set; estimated age, late seventies. Status: warrior, farmer. Purpose: traditional warfare; relations of Katheri (*gaaru*) with Maasai, etc.

77. Muchena M'Ringeera. Four interviews, April-June 1970, Ruiga village, North Imenti. Murungi age-set; estimated age, late eighties. Status: warrior, farmer. Purpose: history of clan (claims ability to trace ancestry back to Mbwa); origins of Meru; relations with Maasai; obligations of ritual alliance (*gichiaro*).

78. Gikabu M'Iteria and Kiagia Njeru. One interview, April 1970, Ithambare village, Miutini. Both Miriti age-set; estimated age, seventies. Gikabu, the elder, acts as spokesman. Status: farmers. Purpose: training for warriorhood.

79. Baigumba Thariaba. One interview, June 1970, Kambi ya Kairanya, North Igembe. Kilamuya (corresponds to Murungi in Imenti); estimated age, eighties. Status: warrior, herder. Purpose: earlier occupants of Igembe; invaders of Igembe; tactics of defense.

80. M'Mukira wa Irembi (Joseph). One interview, March 1970, near Ithambari Primary School, Nkubu, South Imenti. Age-set: Miriti; estimated age, late seventies. Status: warrior, farmer, former teacher. Intelligent; interested in recording Meru past. Purpose: Traditional structure of Njuri ya Biama, South Imenti; Njuri history before colonial era; traditional war; warrior courtship and marriage.

81. Kirimi Nkuruaru. One interview, March 1970, Karaa Market (near Chogoria), Mwimbe. Kiruji age-set; estimated age, fifties. Father and uncles were Ogiek who made *gichiaro* (ritual alliance) with *miiriga* in U. Mwimbe; subsequently served as 'scouts.' Clan: Rukuruku (Mokogodo?) in Kiogiek; Rukinga in Kimwimbe. Purpose: relations of Ogiek with *miiriga* of Mwimbe; in peace (intermarriage, etc.) and war.

82. Karema M'Ringeera. One interview, February 1970, Ncoore village, Northeast Imenti. Murungi age-set; estimated age, early eighties. Status: warrior, herder. Alleged to have been visited by ancestral spirits (*nkoma*); contact with *aathi*. Purpose: traditional spirit worship; *nkoma*, relations with *aathi; kiama kia aathi*.

83. Mburunga Ng'entu. One interview, January 1970, Chogoria village, Mwimbe. Murungi age-set; estimated age, early eighties. Status: warrior, farmer, ex-Chief of Mwimbe, 1930s; reliable on aspects of pre-colonial history, unreliable where his own role is concerned. Purpose: origins of Mwimbe, early (*gichiaro*) relationship to Tigania, Embu; entry of Amuimbe onto Mt. Kenya.